Deleuze, Guattari and the Machine in Early Christianity

Also available from Bloomsbury

Deleuze, Guattari and the Schizoanalysis of Trans Studies, edited by Ciara Cremin

Queer and Deleuzian Temporalities, by Rachel Loewen Walker

Rethinking Philosophy and Theology with Deleuze, by Brent Adkins

Why God Must Do What Is Best, by Justin J. Daeley

Deleuze, Guattari and the Machine in Early Christianity

Schizoanalysis, Affect and Multiplicity

Bradley H. McLean

BLOOMSBURY ACADEMIC
LONDON • NEW YORK • OXFORD • NEW DELHI • SYDNEY

BLOOMSBURY ACADEMIC
Bloomsbury Publishing Plc
50 Bedford Square, London, WC1B 3DP, UK
1385 Broadway, New York, NY 10018, USA
29 Earlsfort Terrace, Dublin 2, Ireland

BLOOMSBURY, BLOOMSBURY ACADEMIC and the Diana logo are trademarks of Bloomsbury Publishing Plc

First published in Great Britain 2022
This paperback edition published 2024

Copyright © Bradley H. McLean, 2022

Bradley H. McLean has asserted his right under the Copyright, Designs and Patents Act, 1988, to be identified as Author of this work.

Copy Right Instants/ Getty Images

All rights reserved. No part of this publication may be reproduced or transmitted in any form or by any means, electronic or mechanical, including photocopying, recording, or any information storage or retrieval system, without prior permission in writing from the publishers.

Bloomsbury Publishing Plc does not have any control over, or responsibility for, any third-party websites referred to or in this book. All internet addresses given in this book were correct at the time of going to press. The author and publisher regret any inconvenience caused if addresses have changed or sites have ceased to exist, but can accept no responsibility for any such changes.

A catalogue record for this book is available from the British Library.

A catalog record for this book is available from the Library of Congress.

ISBN: HB: 978-1-3502-3384-3
PB: 978-1-3502-3388-1
ePDF: 978-1-3502-3385-0
eBook: 978-1-3502-3386-7

Typeset by Newgen KnowledgeWorks Pvt. Ltd., Chennai, India

To find out more about our authors and books visit www.bloomsbury.com and sign up for our newsletters.

Jesus said, 'Those who try to keep their (molar) life will lose it, but those who lose their (molar) life will keep it.'

Lk. 17.33

Contents

List of Abbreviations		viii
Introduction		1
1	The rise of the Christ machines	11
2	Desiring production and early Christianities	21
3	The rhizome: Multiplicities and the virtual dimension of Christ groups	29
4	The autoproduction of a body of Christ without organs	37
5	Territorializations and deterritorializations: On becoming outlandish	45
6	Deterritorialization in the Gospels: A typology of lines	55
7	The stratification of Christ groups in the Roman despotic socius	65
8	Christ groups as social assemblages and abstract machines: Discourse and power	77
9	The God of religion and the schizo God	91
10	The myth of Eve: Falling into, and out of, delusion	99
11	On several regimes of signs and several Christs	113
12	The despotic Christ and the signifying despotic regime of signs	123
13	The passional Christ and the passional subjective regime of signs	135
14	What can Christ's body do?	145
15	Molecular becomings of Christ: Becoming-woman	157
16	Christ becoming-animal: An affair of sorcery	165
17	Christ's becomings-imperceptible: Martyrological, magical and cosmic	175
18	The nomad Jesus and the Galilean war machine	181
Conclusion		193
Notes		209
Bibliography		233
Index		247

Abbreviations

AO	Deleuze and Guattari, *Anti-Oedipus: Capitalism and Schizophrenia*, trans. R. Hurley, 1983.
AO^f	Deleuze and Guattari, *L'Anti-Œdipe: Capitalisme et schizophrénie 1*, 1972.
B	Deleuze, *Bergsonism*, trans. Hugh Tomlinson et al., 1990.
C1	Deleuze, *Cinema 1: The Movement-Image*, trans. H. Tomlinson, 1986.
C2	Deleuze, *Cinema 2: The Time-Image*, trans. H. Tomlinson, 1989.
D	Deleuze and Parnet, *Dialogues II*, rev. edn, trans. H. Tomlinson, 2007.
DI	Deleuze, *Desert Islands and Other Texts 1953–1974*, trans. M. Taormina, 2007.
DR	Deleuze, *Difference and Repetition*, trans. P. Patton, 1994.
DR^f	Deleuze, *Différence and répétition*, 1968.
ECC	Deleuze, *Essays Critical and Clinical*, trans. Daniel W. Smith et al., 1997.
EPS	Deleuze, *Expressionism in Philosophy: Spinoza*, 1992.
ES	Deleuze, *Empiricism and Subjectivity*, 2001.
F	Deleuze, *Foucault*, trans. S. Hand, 1988.
F^f	Deleuze, *Foucault*, 1986.
FB	Deleuze, *Francis Bacon: The Logic of Sensation*, trans. D. Smith, 2003.
IM	Deleuze, *Cinéma 1. L'image-Mouvement*, 1983.
K	Deleuze and Guattari, *Kafka: Toward a Minor Literature*, trans. D. Polan, 1986.
K^f	Deleuze and Guattari, *Kafka – Pour une littérature mineure*, 1975.
L	Deleuze, *Lettres et autres textes*, ed. David Lapoujade, 2015.
LS	Deleuze, *The Logic of Sense*, trans. M. Lester, 1990.
MP	Deleuze and Guattari, *Mille plateaux: Capitalisme et Schizophrénie 2*, 1980.
Neg.	Deleuze, *Negotiations: 1972–1990*, trans. M. Joughin, 1995.
NP	Deleuze, *Nietzsche and Philosophy*, trans. H. Tomlinson, 1983.
PS	Deleuze, *Proust and Signs: The Complete Text*, trans. R. Howard, 2008.
PS^f	Deleuze, *Proust et les signes*, 3º édition, 1973.
PT	Guattari, *Psychoanalysis and Transversality: Texts and Interviews 1955–1971*, trans. Ames Hodges, 2015.

SPP   Deleuze, *Spinoza: Practical Philosophy*, 1988.
TP   Deleuze and Guattari, *A Thousand Plateaus: Capitalism and Schizophrenia*, trans. B. Massumi, 1987.
WP   Deleuze and Guattari, *What Is Philosophy?*, trans. H. Tomlinson, 1994.

Introduction

Michel Foucault once remarked that 'a bolt of lightning has struck that will bear Deleuze's name', with the result that 'a new kind of thinking is possible, thinking is possible anew. ... One day, perhaps, the century will be seen as Deleuzian' (Foucault 1977b: 165). Even if Foucault's 'little remark' was no more than 'a joke meant to make people who like us laugh, and make everybody else livid', as Deleuze himself modestly suggested (NP 4), Foucault's comment nonetheless reflected the extent to which the philosophy of Gilles Deleuze was opening fresh pathways for thought in philosophy, the humanities and social sciences. And we must hasten to mention the considerable contributions of Félix Guattari, who co-authored six books with Deleuze and co-founded the journal *Chimères: Revue des schizoanalysis* with him. Deleuze and Guattari (D&G) are best known for their esoteric, exhilarating, humorous and frequently vulgar *L'Anti-Oedipe*, published in 1972, and its epic companion volume, *Mille plateau*, published eight years later.[1] Guattari contributed many of the key concepts to this so-called 'Capitalism and Schizophrenia' project including the 'machine' and 'schizoanalysis'.[2] For many readers D&G's 'Capitalism and Schizophrenia' project represents the apogee of French poststructuralism.

Of course, Deleuze also published independently of Guattari. The impact of the philosophy of Deleuze on the humanities and social sciences notably includes the study of religion and theology. Lindsay Powell-Jones and LeRon Shults's recent edited volume of essays entitled *Deleuze and the Schizoanalysis of Religion* (2016), and Tony See and Joff Bradley's *Deleuze and Buddhism* (2016) constitute two of many studies devoted to the contributions of Deleuze to the study of religion. Explorations of Deleuze's contribution to the study of academic theology are even more abundant. For instance, the year 2012 alone witnessed the publication of Christopher Ben Simpson's *Deleuze and Theology* (2012), Kristien Justaert's *Theology after Deleuze* (2012), and Petra Carlsson Redell's *Theology beyond Representation: Foucault, Deleuze and the Phantasms of Theological*

Thinking (2012).³ We should not be surprised by this synergy between Deleuzian philosophy and the academic study of religion and theology because, as Peter Hallward observes, Deleuzian philosophy is a philosophy of pure difference, virtuality and immanent transcendence, which manifests the unlimited creativity and power of Being or God (2006: 1). Deleuze's rapprochement with theology is perhaps most evident in his engagement with the philosophy of Søren Kierkegaard (Bouaniche 2014). In *Difference and Repetition* he invests the Kierkegaardian terms, faith and belief, with positive meaning, and he even speaks appreciatively of Kierkegaard's concept of the 'adventure of faith' (DR 95). It is clear that Deleuze invests some religious terms with positive meaning (Bouaniche 2014: 131). What is perhaps even more remarkable is that Deleuze effects a reconciliation of Kierkegaard and Nietzsche based on their shared concept of repetition: he argues that 'there is a force common to Kierkegaard and Nietzsche. … Each … in his own way, makes repetition not only a power peculiar to language and thought, … but also the fundamental category of a philosophy of the future' (DR 5). By uniting Kierkegaard and Nietzsche as philosophers of 'true' repetition against the philosopher of 'false' repetition, namely Hegel, *Deleuze breaks down the long-standing divisions between atheism and theology and, indeed, between materialism and spirituality*. True repetition, regardless of whether it is styled 'Kierkegaardian' or 'Nietzschean', is a spiritual force that overcomes such conventional theoretical divisions. Suffice to say that the philosophy of Deleuze (and potentially Guattari as well) has much to offer those who are engaged in the academic study of theology and early Christianity.

While examples of theology's engagement with the philosophy of Deleuze could be multiplied, it is obvious that a genuine encounter between them is now underway. Kristien Justaert goes so far as to argue that the discipline of theology actually *needs* Deleuze, for only through such an encounter can theology 'recover' from its current problems (2012: 2). In contrast to the discipline of theology, the discipline of Christian origins has not yet encountered Deleuzian philosophy in a serious way. This prompts the question, if the discipline of theology actually *needs* Deleuzian philosophy, as Justaert maintains, then *why does the discipline of Christian origins not have a similar need?*

1. A tale of two origins

Perhaps this lack of engagement with Deleuzian philosophy on the discipline of Christian origins can be traced back to the underlying tendencies of the discipline, which, as I have argued elsewhere, are based on a genealogical model, which contributes synthetic a priori claims to its analysis of early Christianity (McLean 2020: 536–9). This genealogical model orients the discipline towards the task of recovering early Christianity's *lost origins*, with a focus on the historical Jesus of Galilee, or his lost original teachings, the earliest Jesus movement, Pauline Christianity and so forth. Quests for 'lost origins' are generally guided by the historicist logic of genesis, influence and development (McLean 2012a: 55–79, 2012b). Michel Foucault has observed how *the very concept of a lost origin induces a belief in the pure essence of things, and simultaneously gives rise to the impulse to find it*. Before long, a discipline of knowledge forms that is dedicated to its recovery (1977b: 142). Is it possible that the theoretical concept of a lost origin is responsible for engendering the historical quest for early Christianity's lost origins?

The discipline of Christian origins is certainly not unique with respect to its obsession with the silent beginnings of Christianity. Systematic theology also represents Christianity on a genealogical model but within a *transcendental*, rather than historical, framework: it traces 'the Church' backwards to a single point of transcendental origin, a supreme signifier, Jesus Christ, Son of God, as one might trace a mighty oak tree back to the acorn from which it grew. It is easy to interpret Christianity this way. It's comforting and one can do so almost without thinking. But is identifying the origin of Christianity as simple as this? Jürgen Habermas has noted how the reconstruction of history based on historical 'facts' is always 'organized backward from a projected endpoint into a story' (1988: 162).

D&G would say that systematic theology has employed 'tree logic' to represent the past: 'All tree logic is a logic of tracing and reproduction. … It consists of tracing something that comes ready-made' (TP 12). René Descartes famously compared the structure of Western knowledge to that of a tree: 'Thus, the whole of philosophy is like a tree: the roots are metaphysics, the trunk is physics, and the branches that issue from the trunk are all the other sciences.'[4] D&G argue that all Western humanist thought is modelled on what they term 'tree-logic' or 'arborescence'. A survey of the systematic theology's accounts of the origin of Christianity would demonstrate that this 'tree-logic', which traces back historical Christianity to a sui generis transcendental origin, has often served as the accomplice of domination. For it has been employed as a universalist and colonizing discourse to argue that Christianity is superior to all other religions. Hence, even theology can serve as a tool for domination.

Deleuzo-Guattarian 'rhizomatic' philosophy destabilizes all forms of tree-logic and universalist discourses, not to mention the sui generis origins they give rise to.⁵ If the greatest impediment to inter-religious dialogue is Christian theology's exclusivist claim to a sui generis transcendental origin, then D&G's philosophical concept of a 'rhizome' provides a means to facilitate new forms of dialogue and cooperation between Christians and other co-religionists including not only adherents of the five 'world' religions but also queer spirituality (§§ 3, 15.2.1), followers of the sacred spiritualities of aboriginal peoples. For 'rhizomatics' finds its theoretical and practical coherence by means of an exploration of *our relations* to Jews and Moslems, Buddhists and Hindus, to differently gendered people, to migrants and the economically exploited. In other words, *there is an entire micropolitics of rhizomatics*. In short, the Deleuzo-Guattarian concept of a rhizome provides a new space for fostering non-universalist, non-colonizing discourses, as well as for explorations of the *interrelatedness* of these systems of thought. In short, the substitution of D&G's rhizomatic model in place of the genealogical model of theology could facilitate new forms of inter-religious understanding.

In contrast to theology's use of a genealogical model within a *transcendental* framework, the discipline of Christian origins employs a genealogical model within a *historical* framework. But our dream of finding the historical origin of early Christianity has not led to the discovery of a pure historical origin, Jesus of Nazareth, but to an infinite regress of *rhizomatic* relations, from Jesus of Nazareth to Second Temple Judaism, to Jewish apocalyptic and messianic movements, zealots, social banditry, to Pharisaism, the Essenes, Hermeticism, gnosticism, and back to the Maccabean Revolt, the Hasmonean uprising and so forth. In short, the dream of finding the historical origin of early Christianity has become a nightmare. Given the constitutive undecidability and incompleteness of such historical evidence, the genealogical quest for the ever-receding point or origin of early Christianity can never lead to a single historical cause but only to a vast number of possible, interrelated and interdependent causes. The supposed unilateral causes, chronologies and principles of classification have all lost their self-evidence. Indeed, this quest for the historical origin of early Christianity has led to *an expanded network of historical relations, which strongly resembles D&G's philosophical concept of the rhizome!*

Looking back on this disciplinary history with the benefit of hundreds of years of hindsight, we now find ourselves in a position to contemplate the death of the historical and theological tree-logic of a pure origin. But the present predicament of the discipline of Christian origins is more serious than I have described above, for even if the complex historical origins of early Christianity *could* be determined with any degree of specificity, the logic of influence and development is incapable of theorizing phenomena of change, transformation and the emergence of discontinuities in early Christianity. Are the disciplines of theology and Christian origins forever condemned to search for a pure origin that may be more delusional than real? What benefits would ensue if we abandoned the tree-logic of pure origins, and instead employed Deleuzo-Guattarian concept of a 'rhizome' to theorize the emergence of early Christianity? This book constitutes a sustained exploration of this fundamental question.

2. The failure of representational thinking

The quest for pure origins – historical or transcendental – is a form of *representational* thinking: in commonsensical terms, representational thinking presupposes that the concept of 'origin' corresponds to, or *represents*, an actual (historical or transcendental) origin. The representational concept of an 'origin', like all representational concepts, contributes synthetic a priori claims to the production of such knowledge. In general terms, representational concepts function in a variety of ways: as a shared academic logic about causality, as a culturally shared taxonomy or even as a set of shared cultural metaphors, for metaphors also function as concepts (McLean 2013: 371–3, 2015: 47, 2019: 1). As Georges Didi-Huberman observes, scholars who employ representational concepts are generally unaware of the function of concepts in their thought processes: they 'tend to forget to what extent the words used to account for what we see … are ambiguous words, layered by history', lacking 'historical precision and philosophical coherence' (1995: 1). Language, as a 'form of codification', always supplies a kind of structure that determines what is thinkable, and therefore, expressible (Williams 1977: 167). For example, linguistic signification is based on the epistemological assumption that *sameness precedes difference*. Language signifies by means of general concepts that subordinate 'difference' to categories of the 'same'. Such difference is measured in terms of degrees of variation from representational concepts. The epistemological assumption that sameness precedes difference overlooks 'difference in itself', and therefore prevents one from grasping things in themselves (DR 28–30, 138; DI 33). While representational concepts *simulate* the real, by reducing the real to conceptual categories of sameness, such concepts inevitably fail because they *conceal pure difference*. Instead of subordinating difference to linguistic categories of sameness, Deleuze reverses the relation between sameness and difference, positing sameness on the basis of 'internalized difference' (DR 300). In short, he argues that *difference precedes similarity*; different relates 'to different without any mediation whatsoever by the identical, the similar, the analogous or the opposed' (DR 116–17). We cannot achieve a more direct relation to the world, past or present, without first escaping from the prison-house of representational concepts. Faced with the ephemerality of the lifeworld, and the inherent deficiencies of representational concepts, D&G refrain from using traditional representational concepts. In the option of Peter Hallward, this characteristic of Deleuzo-Guattarian philosophy is one of its strengths because the unlimited creativity of the lifeworld cannot be reduced to a linguistic set of representational concepts (2006: 1).

3. Rhizomatic thinking

The invention of nonrepresentational concepts constitutes an essential feature of D&G's philosophical project. Through the invention of new concepts, they set out to create new ways of perceiving and thinking (WP 77–8). As noted above, one such nonrepresentational concept is the 'rhizome' (§ 2.1). In botanical terms, a rhizome is a kind of fungus that lacks a central coordinating structure. In philosophical terms, the concept of a rhizome provides a means of theorizing the lifeworld as a totality of relations. The 'rhizome' concept helps us theorize the 'in-betweenness' between bodies. In a 'rhizome', there are no independent entities but only temporary, ad hoc organizations, which are historically manifested as struggles and adaptations between heterogeneous components. If one can speak of the truth of this concept, it is always the truth of a totality of rhizomatic relations.

Rhizomatic formations are held together by 'machines', or 'machinic processes', which is another important Deleuzo-Guattarian nonrepresentational concept. Any 'body' (structured entity) that couples with another 'body' to produce or draw in a flow is a 'machine'. The historical emergence of early Christianity, considered rhizomatically, would have no discrete point of origin but only a profusion of 'machines' coupled with other machines. From this 'machinic' perspective, Christ groups were defined less by the *interiority* of their beliefs, teachings and practices than by the *exteriority* of their relations to other machines.[6] This book will theorize Christ groups as 'machines', that is, as 'Christ machines' that coupled and exchanged flows with other machines of widely ranging registers, intensities and magnitudes: synagogue-machines, kinship-machines and benefaction-machines, to name a few, resulting in exchanges of material, libidinal and semiotic flows (§ 1). I will argue that machines comprise an unnoticed dimension of early Christianity. As such, machines provide major analytical tool for mapping the historical emergence, change and transformation of Christ groups in the first three centuries of the Common Era.

4. Nonrepresentational concepts

D&G create concepts experimentally based on their empirical intuitions arising from contact with the sciences, psychoanalysis, social sciences, literature and the arts. As Foucault observes, D&G also rehabilitate old concepts from so-called 'minor' philosophic traditions, making 'joyously unorthodox use' of Lucretius, Hume, Spinoza, Nietzsche, Leibniz and Bergson to construct a kind of 'counter-philosophy' to the rationalist tradition of René Descartes and Georg Hegel (preface, AO xvii–xviii). D&G stipulate only one precondition for the creation and rehabilitation of concepts: namely, that such concepts 'should have a necessity, as well as a strangeness, and they have both to the extent they respond to real problems' (Neg. 36). Only through the creation of strange terms can one become 'a foreigner in … one's own language' and ask strange, new questions.

This precondition of strangeness takes us directly to the heart of the problem of the discursive conditions of thought. For, as Foucault has demonstrated, discourse is a practice that systematically constructs its own conceptual objects according to a *system of discursive rules* (Foucault 1973: 229). Such rules determine *in advance* what is thinkable in any age; they determine, in advance, what discursive 'statements' can be 'caught in the true'.[7] In other words, disciplinary 'truth' is always part of a 'regime of truth' (Foucault 1980: 133). With an understanding of the role of systems of discursive rules in the construction of disciplinary knowledge comes a sense of the contingent nature of all disciplinary knowledge and, by extension, of all perceptual worlds: we sense the reality of disciplinary *unreality*. By drawing attention to the operation of discursive rules, Foucault demonstrated the extent to which human knowledge is contingent rather than necessary, constructive rather than reproductive.

From the vantage point of the rules of discourse, it can be argued that what has united the academic discourses of theology and of Christian origins, respectively, over the last few centuries is not the facticity of their disciplinary objects of inquiry but the *discursive conditions* that governed the construction of their disciplinary objects. Therefore, it follows that, if we change our concepts of analysis, as D&G do, then we can also *change what is thinkable and what counts as knowledge* with respect to early Christianity. Thus, D&G's 'strange' new concepts, lacking established disciplinary usages, provide us with new ways of creating knowledge about early Christianity.

D&G's concepts can be said to be 'constructivist' in the sense that they are 'entirely oriented toward an experimentation in contact with the real' (TP 12–13). These concepts are experimental in at least three ways: first, they establish new coordinates and directions for thought. Second, they are not external to objects of thought but actively participate in their construction. And third, their concepts are intended to produce fresh encounters, that is, to form a 'rhizome' with disciplines, texts and histories, the outcome of which is never known at the outset. Thus, through the invention of new concepts and the rehabilitation of old concepts, D&G turn thinking-as-representation (which argues that 'this is that') into thinking-as-experimentation.

The 'rhizome' and 'machine' comprise two of many of D&G's nonrepresentational concepts, including the 'multiplicity' (§ 3), 'body without organs' (§ 4), 'deterritorialization' and 'reterritorialization' (§ 5), 'stratification' and 'destratification' (§ 7), social 'assemblage', 'abstract machine' (§ 8), 'regimes of signs' (§§ 11–13), 'becoming' (§§ 14–17), and 'nomadism' and the 'war machine' (§ 18). Many of these concepts can be arranged in pairs:

rhizomatic formation	arborescent structure (§ 2.1)
plane of immanence	plane of organization (§ 2.3)
body without organs	organism (§§ 4, 7.2.1)
molecular	molar (§ 6.1.1)
planomenon	ecumenon (§ 9.2)
schizo God	God of religion (§ 9.3)
smooth space	striated space (§ 18.2)
war machine	State apparatus (§ 18)

It must be stressed that these paired concepts do *not* compose a set of dualisms. These concepts are reciprocally determined.[8] Each pair of concepts composes a *spectrum* of possibilities for actualization.[9] Since the relations between concepts are ideal, and are not empirically derived, we should *always expect mixtures of them in historical formations* such as early Christianity and the Graeco-Roman world. Indeed, these concepts are actualized/historicized *only* in mixtures, as a kind of synthesis of ideal opposites. But despite their ideal status, these concepts are exceedingly useful because they provide a set of interrelated coordinates that can be mapped onto various kinds of historical formations.[10]

Since Deleuzo-Guattarian concepts always imply other concepts, their meanings cannot be established on the basis of a set of fixed definitions. Instead, their concepts accrue meanings based on a progressive determination arising from their use in addressing specific philosophic problems.

5. *A Thousand Plateaus* and the study of early Christianity

The primary focus of this book is D&G's *A Thousand Plateaus*. *A Thousand Plateaus* does not employ language representationally. Its translator, Brian Massumi, describes this book as 'less a critique' (in comparison with *Anti-Oedipus*) 'than a sustained, constructive experiment' in real time (1992: 4). What is more, *A Thousand Plateaus* privileges the virtual over the actual, 'becoming' over 'being', 'machinic' transformations over static structures, and semiotics over linguistics. The nonrepresentational concepts employed in *A Thousand Plateaus* are particularly apposite to the current dilemma of Christian origins: for as a rhizome-book consisting of plateaus, machines, singularities and non-representational concepts, this book models new modes of thinking that can help the disciplines of both Christian origins and theology rejuvenate themselves and accomplish new tasks which are presently beyond their reach. For the discipline of Christian Origins (or New Testament Studies) is presently fragmented by a wide range of methods, a restricted focus on individual texts and by bifurcated disciplinary approaches that can be traced back to the theoretical division between the humanities and the social sciences. This fragmentation defines the fate of historical reasoning in our own time. The overall effect of this disciplinary fragmentation is that it is nearly impossible to consider early Christianity in its entirety. Perhaps, within the impasse of our present fragmentation is the heralding of a forthcoming event. Deleuzo-Guattarian philosophy, in contrast, is a *theory of everything*: the historically actual and spiritually virtual, the discursive and nondiscursive, the body of the individual and the supra-individual bodies of groups and institutions. Hence, the reach of Deleuzo-Guattarian philosophy far exceeds the reach of any of these fragmented parts.

Instead of chapters, *A Thousand Plateaus* is comprised of 'plateaus' (*plateaux*). What is a plateau? It is a small, revisable 'map' of the world; it is one 'regime of truth' among many. Through its arrangement of fourteen plateaus in relation to one another, *A Thousand Plateaus* facilitates multiple, *simultaneous* perspectives on our world. Every particular perspective is dwarfed by the vast multitude of possible perspectives. As Claire Colebrook observes, this piling up of diverse perspectives illustrates that 'there are different modes of relation and existence' (2020: 330). Through its proliferation plateaus, *A Thousand Plateaus* disavows 'the *prima facie* value of the single system of difference that has forged "the human"' (Colebrook 2020: 332). Rather than treating any one of these plateaus in isolation, we, as readers of *A Thousand Plateaus*, are invited to explore their points of agreement and conflict, to explore not only how these maps reinforce one another but also how they dismantle one another.

Each of the fourteen plateaus can be likened to 'a sort of room that one can leave by going through a door, only to arrive in another room that one won't stay in, and that has doors that lead to other rooms' (K xxvii). As readers, we are invited to enter *A Thousand Plateaus* by any one of these fourteen plateaus and exit by means of any other plateau. In the course of 'walking' from plateau to plateau, our perspective is repeatedly relocated and altered. As Colebrook observes, the cumulative effect is a piling up of perspectives, the disruption of 'the privilege of a single narrative' (2020: 330). Hence, Deleuze describes this book as the 'ultimate anti-system, as patchwork, absolute dispersion' (Neg. 31).

In my recent article, 'What Does *A Thousand Plateaus* Contribute to the Study of Early Christianity?', I argued that the philosophical processes at work in *A Thousand Plateaus* are particularly relevant to the reinvigoration of the discipline of Christian origins (2020). In its first chapter, entitled simply 'Rhizome', D&G describe *A Thousand Plateaus* as a 'rhizome-book' (in contrast to a traditional 'root-book') on the grounds that this book 'forms a rhizome with the world' (TP 11). As I shall demonstrate in the following chapters, *A Thousand Plateaus* can form a rhizome with the Graeco-Roman *world* in which the first Christ groups emerged. All this is to say that D&G have provided us with a toolbox of nonrepresentational concepts and a new modality of thought, which can give rise to new insights. The opportunity is now ours to experiment with them. So, without further delay, let us begin!

1

The rise of the Christ machines

I commend to you our sister Phoebe, a deacon of the Christ machine in Cenchreae … for she has been a patron of many including myself as well. Greet Prisca and Aquila, my co-workers in Christ Jesus, … to whom, not only I give thanks, but also all the Gentile Christ machines. Greet also the Christ machine that meets in their house. … And all the Christ machines send their greetings to you.

Rom. 16.1-5, 16

Machines, they are everywhere! Everywhere you look in the world, one machine is coupling with another and exchanging flows. It's shocking! But this fact of life shouldn't surprise us because machines are *excessively* passional: they're always reaching out to other machines and coupling with them. For machines are always binary, with one machine producing a flow, and the other drawing in the same flow. An infant's mouth is a machine that couples with a breast machine to draw in a flow of milk (AO 13). On a macro scale, the sun is a cosmic machine that couples with our planet's vegetation-machines through intense flows of light. There are no independent machines but only machines coupling with other machines. Machines are also the universal matter of human drives and instincts. A penis machine couples with a vagina machine to transmit a flow of semen so that 'two bodies become *one flesh*', and *this* machinic coupling is even commanded by God: 'For this reason a man shall leave his father and mother and couple with his wife, and the two will become one flesh' (Mt. 19.5, Eph. 5.31).

Everything in the Graeco-Roman world was a machine. Machines operated at micro and macro scales, ranging from pre-individual machines through to progressively larger and more abstract machines. The Christ groups (ἐκκλησίαι) in Rome, Corinth and Cenchreae were all *Christ machines* (Rom. 16.1-16). They too were excessively passional. The Christ machine in Rome coupled with other Christ machines producing and drawing in flows of people (Phoebe, Prisca and Aquila), money and texts (such as Paul's letters).[1] Christ machines coupled with a diverse assortment of other machines including synagogue machines, immigrant association machines, cultic machines and guild machines, as well as, of course, with the great bureaucratic megamachine, which was the Roman Empire (§ 9). From this machinic perspective Christ machines were defined less by their interiority – by their beliefs, teachings and iterative practices – than by their machinic exteriorities. For early Christianity of the first three centuries of the Common Era was exceedingly rhizomatic, consisting of machines connected to machines, which were connected to other machines.

The historical record supports this machinic analysis of early Christianity: the coupling with Jewish, gnostic, pagan, philosophical and magical machines resulted in the formation of diverse groups including Ebionites, Marcionites, Christian gnostics and so-called 'proto-orthodox' groups. The resulting phenomenon was exceedingly rhizomatic. Ebionites revered the Jewish scriptures, and believed that Jesus was a fully human, righteous man (not the Son of God), who taught that Gentiles should become Jews and follow the commandments of Torah; they regarded the apostle Paul as a *heretic*. In contrast, the Marcionites of Asia Minor regarded Paul as a *hero*; they rejected the Jewish scriptures, and believed that the God of the New Testament had sent Jesus to save humanity from this wrathful God (Demiurge) of the Jewish scriptures. So-called 'gnostics', which emerged in places such as Egypt, Syria and Asia Minor, held widely diverse views, some of which were similar to the Ebionites, while others were more like the Marcionites (Brakke 2010; King 2005). Other Christ followers, who would dub themselves 'orthodox' in the fourth century CE, agreed and disagreed with parts of the teachings of all three of these groups. What all these groups held in common was their firm belief that *every other group was heretical* (Betz 1998: 5). *This rhizomatic state of affairs is exactly what one would expect if the first Christ groups functioned as machines.*

1. Machines versus structures

Scholars of early Christianity are accustomed to analysing the Graeco-Roman world based on synchronic *structural* configurations such as the structure of its two primary social institutions, civic structures and kinship structures, the structure of benefaction, and the structure of honour and shame (McLean 2015: 49–51). Such structural analyses tend to represent the ancient world as being relatively *static*. Indeed, structural analyses cannot easily account for historical phenomena *change and transformation*.² Surely, the Graeco-Roman world entailed more than an endless repeating of the same structural configurations, ad infinitum.

Deleuze and Guattari were intensely interested in accounting for how structural configurations undergo change and transformation over time. They recognized that a theoretical model was needed that combines the analysis of synchronic structural configurations with a diachronic, event-oriented analysis that takes into consideration historical contingency, change and especially *structural transformation*. Hence, their philosophy can be situated at the intersection of the structure versus genesis debate. Deleuze's first attempt to account for structural transformation can be found in *Logique de sens* (1969), where he enumerates three minimal conditions for structures in general, the third and most important of which concerns structural transformation.³ His third general condition states that every structure entails a 'differentiator' or 'paradoxical element', which is *internal* to structure, that introduces a principle of movement into structures and generates virtual 'events' (DR 119).⁴

1.1. Guattarian machines

In his article entitled 'Machine and Structure' (1969), Félix Guattari challenged Deleuze's third general condition, gently reproaching Deleuze for what he considered to be his latent structuralist tendencies.⁵ Guattari famously argued that the cause of structural transformation is *external* to structural formations and 'relates … exclusively to the order of the machine' (Guattari 2015: 382, n. 1). Guattarian 'machines' entail the flow of asignifying semiotic 'singularities', or 'particles-signs', that act on structures from their exteriors and generate transformational 'events'.⁶ In short, Guattari argued that structural transformations are not caused by processes which are internal to structures, as Deleuze had proposed, but rather are caused by *machinic processes that are exterior to structural formations*. With this profound insight Guattari reversed the directionality of French structuralism.⁷ If machinic processes can bring about structural transformations, then it follows that *structures are not autonomous systems that are closed off to effects of history*. Historical machinic processes can bring about changes on the virtual plane, which are in turn actualized as historically actual, structural transformations (§ 3.2).

It is difficult to overstate the revolutionary consequences of Guattari's insight. By moving Deleuze's 'differentiator' or 'paradoxical element' from the interiority of virtual structures to their exteriority, Guattari succeeded in accounting for how structural transformation occurs through aleatory, historical/material 'machinic' phenomena. Guattari goes so far as to suggest that machinic processes constitute the silent beginnings of all structures: in other words, 'machinic' processes *pre-exist* structures, and *structures are a secondary effect of them* (Thornton 2017: 462).

The relation between (Guattarian) machines and structures is comparable to the relation between the base and superstructure in Karl Marx's base–superstructure schema, according to which society's economic 'base' (conditions of production, forces of production, relations of production) determines society's 'superstructure' (social consciousness; philosophical, ideological, legal, religious ideas; and corresponding political, legal, educational, religious institutions) (§ 7.1.1, n. 7).[8] Likewise, Guattari argues that machines are responsible for the production of structures (cf. § 2, n. 11).[9]

The analyses carried out in this book are also situated at the *intersection of machines and structures*. In my theorization of Christ groups as 'machines', I will privilege the role of machines over structures, as well as the virtual plane over the historically actual plane of existence, and semiotic exchanges over linguistic meanings. In short, this book will argue that the first Christ groups emerged historically through the structuration of machinic processes and that, once formed, the same Christ groups underwent structural transformations which were brought about by the same machinic processes.

2. Christ followers as machines

Individual Christ followers can also be theorized as the working parts, organs or machines of Christ groups. On the basis of this insight 1 Cor. 12.27 can be translated as follows: 'Now you are the body of Christ and individually parts/machines (μέλη) of it'. These working parts included apostle machines, prophet machines, teacher machines, miracle-worker machines, and an assortment of healing, helping, and guiding machines (1 Cor. 12.28, §§ 4.2.2, 8.2). On the basis of an analogy with the human body, Paul explains at length how these parts are interdependent, as *machines connected to other machines* in the same body of Christ:

> The (human) body is not composed of one machine (μέλος) but many. Now if the foot machine should say, 'Because I am not a hand machine, I do not belong to the body', it would not for that reason stop belonging to the body. And if

the ear machine should say, 'Because I am not an eye machine, I do not belong to the body', it would not for that reason stop belong of the body. If the whole body were an eye machine, where would hearing happen? If the whole body were an ear-machine, where would smelling happen? … If the whole were a single machine, where would the body be at all? In fact, however, there are many machines (μέλη), but one body (σῶμα). … Now you are the body of Christ and individually the machines (τα μέλη) of it. (1 Cor. 12.14-20, 27)

On the basis of this analogy with the human body, Paul asserts there are *no isolated or independent machines* in the body of Christ.[10] For instance, flows of bread and wine interconnected the Christ machines within the body of Christ (1 Cor. 11.20-26). This machinic dimension of Christ groups could also be highly problematic, as evidenced in the notorious case of the Christ-follower machine who coupled (κολληθήσεται) with a sex-worker machine (1 Cor. 6.15-20): in the moment that these two machines were connected by a flow, Paul declares that they were temporarily organized as 'one body' (ἓν σῶμα) and 'one flesh' (σάρκα μία). In other words, the man and sex worker temporarily became *one machine*. Why was this a problem? Paul argues that since this Christ follower was also one of the machines of the body of Christ, therefore through his coupling with the sex worker, she was connected *through him* to all the other machines of the body of Christ! In a state of outrage, he asks, 'Shall I take the machines (τα μέλη) of Christ and make them machines of a sex worker?' Never! You know that anyone that couples with a sex worker becomes *one body* with her, for the scripture says, 'The two will become *one flesh*' (1 Cor. 6.15a-16).

The specific case of the coupling of a Christ-follower machine with a sex-worker machine illustrates a general principle that is applicable to machines in general: the human body, as a machine, is connected to countless other machines and functions transversally with them through flows of intensities that obscure all bodily boundaries. We have abundant historical evidence that Christ machines were excessively social; they were constantly coupling with other machines and exchanging flows. For example, the Christ-follower machines in Corinth were *porously connected* to an expanded network of other machines besides sex-worker machines, including occupational-guild machines (1 Cor. 4.12; 1 Thess. 2.9; 2 Thess. 3.8; Acts 20.34), judicial-court machines (1 Cor. 6.1-8), sacrifice machines (1 Cor. 8.1–11.1), synagogue machines and kinship machines, to name but a few.

That which is true of individual Christ followers is equally true of Christ groups as a whole: every Christ group was a machine that coupled with other machines of widely ranging registers, intensities and magnitudes resulting in semiotic flows between groups, institutions and sociocultural processes. There is no privileged point of view from which the scholar of early Christianity can observe these countless machinic couplings and exchanges of flows. All we can do is marvel at this vast web of machines connected to machines, connected to more machines, the sum of which constituted the social production of the Graeco-Roman bureaucratic megamachine.

3. Christian texts as little non-signifying machines

Early Christian texts were also machines: a Gospel or Pauline letter is a *literary machine* that coupled with other literary machines and social machines and exchanged semiotic flows (§ 8.3). Needless to say, this machinic dimension of early Christian discourse is overlooked by traditional exegesis, which is based on a communication model. It entails a focused questioning of the document considered as *linguistic* containers of information. Through the practice of exegesis, it attempts to extract – to bring 'out' (ἐξ) – from a text this information and represent it in contemporary language.

However, every Christian text possessed a *semiotic* dimension in addition to its linguistic content and, through this semiotic dimension, it accomplished *strategic effects* such as the discipline and normalization of human bodies (2 Tim. 3.16-17, Heb. 4.12, § 8). Deleuze and Guattari argue that this strategic effect of discourse is coextensive with language itself: every statement (*énoncé*) is an 'order-word' (*mot d'ordre*) that has pragmatic effects the moment it is enunciated: 'The elementary unit of language – the statement – is the order-word. ... Language is made not to be believed but to be obeyed, and to compel obedience. ... Language is not life; it gives life orders' (TP 76). Hence, Deleuze speaks of the 'tyrannical, terrorizing, castrating character of the signifier' (Neg. 21).

When Jesus rebuked the wind and waves with an order-word – 'Quiet! Be still!' – the wind immediately 'died down and it was completely calm' (Mk 4.39). When he cursed a fig tree, 'May no fruit ever come from you again!', it 'withered at once' (Mt. 21.18-19).[11] Communication in the form of observations, questions, requests, warnings and promises also has strategic effects, which are tied to social obligation and obedience (TP 79).[12] Through early Christian literary machines (discourse), semiotic forces were injected into the bodies of Christ followers. All this is to say that discursive utterances entailed more than information: all early

Christian writings *functioned as literary machines* in relation to a tangled mass of other machines (bodies) of Christ followers.

By virtue of this semiotic dimension, early Christian texts are *not reducible to the information they communicate*. Such 'information' was always embedded in non-informational processes: 'Information is only the strict minimum necessity for the emission, transmission and observation of orders as commands' (TP 76). An early Christian text is not primarily a semiotic medium for the storage and retrieval of information. For all signifying content is generated by non-signifying processes (NP 26; Massumi 1992: 41–5). Fundamentally, every early Christian text is a non-informational and nondiscursive expression of force. For example, Paul's discourses on circumcision (περιτομή) and 'uncircumcision' (ἀκροβυστία) entailed more than information about Jews and Gentiles: 'circumcision' and 'uncircumcision', and the discourses in which these terms were embedded, functioned *machinically* in the determination of the coordinates of Jewish and Christian bodies, within a specific sociocultural network of power. Therefore, early Christian discourse conveyed something *more than* that which was signified by it, and this 'something more' was *performative force*, which constituted the virtual 'unsaid' of every text (§ 14.1.1).

For example, the Graeco-Roman 'Lives' of Plutarch, Philostratus, Suetonius and Tacitus always conveyed something *more than* that which was signified by language. These 'lives' *promoted the values of their heroes* (Burridge 2004: 117). In a similar fashion, the canonical Gospels, as Christianized adaptations of the Graeco-Roman 'Lives' genre, likewise had strategic effects of human bodies through the promotion of the life of Jesus Christ as a 'hero' of God. As Richard Burridge observes, 'the combination of stories, sayings, and speeches found in the Synoptic Gospels are very similar to the basic literary units used by βίοι' (2004: 198). In the concluding section of the Gospel of John, its author explicitly acknowledges this strategic purpose: 'these are written that you *may believe that* Jesus is the Messiah, the Son of God' (Jn 20.31). Even if we lacked this explicit admission of the author's strategic purpose, we could have discerned it from the prologue (Jn 1.1-18), and from every chapter thereafter, which repeatedly tells the reader that Jesus is from God, and that if you believe in him, *you must follow his example* (Jn 14.15, 23, 31, 15.9-11). Thus, the meaning of early Christian Gospels was not determined solely by their literary meanings because such texts functioned as machines in relation to their exteriorities. As I shall explain in Chapter 8, every Christian text was a 'little non-signifying machine' that coupled with a vast array of nondiscursive social machines, and thereby exercised strategic functions with respect to the bodies of Christ followers

(§ 8.3). A schizoanalysis of early Christian texts, considered as little machines, subordinates linguistics to semiotics, and connects linguistic information to its strategic purposes. Deleuze contrasts the traditional exegetical approach to reading a book with such a schizoanalytic approach:

> There are, you see, two ways of reading a book. You either see it as a box with something inside and start looking for what it signifies, and then if you're even more perverse or depraved you set off after signifiers. And you treat the next book like a box contained in the first or containing it. And you annotate and interpret and question, and write a book about a book and so on and on. Or there's the other [schizoanalytic] way: you see the book as a little non-signifying machine, and the only question is 'Does it work, and how does it work?' (Neg. 7–8)

Thus, schizoanalysis replaces traditional exegesis' attempts to recover the meaning (informational content) of a text with an analysis of how the *discursive* production of meaning functioned in relation to *nondiscursive* social machines of widely ranging registers, intensities and magnitudes (§ 8). What difference would it make to our understanding of the New Testament if scholars abandoned exegesis and took up a schizoanalytic approach instead? What difference would it make if we asked, with what machines did such and such a text (as a literary machine) couple and exchange intensities? With what other machines did literary machines function?

Conclusion

Everywhere one looks in the Graeco-Roman world, one machine couples with another and exchanges flows. This phenomenon should not shock us because machines are *excessively* passional: they are always reaching out to other machines, and coupling with them, with one machine producing a flow, and the other drawing the flow in. The Deleuzo-Guattarian concept of a 'machine' provides scholars with a new tool for the exploration of the intensive relations between Christ groups and other groups and institutions in the ancient Graeco-Roman world. 'Machines', or machinic processes, are an unnoticed dimension of early Christianity. The first Christ groups can be theorized as machines that coupled with countless other machines of widely ranging types and magnitudes. The theorization of Christ groups as machines highlights the primary role of asignifying semiotic flows in the genesis, change and transformation of Christ groups. Indeed, the history of early Christianity can be told as *a history of machines unceasingly coupling and uncoupling with other machines.*

Christ groups were not uniformly machinic in character. They also actualized many different types of structures. Hence, the analytic method of this book is focused *at the intersection of machines and structures*. But this book will also argue that the sociocultural and discursive structures actualized by early Christianity were *subordinate* to machinic processes, and a secondary effect of them. Even the *signifying* structures in early Christian discourse were dependent on *asignifying* machinic processes. In other words, machines, not structures, constitute the starting point for mapping the genesis, diversification and transformation of early Christianity.

Early Christian texts were also machines: each of the twenty-seven texts of the New Testament functioned as a 'little non-signifying machine' that exchanged semiotic flows with other machines. Early Christian texts composed semiotic flows as much as they embodied linguistic codes. These exchanges of semiotic flows were primarily *productive and non-informational*: informational content functioned as an extension of nondiscursive machinic processes. Through early Christian literary machines (discourse), semiotic forces were injected into the bodies of Christ followers. All this is to say that discursive utterances entailed more than information: all early Christian writings *functioned as literary machines* in relation to a tangled mass of other machines (bodies) of Christ followers.

By virtue of their machinic character, early Christian texts possessed a *surplus of exteriorities*: they coupled with a vast array of discursive and nondiscursive machines, through which they participated in a variety of strategic functions including the regulation, discipline and normalization of human bodies. If we grasp the machinic character of early Christian texts, we will never again ask the exegetical question, what do they mean?, nor will we look for anything to understand them, but instead, we will ask, with what other kinds of machines did they function?

One such 'strange' new concept is the 'machine'. What difference does the concept of the machine make to our understanding of the structurality of life? By drawing attention to the central role of *machinic processes* in the historical emergence and diversification of Christ groups and their texts, this book will challenge many of the general tendencies of the disciplines of Christian origins and theology, at least to the extent that these disciplines prioritize the structure of their beliefs or their transcendental origin. For what could a Christ *machine* possibly be, if it is reduced to the static set of beliefs or supraterrestrial metaphysical influx? The Christ groups of the first three centuries were not corrupted versions of a prior unity established by a metaphysical influx from a transcendental plane: they were machines composed within multiplicities, each of which was a purely differential field that did not reference a prior unity. If we truly grasp the machinic character of Christ groups and their texts, our two primary questions will be, with which machines did they couple? and, what types of flows did they exchange?

2

Desiring production and early Christianities

And when men had multiplied on the earth, in those days, beautiful and attractive daughters were born to them. And the Watchers, the sons of heaven, saw them and desired them. And they said to one another, 'Come, let us choose for ourselves wives from the daughters of men'. … These Watchers and all the others with them took for themselves wives from among girls, such as they chose. And they began to have sex with them.

1 En. 6.1-2, 7.1, 8.2

When the angels in heaven, the so-called 'sons of heaven', gazed on the beautiful daughters of mortal men, they were overwhelmed with *desire*. So overcome were they that they descended to earth and had sexual intercourse with them. This myth, recounted in Gen. 6.1-4, and subsequently expanded in *1 En.* 6.1–8.2, has much to teach us about human desire, as theorized by Jacques Lacan.[1]

However, Lacan argues that human desire has nothing to do with the lack (*manque*) or privation of an empirical object. For the object of desire is an *empty* position because the true 'object of desire' (*objet a*) is a phantasmatic object produced by the symbolic register, especially by language as Other (*Autre*) (Lacan 1977: 286–7) (§ 9). Lacanian theory, as applied to the angels in heaven who gazed on the daughters of mortal men, would argue that the daughters did not function as the empirical objects of the Watchers' desire but only as a kind of screen upon which they projected their phantasmatic objects of desire (*objet a*).

1. The unattainable object of desire

'*Objet a*' is Lacan's algebraic shorthand for the object-cause of desire, with '*a*' in '*objet a*' standing for '*l'autre*' (the other).[2] The object-cause of desire is unattainable because '*objet a*' is not a physical, empirical object – such as the aforementioned beautiful daughters – but an object that is constructed through fantasy. As Slavoj Žižek observes, it is 'through fantasy, we learn how to desire' (1992: 6). By virtue of its phantasmatic character, *objet a* is an embodiment of a lack. As Žižek examples, *objet a* is

> a strange object which is not only lacking, never fully here, always eluding the subject, but is in itself nothing but the embodiment of a lack. That is to say, since the subject is the self-appearing of nothing, its 'objective correlate' can only be a weird object whose nature is to be the embodiment of nothing, an 'impossible' object, an object the entire being of which is an embodiment of its own impossibility, the object called by Lacan *objet a*. (2016b: 81)

Returning to the case of Gen. 6:1-4, the object-cause (*objet a*) of desire was not the beautiful daughters of men. These daughters only *set the desire of the angels into motion*. Through their *gaze* on these daughters, the angels established the coordinates of the construction of their phantasmatic objects of desire. It is remarkable, indeed, that *1 Enoch* actually refers to these angels as the 'Watchers' (ἐγρήοροι), a designation that underscores their preoccupation with watching – with *gazing on* – the lovely daughters of men.³ Through the gaze, their desire was organized backwards on the basis of their prior fantasy. Indeed, the gaze always entails misrecognition: the Watchers mistook the daughters for their spectral objects of desire.⁴ In truth, their spectral object of desire was unattainable.

To be precise, the failure of the Watchers' desire resulted from a *double* misrecognition. The first misrecognition occurred when the Watchers' gazed at the girls and mistook their bodies for their own spectral objects of desire. A *second* misrecognition occurred when the angels, having had sexual intercourse with the girls, and experiencing their desire unsatisfied, blamed the girls for their failure of desire. But, in point of fact, the desire of the Watchers could never have been satisfied because it was founded on lack.⁵ Lacan argues that what is lacking is not only the object-cause (*objet a*) of desire but the very 'being' of the subject: for 'the lack is the lack of being (*manque à être*) properly' (1988: 223). There is no ontological subject of lack. Subjectivity mistakenly traces the human experience of lack back to a unified *subject* of this experience, but no such subject exists. *Through the idealization of lack, the 'subject' of lack is produced*. In other words, the subject of desire is *produced* through a positivization of an absence.

Despite their many criticisms of Lacanian theory in *Anti-Oedipus*, D&G do not, in fact, contest Lacan's theorization of human desire in terms of lack. They too argue that 'the reality of the object, insofar as it is produced by desire, is thus a *psychic reality*', that is, Lacan's '*objet a*' (TP 25, original emphasis). In point of fact, D&G draw tremendous inspiration from Lacan's psychoanalytic theory. And, as I shall explain in the forthcoming chapters, many of their key concepts including territorialization, deterritorialization, and stratification are dependent on Lacanian psychoanalytic theory.[6]

Even in the case of Lacanian 'desire-as-lack', there are significant connections. D&G do not contest that through the capture of human desire, a child becomes trapped in a 'mommy-daddy-me' universe (AO 286; Flieger 1999). However, rather than theorizing 'desire-as-lack' as an ontological and ahistorical human condition, as Lacan does, D&G interpret 'desire-as-lack' as the result of historical forms of social production. Human beings are not ontologically 'Oedipal'. They argue that human desire has always been co-opted and organized by the dominant form of social production in relation to the specific form of surplus value (*plus-value*) in any given historical period. In the case of the Roman Empire, this surplus value took the form of a 'despot-god' (emperor) who was affiliated to a 'despotic signifier' (chief god) (§ 7.2). Hence, in anthropomorphic formations, 'social production is purely and simply desiring production itself under determinate conditions' (AO 29). In essence, D&G argue that what Lacan puts forward as the ontological and ahistorical *truth* desire is not an inescapable truth of human existence but a sociohistorical condition that can be reversed by disrupting the processes of social production that overcoded desire in the first place (§§ 7, 10). By implication, there is an *exteriority* to human 'desire-as-lack' where *desire lacks nothing*. Apart from socially produced desire, such desire is free of human needs, demands and wants. Indeed, desire, outside the human economy of lack, is even free of desiring subjects (§§ 7, 9, 12).[7]

2. Cosmic desire and historical-libidinal materialism

In *Anti-Oedipus* D&G enunciate a primary principle of their entire philosophy: namely, that the entire cosmos is animated by desire. Everywhere one looks in the Graeco Roman world, one machine couples with another and exchanges *flows of desire*: '*There is only desire and the social, and nothing else*' (AO 29, original emphasis). Such desire is machinic: it is productive. Desire is always 'desiring production' (*production désirante*). Desire is a cosmic force that *produces* relations and connections between all kinds and magnitudes of machines (TP 229). Desire is neither an appetite for satisfaction, nor a feeling of privation: it is *the* power of inorganic Life to form new connections (Zourabichvili 2004: 84). Indeed, desire is the very power of cosmos to form new connections. Thus, as the pre-Socratic philosopher, Heraclitus, famously observed, 'Everything flows and nothing remains the same' (Πάντα χωρεῖ καὶ οὐδὲν μένει).[8] On the first page of *Anti-Oedipus*, D&G describe in graphic language the magnificent spectacle of cosmic desiring production. Desiring production is

> at work everywhere, functioning smoothly at times, at other times in fits and starts. It breathes, it heats, it eats. It shits and fucks. ... Everywhere it is machines – real ones, not figurative ones: machines driving other machines, machines being driven by other machines, with all the necessary couplings and connections. (AO 1)

This erotic spectacle of desiring production was apparent in every aspect of the Graeco-Roman world: all that was observable and unobservable in the ancient world – the cultural and natural, the human and animal, the knowable and unknowable, all that was pagan, gnostic, Jewish and Christian – was interconnected by flows of desire. Hence, if you were to ask D&G what connected the first Christ machines to everything else around them, they would surely have answered, without equivocation, in one word: desire! The first Christ machines emerged at the intersection of countless flows, and they developed and diversified over time through the regulation, organization and repression of these same flows of desire.

2.1. Historical-libidinal materialism

D&G's sources of inspiration for their conceptualization of desiring production were many including Nietzsche's global concept of life as a 'will-to-power' (*Wille zur Macht*), Marx and Engel's historical materialism and Freud's analysis of libidinal drives.[9] You might ask, why Nietzsche, Freud and Marx? Why these three? In the 1960s, French theory produced a kind of composite of Nietzsche, Freud and Marx, known by the acronym 'NFM'. This so-called 'NFM construct' first appeared in the writings of Michel Foucault, who grouped them together as three 'masters of suspicion' in his 1964 essay 'Nietzsche, Freud, Marx' (1990: 59–67). According to Foucault, Nietzsche's *Birth of Tragedy*, Marx's *Capital* and Freud's *Interpretation of Dreams* caused three 'inexhaustible wounds' in Western discourse, the last of which was Freud's discovery of the unconscious as the basis of consciousness (1990: 59–61).[10]

We can divide D&G's adaptation of this 'NFM construct' into three stages. First, building on Freud's analysis of libidinal drives, they argue that desire works by constructing multiple relations, and consequently that desire is always desiring *production*: it always entails flows between 'desiring machines' (*machine désirante*) (AO 26).¹¹ Next, D&G interpret Freud's psychoanalytic investigation of the libidinal drives and the unconscious on the basis of Marxist historical materialism, insisting on the libidinal nature of *groups*, and the *social* nature of the unconscious.¹² This theoretical move was anticipated in the publications of Guattari, who applied the analysis of individual subjectivity to *group* subjectivity, which, he argued, 'possesses its own laws', forms of transference, fantasy and resistance (Guattari 2015: 93–4, 130, § 10.2, n. 11). Finally, D&G subsume Freud's analysis of libidinal drives, and Marx's historical materialism, within Nietzsche's 'will-to-power' as a global concept. Deleuze defines Nietzsche's 'will-to-power' as 'the element from which derive both the quantitative difference of related forces and the quality that devolves into each force in this relation'. Hence, on this basis, Deleuze argues that Nietzsche's 'will to power' reveals 'the principle of the synthesis of forces' (NP 46).¹³ Nietzsche conceptualized natural existence as an interplay of the forces of the 'will-to-power', which are variously active or reactive, 'dominant or dominated depending on their difference in quantity' (NP 53). Through the interplay of forces, Nietzsche envisaged the emergence of new possibilities for living.

In *Anti-Oedipus* and *A Thousand Plateaus*, Nietzsche's active and reactive forces function as a general framework for both Marx's base–superstructure schema (§ 1, n. 7, § 7, n. 11) and Freud's unconscious–consciousness schema (§ 14.1.2, n. 4). John Protevi terms this 'NFM' amalgamation in Deleuzo-Guattarian philosophy, 'historical-libidinal materialism' (Protevi 2001: 4–5). From the perspective of historical-libidinal materialism, all ideas and ideologies, and all libidinal attachments, including the libidinal nature of groups and the social nature of the unconscious, are *instantiations of desiring production*.¹⁴ In historical terms, desiring production has always been repressed, co-opted and organized by the dominant forms of social production.

The concept of historical-libidinal materialism is directly applicable to the Roman Empire, in which, desire always possessed historical, libidinal and material coordinates: everything was bound together by the management, regulation, control and repression of *flows of desire*: flows of cargo (amphorae of wine, grain, fish products, olive oil, slaves, chests of money and texts) from port to port; flows of legionaries and auxiliaries between Roman provinces and colonies; flows of marriageable women between families and clans; flows of official communications, edicts, tax documents, private letters and literary, philosophical and religious texts, between cities; and flows of libidinal energy – of anger, greed, lust and love, jealousy and joy – between peoples. Indeed, all that was visible and invisible in the Roman Empire was connected by desiring production. The historical emergence of early Christianity was part of this erotic *'productions of productions'*, 'of actions and of passions; … productions of consumptions, of sensual pleasures, of anxieties, and of pain' (AO 4).

3. The plane of immanence

The sum of all processes of desiring production constitutes the 'plane of immanence' (*plan d'immanence*).[15] This plane, also termed the 'plane of univocity' (*plan d'univocité*), is univocal, one-storey universe that *does not distinguish between immanence and transcendence*.[16] In other words, there is no transcendental-outside to the plane of immanence, there is no infinity that supersedes its 'finity' (Barber 2009, 2010; Niemoczynsk 2013; Sherman 2009). Of course, systematic theology is premised on the principle that God and human beings inhabit *different* planes: such theologians imagine that God abides in a supraterrestrial, transcendental plane of eternal essences (with the heavenly Logos, angels and archangels, the Good, the True) whence he oversees the terrestrial plane of human existence.[17] But D&G's plane of immanence allows no such distinction between planes. Being free of the ontological dualism of Plato – free of the logic of eternal essences versus material copies (simulacra, phantasms) – the plane of immanence is populated solely by 'copies' that do not refer to essences beyond them. In other words, every 'copy' *embodies pure difference*.[18] As Arnaud Bouaniche explains,

> To establish a plane of immanence is to construct a space of thought in which there is no transcendent element, that is to say, no One, the True, the Good, God, Reason, Subject of superior categories that would dominate and organize everything, etc. In this disintegration of transcendence, there are only multiplicities: affects, forces, signs, tendencies, etc., so many events and processes, which populate a universe, henceforth completely decentered, a-subjective and anarchical, in which processes are evaluated according to their intensity and their, more or less expansive, creative ability. (2007: 55)

Even God belongs to the plane of immanence. God is a continuously differentiating life force that produces endless becomings, each of which manifests the creative, immanent force of Being.[19] However, Deleuze does not dispense with the concept of transcendence altogether. Rather, he accords transcendence a derivative status by *defining transcendence in terms of immanence*: transcendence is that part within Being that escapes human comprehension: it is the plane of immanence that 'must be thought and that which cannot be thought. It is the nonthought within thought … it is immanence' (WP 59). Thus, transcendence is a secondary phenomenon that is produced by, and within, the plane of immanence itself. In short, immanence and transcendence are 'functives (*fonctifs*) of the same function (*fonction*)'.[20] In short, 'transcendence' is another term for unpresentable, unthinkable, mysterious difference and repetition, of the 'eternal return' of difference through repetition. Hence, it is possible to think metaphysically, as Deleuze does, without grounding thought in the ontological dualism of Plato (or Neoplatonism), and in the dualism of essences versus copies.

If you are having difficulty imagining this plane of immanence, it is because this plane is unthinkable; it is a plane of pure difference that subsists on the exteriority of human thought and linguistic categories (TP 255). Nevertheless, this plane was always working in our constructed social world. In the Graeco-Roman world, it was everywhere, and people were immersed in it, but it remained imperceptible. On this plane all the desiring machines of the Graeco-Roman world mingled and conjugated; every point on this plane was an 'in-between', which was not a place but a set of connections that could be established between desiring machines (D 12). Through the historical period when the first Christ groups emerged, the plane of immanence was always working in the background, as the great orchestrator of pure difference and new becomings.

Owing to the hyperfusional character of the plane of immanence, the historical phenomena that we commonly term 'early Christianity' cannot be condensed into a unified narrative, nor can it be traced back genealogically to a single (historical or transcendental) point of origin. We must be sensitive to the parallel development of heterogeneous forms, ad hoc arrangements and, more generally, the ephemerality of their culturally specific manifestations of early Christianity. In short, we must always speak of early Christiani*ties*, not early Christianity.

This is not to imply that these early Christianities consisted *solely* of machinic processes. They did not. As I shall explain, the desiring production of Christ groups was continuously being coded ('territorialized', § 5), overcoded ('stratified', § 7) and organized into social assemblages (§ 8) and regimes of signs (§§ 10–12). Nonetheless, the plane of immanence was also operating in the background of these processes of structuration, decoding them and triggering fresh 'becomings' (§ 9). Hence, the desiring production of the plane of immanence served as the ultimate cause of the historical emergence of Christ groups, as well as the cause for their unceasing historical transformations and diversifications that followed.

Conclusion

Jacques Lacan theorized all human desire in terms of lack but not as the lack of an empirical object, for the object-cause of desire (*objet a*) is always an *empty position*. It is a phantasmatic object produced by the symbolic register. D&G do not contest Lacan's theorization of desire in terms of lack. But instead of treating 'desire-as-lack' as an ontological human condition, they theorize it as an *historical* effect of social production. They argue that, apart from social production, desire is always desiring *production*. Pure desire lacks nothing: it is a cosmic force that produces connections between all kinds and magnitudes of machines. All that was observable and unobservable in the Graeco-Roman world was interconnected by flows of desiring production, and Christ machines emerged at the intersection of these flows. Hence, *the history of the emergence and growth of early Christianity is a history of desiring production.*

The totality of all desiring production constitutes the plane of immanence, which is a one-storey universe that does not distinguish between immanence and transcendence. This plane was continuously working in the background of the Graeco-Roman world during the period in which the first Christ groups were emerging. Owing to the hyperfusional character of the plane of immanence and desiring production, the historical phenomena, which scholars commonly refer to as 'early Christianity', cannot be condensed into a unified narrative. The historical emergence of Christ groups entailed heterogeneous forms, ad hoc arrangements and an ephemerality of culturally specific manifestations.

The concepts of desiring production and the plane of immanence provide new tools for the analysis of the historical emergence and diversification of Christ groups (Christianities) in the first three centuries of the Common Era. The role of desiring production in the history of early Christianity raises new questions about the *types* of flows that connected Christ machines to other machines and, specifically, new questions concerning how these flows were variously coded (territorialized and stratified) by the social production of the Graeco-Roman megamachine, and decoded (deterritorialized and destratified) by the plane of immanence.

3

The rhizome: Multiplicities and the virtual dimension of Christ groups

Jesus said, 'To what should I compare the kingdom of God? It is like yeast that a woman took and mixed in with three measures of flour until all of it was leavened.'

Lk. 13.20-21

The Gerasene demoniac would tell you, if you dared to ask him, that we are never far from multiplicities. For he was overtaken by a multiplicity (*multiplicité*) of demons – five thousand of them – which made for a very crowded body! And his experience was not unique, for there were countless multiplicities in the Hellenistic world, and people both feared and loved them. Farmers feared them: a multiplicity of weeds could *take over* a field of wheat, and these weeds could not be uprooted from the field without 'uprooting with wheat along with them' (Mt. 13.25-30). But not all multiplicities are so fearful. Christ even compares the spread of the kingdom of God to a multiplicity of yeast that *takes over* a lump of dough (Lk. 13.20-21). He declared that the kingdom of God spreads like a culture of yeast that *infects* a lump of dough, when yeast, wheat and water are mixed (Lk. 13.20-21, § 3). Jesus' teachings were like a contagion of yeast that *infected* those who listened to them (§ 16.1).

Our lifeworld abounds in multiplicities: crabgrass, clouds and crowds, waves and storms, a pack of wolves, a swarm of rats, a colony of ants, a murmuration of birds and a legion of demons are all multiplicities (§ 14.2). Once you become aware of multiplicities, you see them everywhere! They are over your head and under your feet. Some are relatively stable and enduring, like a field of weeds, while others are fleeting, like a leaven of yeast dispersed throughout a lump of dough. From waves to wolves, people to plants, music to molecules, the world is comprised of nothing but multiplicities. Hence, we should not be surprised when D&G tell us that their philosophy is nothing but the theory of multiplicities.

> All we talk about are multiplicities, lines, strata and segmentarities, lines of flight and intensities, machinic assemblages and their various types, bodies without organs and their construction and selection, the plane of consistency, and in each case the units of measure. (TP 4)

What is a multiplicity? In its most basic sense, a multiplicity is a purely differential field – a bloc of becoming – *that does not reference a prior unity* (§ 14.2). A multiplicity is a multidimensional, dissymmetrical, differential field of intensities, flows, events and processes whose total number of dimensions is always in flux. D&G's philosophical concept of a multiplicity provides a tool for mapping the *interrelatedness* of social movements, groups and systems of thought.

To be sure, the concept of a multiplicity is easily misunderstood. For D&G employ the concept of the multiplicity in ways that are entirely different to such simplistic notions of essence or complication. A multiplicity lacks a stable essence: it is not an organic unity that becomes complicated over time; it entails nothing but temporary organizations and ever-changing dimensions. Your life, considered as a multiplicity, has 'the individuality of a day, a season, a year, a life (regardless of its duration) – a climate, a wind, a fog, a swarm, a pack (regardless of its regularity)' (TP 262).

The concept of a multiplicity is inextricably tied to the concepts of a 'machine' and desire (§§ 1–2). *For machines, desire and multiplicities are three aspects of the same bloc of becoming.* Machines are not discrete essences that couple to other machines through flows of desire: there are only machines that function in relation to other machines, which collectively compose the dimensions of a multiplicity, without centre or periphery, essence or unity. A multiplicity is defined by the number of its dimensions (machines) at any point in time. Since the number of dimensions is always changing, the multiplicity itself 'is continually transforming itself into a string of other multiplicities' (TP 249).

This concept of a multiplicity provides a tool for theorizing the complex interrelationality of Christ machines to other machines. While Christ machines, synagogue machines, temple machines and so forth *did not reference a prior unity*, 'the' Graeco-Roman world, they did belong to the same multiplicities. Christ groups, being machines, were likewise composed within multiplicities through flows of desire. The relation of Christ machines (and other machines) to the multiplicity they composed took the form of a 'disjunctive synthesis', in other words, in terms of a balance between a *disjunction* of machines (a disorganization of machines) and their propensity towards *synthesis* (an organization of machines) into a single multiplicity (§ 4.2.2). Owing to the unceasing nature of this process of disorganizing and organizing, of disjunction and synthesis, the distinction between a multiplicity as a disjunctive body and as a synthesis was in a state of constant negotiation. The disjunctive synthesis of a multiplicity is irreducible. Thus, to analyse Christ groups in terms of multiplicities requires that we refuse everything that presents itself in the form of a simplistic alternative of the one versus the multiple, one multiplicity versus a profusion of machines.

If early Christ groups can be said to possess one essential truth, it was the truth of the one and the multiple, which is to say, the *truth of disjunctive synthesis*. To discover this truth, we must search for the cycles of organization and disorganization of intensive connections between Christ machines and other machines within multiplicities. Therefore, Christ groups must be analysed at the level of a multiplicity (bloc of becoming), in a constant state of *disjunctive synthesis*, and not at the level of an individual Christ machine (e.g. the 'Corinthian church', the 'Philippian church', the 'Thessalonian church'). Christ machines should always be analysed in relation to the multiplicities in which they were composed.

1. On the danger of ignoring multiplicities: The lesson of the Wolf-Man

In the second plateau of *A Thousand Plateaus*, entitled '1914: One or Several Wolves', D&G discuss multiplicities in relation to one of Sigmund Freud's most famous patients, known by the pseudonym the 'Wolf-Man'. One night, while this patient slept in bed, he dreamt that he saw a pack of wolves – a *multiplicity* of wolves – sitting in the tree outside his bedroom window. As D&G observe, what could be more expected that a *multiple* of wolves, for all wolves come in packs (§ 16): 'What would a lone wolf be? … The wolf is not fundamentally a characteristic or a certain number of characteristics; it is a "wolf machine", "a wolfing"' (TP 3, 239). Despite the predictable nature of this *pack* of wolves, Freud considered this pack *a problem* to be solved. For he expected a single wolf, a potent symbol, that could be traced back to a single referent, the Wolf-Man's father, whom the Wolf-Man had accidentally spied having sexual intercourse with his mother, 'from behind', like a wolf. In Freud's view, the *father* was the root cause, the origin, of his patient's psychiatric illness. On the basis that it all leads 'back to daddy', Freud traced this multiplicity of wolves back to a lone wolf, with a *single, essential meaning* (TP 35).[1]

D&G argue that Freud consistently reverts to such essential meanings: 'the father, the penis, the vagina, Castration with a capital C' (TP 27). They term this tendency 'Oedipal mystification' and sarcastically ask, 'Who is ignorant of the fact that wolves travel in packs? Only Freud. Every child knows it' (TP 8). The case of the Wolf-Man serves as a reminder to us of the danger of ignoring multiplicities. Freud's predilection for tracing a pack of wolves back to a single wolf caused him to overlook the *movements of the pack, of a multiplicity*. The case of the Wolf-Man reminds us that a pack of wolves is simultaneously one *and* the multiple, a synthesis and disjunction, a multiplicity *and* a pack of machines.

Like Freud, who considered a pack of wolves a problem to be solved, systematic theologians consider the diversity of early 'Christianity' as a problem requiring a solution: somehow, we must find a way to trace this ancient pack of Christ groups – Adoptionists, Macionites, gnostics and 'proto-orthodox' – back to a lone wolf, Jesus Christ, and assign this wolf a single, unchanging meaning, the son of the *Father*! 'Yes, of course there are Oedipal statements everywhere', even in theology (TP 36), especially in systematic theology! Even theologians are under the spell of Oedipal mystification.

But D&G remind us that an ancient pack of Christ groups is *not a problem to be solved*: for a multiplicity and machines *are co-extensive with each other, a disjunctive synthesis*. Therefore, Christ machines, in all their historical diversity, are not the visible remnants of a lost origin. Their teachings are not corrupted versions of a lost, essential truth. Indeed, such concepts are sterile and unproductive. Christ groups, being machines, were composed within various multiplicities, purely differential fields of disjunction and synthesis that did not reference a prior unity.

2. Virtual Christianity

Deleuze brings into play another distinction, and in a rather surprising way: the distinction between the virtual and the actual. Deleuze declares not only that his philosophy is nothing but 'the theory of multiplicities' but also that every multiplicity is 'composed of actual and *virtual* elements' (D 148, emphasis added). Indeed, *the* primary characteristic of a multiplicity is its virtuality. My previous discussions of machines (§ 1) and desiring production (§ 2) may have imparted the impression that Deleuzo-Guattarian philosophy is a materialist philosophy, the impression that D&G are only interested in what is materially actual. But this is not the case: the primary focus of D&G's philosophy is neither matter, nor the actual, but that which is *beyond* matter and the actual, but *not beyond the real* (Boundas 1996; Lévy 2007; Pearson 2002).

D&G theorize *the virtual as fully real*. Indeed, theirs is a philosophy that privileges the virtual over the actual, just as it privileges machinic processes over static structures (§ 1), and 'becoming' over 'being' (§ 15). The historically actual, including historically actual Christ groups, emerged from a restructuring of *virtual* relations. As I shall explain below, events on the virtual plane of a multiplicity are continuously being actualized, materialized, manifested, indeed 'incarnated', on the historical plane of organization.

Deleuze's starting point for this theorization of the virtual plane of a multiplicity was provided by a passage in Marcel Proust's *Le Temps retrouvé* (*Time Regained*), the last volume of his *À la recherche du temps perdu*. In this passage the narrator describes virtual states of resonance in relation to memory. He speaks of a 'veritable moment' of the past which is reborn in the present when a sensation such as a noise, scent or sense of touch 'is mirrored at one and the same time' in the past and present allowing one to apprehend the pure 'essence of things' – an eternal instant that never passes – that is 'liberated from the contingencies of time', which is neither past nor present but 'a fragment of time in the pure state' (Proust 1981: III, 905, 924–5).

> But let a noise, or a scent, once heard or once smelt, be heard or smelt again in the present and at the same time in the past, real without being actual, ideal without being abstract (*réels sans être actuels, idéaux sans être abstrait*), and immediately the permanent and habitually concealed essence of things is liberated and our true self ... is awakened and reanimated as it receives the celestial nourishment that is brought to it. A minute freed from the order of time has re-created in us, to feel it, the man freed from the order of time. (Proust 1981: III, 905–6)

On the basis of Proust's distinction between the real and the actual – that which is 'real without being actual' – Deleuze developed the truly remarkable metaphysical concept: the *non-actualized real*. In *Difference and Repetition* he argued that what Proust specifically says about the virtual in relation to memory is uniformly true of the virtual in general: that 'the virtual is opposed not to the real (*réel*), but to the actual (*actuel*). The virtual is fully real (*pleine réalité*) in so far as it is virtual, despite not necessarily being actualized'.[2] What kind of metaphysics does this non-virtual 'real' imply?

At the outset, two points must be made. First, Deleuze's concept of the virtual as 'fully real', and his reference to the 'essence of pure things', in no way implies a return to the ontological dualism of Plato, with its separation of existence and essence (§ 3.3).³ Deleuze is not a Platonist. As previously discussed, Deleuzian philosophy makes no distinction between immanence and transcendence, existence and essence, or the singular and the universal. The virtual and actual are asymmetrical aspects of the *same* processual plane of immanence, which is a univocal plane, without any assignable limit between them (§ 2.3). What is more, the threshold between virtuality and actuality is always fluctuating, uncertain and in constant negotiation (Droit and de Tonnac 2002). The difference between the virtual and actual entails only the rates of the emission and absorption of singularities: the virtual consists of singularities that are in continuous motion, whereas the actual entails a 'kind of coagulation of the virtual', a temporary organization of it, in which the rates of motion have been slowed to zero (DR 208).⁴ On the virtual plane, the emission of singularities occurs in a period of time that is shorter than the 'shortest continuous period imaginable'. As Deleuze explains,

> It is this very brevity that keeps them subject to a principle of uncertainty or indetermination. The virtual, encircling the actual, perpetually renew themselves by emitting yet others, with which they are in turn surrounded and which go on in turn to react upon the actual. (D 148)

Second, the fact that Deleuze is not a Platonist in no way implies that he is a materialist. As noted above, the primary focus of Deleuze's ontology is not matter but that which is *beyond* matter – but *not beyond the real* – namely, the *virtual as fully real*. The virtual plane conditions the actual plane, such that changes on the virtual plane give rise to changes on the actual (historical) plane of organization. Every actualized material thing – including human beings, groups and larger collectives – possesses a virtual dimension. Hence, actualized things without this virtual dimension do not exist.

> Purely actual objects do not exist. Every actual surrounds itself with a cloud of virtual images. This cloud is composed of a series of more or less extensive coexisting circuits, along which the virtual images are distributed, and around which they run. (D 148)

By extension, in the case of the Graeco-Roman world, *purely actual Christ groups did not exist*. Needless to say, scholars of Christian origins are unaccustomed to theorizing the virtual (non-actualized) dimension of Christ groups in the Graeco-Roman world, for they deal only in historically actual entities. But if purely actual Christ groups *did not exist*, do such scholars have a theoretical blind spot? If the historical 'real' of Christ groups was an actualization, or crystallization, of their virtual ('spiritual') dimension, what is lost by ignoring their virtuality? Surely, such an investigation is compromised from the outset. What is gained by overlooking the most fundamental aspect of early Christianity?

For all that was observable and unobservable on the historical plane of the Graeco-Roman world, including Christ groups in all their diversity, involved the actualization of the virtual dimension of life. These diverse actualizations *never exhausted all the possibilities afforded to Christ groups by their virtual dimension*: a portion of the virtual always escaped full actualization in any moment of time. This unactualized virtual was not lost, but simply went into hibernation; it can be termed a 'non-potentiated option, that falls asleep, in an ontological slumber' (Braidotti 2019: 470).

Why does this non-potentiated option of Christ groups matter? It is by virtue of these non-potentiated options that unexpected 'events' occurred in the Graeco-Roman world, such as the transformation of Jewish and gnostic groups into a diversity of Christ groups. All this is to argue that the primary index of Christ groups, considered as machines, composed as dimensions within multiplicities, was their virtual dimension, and their non-potentiated options, which predisposed them towards change and transformation.

Conclusion

The Graeco-Roman world abounded in multiplicities. A multiplicity is a complex structure that does not reference a prior unity: it is simultaneously one *and* the multiple, a synthesis and disjunction of machines interconnected by desiring production. The concept of a multiplicity provides a tool for theorizing the complex inter-relationality of Christ machines to other machines within the Graeco-Roman world. All Christ groups, as machines, were composed within multiplicities, by virtue of which they were perpetually in flux, adjusting themselves to the shifting presence of other machines within the same multiplicity. These Christ groups possessed no essence, but only *dimensions*, lines of intensity and lines of segmentarity. For this reason, continuous transformation was the pure state of Christ machines.

Owing to the continuous process of disjunctive synthesis, the dividing line between a multiplicity as a disjunctive body of many machines, and a multiplicity as a synthesis of machines, is in a state of constant flux. Therefore, to analyse Christ machines in terms of multiplicities requires that we refuse everything that presents itself in the form of a simplistic alternative of the one and a multiple: Christ groups should be mapped simultaneously in terms of the multiplicities (blocs of becoming) in which they were composed *and* as individual machines in relation to other machines.

Christ groups of the first three centuries were not corrupted versions of a prior unity. They were machines composed within multiplicities, each of which was a purely differential field *that did not reference a prior unity*. Thus, the truth of early 'Christianity' is a *truth of disjunctive synthesis*, which is the truth of the one *and* the multiple. Therefore, the task of the theologian and scholar of early Christianity alike is not to recover Christianity's prior (transcendental or historical) unity but instead to investigate the rhizomatic relations, in all their specificity, that connected Christ machines to other machines within a vast range of magnitudes of multiplicities. For the rhizome helps us theorize the 'in-betweenness' between bodies.

The most notable feature of all these multiplicities was their *virtuality*. For every multiplicity had a virtual ('spiritual') dimension that was fully *real*, even when it was not actualized. Purely *actual* Christ groups did not exist: all Christ groups were composed within multiplicities, as *a manifestation of actual and virtual elements*. In these Christ groups, there was always a portion of the virtual that *escaped* actualization in any given moment; many virtual possibilities were non-potentiated. Owing to this surplus of non-potentiated, virtual options, *the proliferation of differences between Christ groups in the first three centuries was inexorable*. Consequently, it is not possible to speak of 'early Christianity' as a unified movement but only of an ever-changing diversity of early Christiani*ties*. The remainder of this book constitutes a sustained exploration of the virtuality of Christ groups within various types of multiplicities. Each chapter is devoted to an exploration of how the virtual dimension of Christ groups played a role in their historical emergence, transformation and the diversification over the first three centuries of the Common Era.

4

The autoproduction of a body of Christ without organs

Now you are the body of Christ and individually organs of it.

1 Cor. 12.27

In *Anti-Oedipus*, D&G playfully pose the Freudian question, 'Which comes first, … the father and mother, or the child?' (AO 273). We might riddle them back and ask, which came first, Christ or Christ groups? If you were to pose this riddle to a traditional theologian, you will quickly discover that he gives primacy to a preexistent, transcendental Christ, the Son of the *Father*. And so, once again, we're back to Oedipal mystification! Everything leads back to daddy!

But since the plane of immanence is a univocal plane of existence, which does not distinguish between the immanence and transcendence, we cannot accept a theological solution based on transcendental influxes and the ontological dualism of Plato (§ 2.3). Hence, I insist on posing my riddle again: which came first, Christ or Christ groups? Of course, the correct answer is neither: both were formed immanently through *autoproduction* without reference to a transcendental plane. In this chapter I will argue that the formation of every Christ group can be mapped immanently as the formation of a 'body *of Christ* without organs', which is to say, as a self-organizing system, without reference to a transcendental plane.

The concept of a Christ group as the 'body of Christ' is very ancient and can be traced back to the writings of the apostle Paul, who, in 1 Cor. 12.27, declares to Corinthians that they are collectively the 'body of Christ' (σῶμα Χριστοῦ) and individually 'organs' (τα μέλη) of it (1 Cor. 12.27).[1] Similarly, in Rom. 12.4-5, Paul proclaims that 'we, who are many, are one body in Christ (ἐν σῶμα ἐν Χριστῷ) and individually "organs"/"machines" (τα μέλη) in relation to each another' (Rom. 12.4-5). In this chapter I will argue that this Pauline 'body of Christ' can be mapped as a Deleuzian 'body without organs' (*corps sans organes*), which is a type of multiplicity formed immanently through autoproduction.

This application of the concept of a 'body without organs' to Pauline theology is defensible, even on Deleuzo-Guattarian grounds, for in *Anti-Oedipus* D&G explicitly assert that 'Christ's body is engineered on all sides and in all fashions, pulled in all directions, playing the role of a full body without organs' (AO 369). This chapter will argue that the Deleuzo-Guattarian 'body without organs' is ideally suited to mapping the 'body of Christ' because a 'body without organs' is not restricted to individuals but is equally applicable to supra-individual bodies such as groups, associations, cities and even the Roman Empire as a whole. Indeed, when considered in terms of autoproduction, there is no substantive difference between these different manifestations of a 'body without organs'. Every Christ group, such as those that formed in Corinth, Rome, Philippi and Thessaloniki, can each be theorized as a 'body *of Christ* without organs'.

1. What is a body without organs?

The term 'body without organs' (*corps sans organes*), a strange and unfamiliar concept to be sure, was coined by the avant-garde, surrealist poet and playwright Antonin Artaud in his radio play entitled, '*Pour en finir avec le jugement de dieu*' ('To Have Done with the Judgment of God'). The sixth plateaus of *A Thousand Plateaus*, entitled 'November 28, 1947: How Do You Make Yourself a Body without Organs?', actually contains an oblique reference to Artaud's play, which was recorded for broadcast on 28 November 1947. In this play, Artaud transcribes the words, stammers and cries of a suffering, tortured body that refuses any transcendent intervention. Artaud refers to the human body as 'this ill-assembled heap of organs', a 'badly constructed' body, which has been produced by the 'judgment of God':

> Man is sick because he is badly constructed. We must make up our minds to strip him bare in order to scrape off that microorganism (*animalcule*) that itches him mortally, god, and with god his organs. When you will have made him a *body without organs*, then you will have … restored him to his true freedom. (Artaud 1976: 571, emphasis added)

Artaud's play enacts a kind of *ontological revolt* by which the body is freed from the judgment of God by becoming a body *without* organs. D&G converted Artaud's poetic figure of a free 'body without organs' into a philosophical concept with several interrelated meanings. In *Anti-Oedipus* they devote several chapters to theorizing a 'full' body without organs as a disorganized body of pure intensity. A human body, considered as such a body without organs, is an intense body with 'disorganized' – or de-organized – body, one which is profoundly connected to the plane of immanence. This 'body without organs' actually *does* possess organs, but its organs have yet to be '*organ*-ized' by 'the judgement of God' according to the specific requirements of social production (§ 7.1); organs are attached to the body 'as so many points of disjunction, between which an entire network of new syntheses is now woven, marking the surface off into co-ordinates, like a grid' (AO 12). This high-intensity 'body without organs' is a loose cluster of machines/organs, held together only by desiring production. In this chapter, my question is, could individual Christ groups have begun as such an intense, loosely bound cluster of organs?

2. The three passive syntheses of autoproduction

Over the course of time the relatively homogeneous 'body without organs' undergoes internal differentiation in the form of three passive syntheses, beginning with a connective synthesis, followed by disjunctive synthesis and subsequently by a conjunctive synthesis.[2]

2.1. Connective synthesis

Through connective synthesis, a 'body without organs' is formed, as a loosely bound cluster of organs outside of any determined state. This undifferentiated body lacks clearly defined boundaries. Its organs (machines) connect to, and disconnect from, other organs (machines) – both internal and external – through intensive flows, unhindered by internal repression or external regulation. *This 'body without organs' constitutes a field of molecular forces, which interact with other bodies, as a field of forces. These forces differentiate themselves immanently at a molecular level without reference to molar bodies or transcendental causes.* In point of fact, this 'body without organs' *does* possess organs: as noted above, the modifier, 'without organs', simply indicates that the connections between the body's organs/machines and the organs/machines on the *exterior* of the body are just as significant as the connections between the organs *within* the body.

The Corinthian 'body *of Christ* without organs' may have begun as such undifferentiated body. During a connective synthesis, it would have had no fixed boundaries between insiders (organs/machines) and outsiders (other machines including individuals, groups and institutions).[3] Indeed, there is ample evidence to suggest that Christ follower-machines had connections to synagogue machines, pagan-cult machines and trade-guild machines, not to mention the famous case of the connection with a sex-worker machine (§ 1). This undifferentiated 'body of Christ without organs' would even have facilitated ad hoc couplings with these exterior machines, rather than repressing such connections based on religious beliefs or laws. Owing to the absence of fixed boundaries, this 'body of Christ without organs' would have had the status of 'being there' and 'not being there' at the same time.

2.2. Disjunctive synthesis and the creation of surplus value

The term 'disjunctive synthesis' may seem self-contradictory, for the term 'synthesis' implies an organization of parts into a whole, whereas disjunction implies the opposite, a disorganization of parts.[4] As previously discussed, this apparent contradiction captures the very essence of a multiplicity, which is simultaneously one and many (§ 3).

During the second passive synthesis, the 'body without organs' develops distinct boundaries on the basis of the accumulation of recordings of past 'good' and 'bad' flows.[5] Habitual flows are collectively recorded in the raw substance of the 'body without organs' as a kind of 'memory'. For example, in the case of an infant (as a body without organs), flows of breast milk into its mouth-machine and flows of faeces out of its anus-machine are experienced as 'good' flows. The infant's body develops a kind of memory of such good flows and accords the organs (machines) responsible for such 'good' flows with higher value, while the organs that produce 'bad' flows are simultaneously repressed. Through this mechanism, the chains of interconnected organs/machines formed during the (first) connective synthesis are reinforced and are incorporated into interconnected networks of organs (AO 75–83). Despite the fact that this so-called 'memory' of past flows consists of nothing but an accumulation of past recordings of flows, this memory nonetheless gives rise to *the illusion of a surplus value (plus-value), which exists apart from, and in addition to, the organs themselves* (AO 13, 326–7, TP 153). This surplus value is produced by the organs and is dependent on them. Nonetheless, over time it accrues the value of the *quasi-cause* of the entire body, that is, the status of a 'body *without* (need of) organs'.

Depending on the type of body in question, this surplus value may be construed as a body's inner self, soul or life source, or, in the case of a group, the group's founder (§ 7.2.2). In the case of the Roman Empire or kingdom, this surplus value takes the form of an emperor, king or pharaoh (§ 7). In the case of the Corinthian 'body *of Christ* without organs', the selection of good flows (flows benefaction, eucharistic bread and wine, apostles) and the repression of bad flows (flows of sacrificial meat, flows with sex workers) not only resulted in the formation of a body (Christ group) with distinct boundaries, but it simultaneously created a *surplus value* – a Christ without organs – which is to say, a body of Christ *without need* of organs (members). This surplus value 'Christ' seemed to have an autonomous existence apart from the organs that created it. Over time, this surplus value came to be regarded as the very life source of the group.

As noted above, the body that is formed through disjunctive synthesis entails *both* a disorganization and synthesis of parts. It is both a disjunctive 'body without need of organs' (in terms of the self-sufficiency of the surplus value) *and* a synthesized 'body without discrete organs' (in the sense that all organs are organic extensions of one surplus value). Owing to its polarized character, *a conflict may arise between this surplus value and its organs*. At its so-called 'paranoiac' pole, the surplus value repels its organs, while at its so-called 'miraculating' or 'attractive' pole it attracts them.[6] At its *paranoiac pole*, this body can truly be said to be 'without organs' because it has repudiated them as foreign objects; this paranoiac surplus value seems to shout, 'You're out to get me! I don't need you! I hate you!' Its organs are attached to it as mere *points of disjunction* (AO 18). But this disjunction comes at a price, for by virtue of being disconnected from the intensity of its organs, the paranoiac body without organs loses all its intensity (TP 150).

We have evidence of the paranoiac pole of the Corinthian 'body of Christ without organs' in 1 Cor. 11.3, where Paul states, 'Christ is the head of every man, and the man is the head of a woman, and God is the head of Christ' (§ 7.3.1). This paranoiac Christ repelled his organs (members) as persecuting objects. In this disjunctive form, Christ, as surplus value, seems to have an existence apart from the individuated organs/machines of the body. The result is a low-intensity, paranoiac body, one in which Christ seemed to have an autonomous existence apart from the flows from the organs that created him. All relations and flows in this Christ group converged upon this paranoiac Christ, who was vertically filiated to God as 'the head of Christ' (§ 11.2).

This paranoiac 'body without organs' is also evident in many voluntary religious associations of the Hellenistic period. As a case in point, let us consider the association of silver miners in Laurion (Attica) dedicated to the lunar god, Mēn Tyrannos (king Mēn).[7] According to its sacred laws, this god 'chose' the founder of this association, Xanthos, while he lay sleeping and charged him with the authority to establish a cultic association, to engrave his sacred laws on a stele and to oversee all aspects of the association. By virtue of being chosen by Mēn Tyrannos and vested with authority, Xanthos functioned as a surplus value of the body (§§ 4.2.2.3, 7.2.2). In short, Xanthos functioned as the *surplus value* of a 'body of Mēn without (need of) organs' through the repetition of flows produced by cycles of sacrifices, purifications, oaths and punishments, which collectively repressed and organized the desiring production of individual members (organs). He determined how all the organs (members) functioned in relation to each other within the association. Thus, at its dominant paranoiac pole, obedience to the group's sacred laws was equated with obedience to Xanthos.

While this association dedicated to Mēn Tyrannos, like all Hellenistic associations, had its own distinctive characteristics, these characteristics should not distract us from their similarity with respect to the process of autoproduction: the beginning of every Hellenistic cult can be traced back to a 'body without organs' formed through connective synthesis, which subsequently developed a surplus value, in the form of its founder, through a disjunctive synthesis. The relation of this founder to the members of the cult was 'paranoiac' in character.[8] Regardless of identity of this founder, his effect on the group remained the same: the oscillation of the body without organs between paranoiac and attractive poles, between being one multiplicity and multiple machines (§ 3).

In contrast to the paranoiac body without organs, at its *attractive pole* the same surplus value is one with its organs, so that these organs seem to emanate from it as its originating cause: this 'miraculating' surplus value seems to say, 'You need me! You can't survive without me!' *This* body can also be said to be 'without organs', but in a different sense: the individuality of each organ has been repressed through its amalgamation within a unified body without organs. All that remains of the organs are the functions that they contribute to the surplus value. By virtue of being connected to the intensity of its organs, this surplus value increases in its own intensity.

In the case of the Corinthian 'body of Christ without organs', there is evidence of the attractive pole of this group in 1 Cor. 12.14-28, which states that individual 'organs' – the apostles, prophets, teachers, workers of miracles, healers, helpers – were all *integrated* parts of the *same* body of Christ and together *performed essential functions* for the benefit of the body as a whole. As previously discussed, Paul discusses this 'attractive' 'body of Christ without organs' on the basis of an analogy with the human body: all these 'organs' are deemed to be extensions of Christ (as surplus value) and every organ transmitted intensities to the body as whole (§§ 1.2, 8.2).

2.3. Conjunctive synthesis

In the third passive synthesis, termed a *conjunctive* synthesis, the first and second passive syntheses are conflated. When aleatory forces arising from the ebb and flow of chance occurrences, calamities and social crises inject intensities into the 'body without organs' of the second passive synthesis, this body is sometimes propelled into a zone of sensitivity in which a bifurcation, or 'schiz', can cause it to reorganize on a molecular level.[9] Thereafter, it distributes its flows and intensities in ways that do not conform to the connective synthesis of the first passive synthesis or the disjunctive synthesis of the second passive syntheses (TP 44). This intense body is capable of distributing its own flows and intensities in ways that do not conform to previous patterns. Such a conjunctive synthesis is always possible because the body without organs is always vacillating between the forces that 'stratify it and the plane that sets it free' (TP 161). Each of the three passive syntheses entails its down dangers, including the conjunctive synthesis: as D&G warn, 'If you free' the body without organs 'with too violent an action', it can become 'plunged into a black hole, or even dragged toward catastrophe' (TP 161). Evidence of the Corinthian 'body of Christ without organs' having *successfully* undergone a conjunctive synthesis would take the form of this group dismantling some of its internal structures of self-repression and experimenting in new ways of living together, and living in relation to society at large.

Conclusion

The Deleuzo-Guattarian 'body without organs' is a multiplicity formed through autoproduction, without reference to a transcendental plane. The concept of a 'body without organs' is ideally suited to mapping a Christ group, considered as a Pauline 'body of Christ', because a body without organs is not restricted to individuals but is equally relevant to supra-individual bodies such as groups, voluntary associations and cities. The historical emergence of a Christ group, considered as a 'body *of Christ* without organs', can be theorized in immanent terms as the product of three passive syntheses. In the first passive synthesis, termed a 'connective synthesis', an undifferentiated 'body of Christ without organs' was formed, consisting of a loosely bound set of organs (members/machines). In this connective synthesis, the resulting 'body without organs' is constituted as a network of forces, differentiated from other networks of forces, without reference to molar bodies. These organs function in a fragmented or non-unified body, for this 'body of Christ without organs' was little more than a loose cluster of machines, lacking fixed boundaries between insiders (organs/machines) and outsiders (other machines including individuals, groups, institutions).

In the second passive synthesis, termed a 'disjunctive synthesis', habitual flows of intensities between organs were recorded in the raw matter of the body as a kind of residual 'memory', through which a *surplus value* Christ emerged. Over time this surplus value accrued the status of that quasi-cause for the Christ group as a whole. The 'body of Christ without organs' produced by disjunctive synthesis was a bipolar body: being simultaneously a disorganization *and* synthesis of parts, it oscillated between paranoiac and attractive forms, between disjunction and synthesis. At its paranoiac pole, this was a low-intensity body that seemed to be truly *without organs*, or at least seemed to exist *without need* of organs (1 Cor. 11:3). But, at its attractive pole, this same body functioned as a high-intensity, *unified* body of Christ '*without* (discrete) organs', in the sense that all organs were organic extensions of the same surplus value (1 Cor. 12.27). Thus, the 'body of Christ without organs' of the second passive synthesis existed in a state of *constant contradiction*, with members (organs) being alternately repressed and organized by its paranoiac and attractive forms of its surplus value respectively. But this 'body of Christ' of disjunctive synthesis was not necessarily the end of the story. Even the body without organs produced by disjunctive synthesis preserved limited degrees of freedom and creativity. For this reason, the scholar must always be alert for signs of a conjunctive synthesis, through which the primordial desiring production of a body of Christ without organs was renewed.

5

Territorializations and deterritorializations: On becoming outlandish

A man planted a vineyard, put a fence around it, dug a pit for the wine press and built a watchtower; then he leased it to some tenants and went to another country. When the season came, he sent a slave to the tenants to collect from them his share of the produce of the vineyard.

Mk 12.1-2

A Deleuzo-Guattarian 'milieu' is a disorganized multiplicity. Imagine yourself standing on the seaside, with your hair blown by the wind, skin warmed by the sun and your toes planted into the sand: this is how it feels to be enclosed in a milieu.[1] The vast range of forces that inhabit this seaside milieu flow unimpeded between the sea, beach, sky and your porous body, without clearly demarcated boundaries: for '*there is no line separating earth and sky*' and one's body (TP 382). For the processual ecology of the life resists territorialization by ceaselessly giving birth to flows that deterritorialize human bodies. In his *Recherche*, Proust refers to the 'play of unstable forces' at the seaside, in which the sea becomes land and the land sea, which together 'recalls that perpetual re-creation of the primordial elements of nature' (Proust 1981: I, 967). This image of the 'play of unstable forces' vividly captures the concept of a Deleuzo-Guattarian 'milieu'.

'Territorialization' is a process of coding or colonizing a milieu (multiplicity).[2] The result of such a coding is a 'territory', which is space that has been sliced out of a milieu. In contrast to milieus, territories are artificial. Territorializations 'bite into' the milieus of the earth and *code* them as 'reality' (TP 323). Milieus are coded ('arborific') spaces with fixed points and outer boundaries. The 'parable of the tenants' records some of the required steps for territorializing a milieu and converting it into a territory (vineyard) (Mk 12.1-2).[3] First, purchase a plot of natural land (a milieu) whose soil is appropriate for viticulture. Second, *code* this land through the construction of a wall to mark its *outer boundaries*. Third, erect a stone watchtower as a *fixed point*, with guards to keep watch over the boundaries of the vineyard. Fourth, plant the plot of land with rows of vines. And finally, lease the vineyard to tenants.[4] When all these steps have been completed, a territory has been successfully created through the colonization of a milieu.

Every dimension of human life is territorialized. Familialist territories (daddy–mommy–me territories) provide us with a sense of stability, security and familiarity. We also inhabit dwellings, physical spaces that have been territorialized into rooms, each individually coded for specific functions. Our territorialized dwellings are arranged along roads, which territorialize dwellings into neighbourhoods, and neighbourhoods into cities. The people who inhabit these dwellings, neighbourhoods and cities work in fields, factories and firms, which have been territorialized for specific purposes.

To various degrees, our beliefs, values, morals, religions and most private convictions are all coded through the territorialization as well. Our existential territories are formed through the demarcation of a boundary between an (imaginary) 'subject' in relation to an Other, and between the 'organism' in relation to the State apparatus (§§ 7, 10). For the 'subject' and 'organism' are both 'molar' formations produced by *capture* of our molecular bodies by external forces (§ 6.1.1). The resulting existential territories constitute a kind of habitat where the unconscious feels 'at home' (*chez moi*) in its habits, routines, rituals and libidinal investments. From this existential perspective, it is remarkable that, however impoverished these existential territories may be, we generally habituate to them, and prefer them to our lost milieus. To one degree or another, we learn how to be 'at home' in our existential territories, to be 'at home' in our repressive states, religious delusions and overwrought obsessions. These existential territories are at least familiar to us. We are therefore less fearful of them than the unterritorialized milieus that lay beyond them.

The above comments on the territorialization of our lives in no way implies that territorialization is a distinctly *human* process. Far from it. For territorialization is fundamentally an *animalistic* process. Indeed, the possession of a territory constitutes a primary condition for every animal (§ 16.1). As Jesus himself observed, foxes and birds each have their distinct territories: 'Foxes have dens and birds of the air have nests' (Mt. 8.20, Lk. 9.58). Not only foxes and birds but every animal – including *human* animals – possesses their own territories. A territory is a circumscribed space where an animal emits its characteristic signs to other animals; a 'bird sings to mark its territory' (TP 312), while other animals mark their territories with oily scents and fetid scats, paw tracks, howls and screeches, warning other animals who would enter their territories to beware.

1. The territories of the Graeco-Roman world

The Graeco-Roman world constituted countless interlocking and overlapping territories. Civic territories and kinship territories were coded in terms of genealogy, gender and social status. In public spaces, territories constructed for offering sacrifices to gods were separated from territories designated for the burial of the dead. Likewise, temples, amphitheatres, gymnasia, military barracks, synagogues, trade guilds and households each possessed their own types of territory. The first Christ groups emerged within specific territories, which overlapped with the territory of households, cities and Empire. For example, the territory of the Christ group in Corinth overlapped with the territory of the private homes of wealthy members, such as Stephanas (1 Cor. 1.16) and Gaius, who hosted the whole church (ὅλης ἐκκλησία, Rom. 16.23) in his house.

As the case of Christ groups illustrates, the concept of territory cannot be equated with a mere physical space. First and foremost, a territory is a *set of structural relations that control, regulate and repress flows of desiring production*. Returning to the parable of the tenants, at the level of viticulture, the territory of the vineyard was held together by *relations and flows* between vines, soil, rain, water wheels, labourers and the sun. At an economic level, the same vineyard was held together by *flows of money*; for vineyards were labour intensive and tenants normally hired permanent labourers, not only during the harvest season but also for such day-to-day tasks as pruning, grafting vine shoots, weeding, hoeing, burning brush and guarding the estate (Kloppenborg 2006: 279–96). As the parable of the vineyard attests, the viability of a vineyard was also predicated on the *flow of payments* to the landlord in the form of crop-shares, which may have amounted to about one-half to two-thirds of the crop (Kloppenborg 2006: 306). We can also speak of non-monetary relations such as the relation between the landlord and tenants, which, in the parable, was mediated by a *flow* of messengers – slaves and the landlord's son – who facilitated flows of communication.

A convenient starting point for the elucidation of the territories of the Graeco-Roman world is provided by three sets of structural relations: first, the relations entailed in the two primary social institutions of the Greco-Roman world, political groupings and kinship structures; second, the relations entailed in the practice of benefaction, which functioned as the primary pattern of social interaction; and third, the relations entailed in the allocation of honour and shame, which jointly functioned as the primary values of ancient society (McLean 2015: 49–51). These three sets of structural relations criss-crossed other sets of relations, including the relations between genders, social classes (free, freemen, slaves), ethnicities (Gentiles, Jews, foreigners), all of which required regulation with respect to cultural codes for communal eating, marriage, sexual intercourse, child bearing and dealing with predictable impure flows (menstruation, miscarriage, contact with a corpse).

The territory of a Christ group likewise entailed more than a physical space: each Christ group was composed by a complex interrelation of physical places of assembly and iterative practices ('visibilities'), such as meetings on the first day of the week for prayer, singing, the 'Lord's Supper' and agape meals (§ 8.3).[5] Of course, these territories were also coded in terms of gender, ethnicity and social status (despite Paul's own aspiration to do away with such coding (Gal. 3.28)), which overlapped with the coding of human bodies in society at large. As a case in point, there is good evidence that the internal territorialization of the members of the Corinthian Christ group reflected the territorialization of Corinthian society at large, with the majority of members from the lower classes mixing with a few influential members from the upper classes.[6]

2. Deterritorialization and reterritorialization

The primary focus of Deleuzo-Guattarian philosophy is not processes of territorialization but how territories are destabilized, and how territories participate in event-oriented processes of change and discontinuity, rupture, break, mutation and transformation. In short, D&G are primarily interested in machinic processes of *deterritorialization* by machines, not in processes of territorialization[7]: 'Machines are always singular keys that open or close an assemblage, a territory' (TP 334). To be 'deterritorialized' is to become abstracted from a set of structural relations and the flows they regulate.

In literal terms, deterritorialization entails 'the movement by which one leaves the territory', 'it is the operation of the line of flight' (TP 508). In other words, deterritorialization entails becoming 'outlandish'.[8] The Gospel of

Matthew narrates how three sorcerers left their territory in the East and became 'outlandish' in pursuit of a deterritorialized star (Mt. 2.1, 11). The paradigmatic example of deterritorialization is the story of the Exodus of the Hebrew people, who were deterritorialized from the territory of Egypt and adopted an 'outlandish' life of nomadic wandering for forty years (Exod. 13.17-21). In point of fact, deterritorialization is often followed by *reterritorialization*, whereby one leaves a territory by entering a different territory. As the book of Joshua attests, even the Hebrew nomads who wandered the desert were eventually *reterritorialized* in the southern Levant, the 'Land of Canaan'. Thus, territorialization, deterritorialization and reterritorialization are all *relative and interrelated processes*. Every aspect of Christ groups of the Graeco-Roman world was subject to territorialization, deterritorialization and reterritorialization, and all four canonical Gospels are likewise criss-crossed by mixtures of territorialization, deterritorialization and reterritorialization (§ 6).

D&G's best known example of deterritorialization and reterritorialization is the interaction of an orchid with a wasp. Prior to their interaction, the bodies of the orchid and wasp constitute separate machines. But when the wasp alights on the orchid, and these two machines enter a mutual zone of proximity, they temporarily couple and form an orchid-machine 'assemblage', whereby a flow of pollen passes between them (TP 10–11, § 8.1-2). Through this transfer of pollen, both machines participate in asymmetrical processes of 'becoming'. From the perspective of the wasp, this transfer of pollen enacts a kind of territorialization of the orchid's bodily power onto its own body. However, from the perspective of the orchid, the body of the orchid is *reterritorialized* through the same transfer of pollen: for the wasp becomes an extension of the territory of the orchid. The body of the wasp becomes a 'liberated piece of the orchid's reproductive system' (TP 293). This territorialization and reterritorialization is a *non-reversible* event in which the identities of both bodies are permanently changed: through intra-action, the body of the orchid is reterritorialized while the body of the wasp is simultaneously deterritorialized.

3. A typology of deterritorialization

D&G developed a typology of deterritorialization that includes four virtual, semiotic functions: namely, a generative, transformational, diagrammatic and machinic function. Owing to the virtual dimension of the plane of immanence, all four of these functions are virtually available within every territory.

3.1. The generative function

Generative (*génératif*) deterritorialization (or 'relative *negative* territorialization') entails processes in which a territory changes in order to *maintain and reproduce* itself. As I shall discuss in Chapter 12, the 'signifying despotic regime of signs' undergoes generative deterritorialization through the removal of all that threatens structure.

3.2. The transformational function

In the case of transformational deterritorialization (also termed 'relative *positive* territorialization'), deterritorialization is followed by reterritorialization into another territory. For example, the aforementioned example of the asymmetrical interaction of an orchid and wasp entails a transformational deterritorialization: when the wasp deterritorializes – flies away – carrying away the orchid's pollen, it is subsequently *reterritorialized* by another orchid. Transformational deterritorialization is by far the most common form of deterritorialization in early Christianity. The Synoptic Gospels record the lives of many reterritorialized persons. In the story of Mary and Martha, Mary is *deterritorialized* from the gendered territory of the kitchen to be *reterritorialized* in the territory of men, where she sits at the feet of Jesus (Lk. 10.38-42, § 6.1.2). Jesus *deterritorialized* from his Lower Galilean territory of kith and kin and *reterritorialized* in the Gentile territories of Tyre (Mk 7.24-29) and in the Decapolis (Mk 5.1-20). Jesus also deterritorialized and reterritorialized kinship groups as the primary locus of societal relations: he rhetorically asked the crowd gathered around him, 'Who are my mother and brothers?', and then answered his own question, 'whoever does the will of God is my brother, sister and mother' (Mk 3:31-35) (§ 17.1). With this pronouncement, he *reterritorialized* the very concept of a 'familialist' territory within an expanded social field: he teaches that those who would follow him must take up a life of deterritorialization, the risk of leaving the safety of one's familial territory and entering foreign territories where the Gentile 'other' emits strange signs. Reterritorialization is also attested in primitive Christian theology: the Christ hymn, passed on by Paul in his Letter to the Philippians, describes Christ as *deterritorializing* from on high (where he was 'on an equality God') and *reterritorializing* on earth in 'the form of a slave' (Phil. 2.5-11). Almost anything can function as a territory that replaces an abandoned territory. As I will explain in Chapter 13, in the case of the post-signifying 'passional subjective regime of signs', the prophet is reterritorialized by his point of subjectification, namely, the Hebrew God (§ 13.1.2).

3.3. The diagrammatic function: Becoming outlandish

In the case of diagrammatic deterritorialization (or 'absolute reterritorialization'), deterritorialization is *not* followed by reterritorialization in another territory. Instead, deterritorialization is followed by a 'line of flight' (*ligne de fuite*) that undermines the formation of a new territory (§ 6.1.4). Lines of flight introduce dynamism, complexity and chance into territorialized formations. In literal terms, to deterritorialize *diagrammatically* is to leave one's land and remain *without a territory*, in other words, to become 'outlandish'. The Hebrew people deterritorialized from Egypt to adopt an 'outlandish' life of nomadic wandering for forty years; they followed an *outlandish* God, who dwelt in a tent (*mishkān*), a portable shrine, which they carried through the desert (Exod. 25–31, 35–40). Likewise, the patriarch Abraham became *outlandish* when he set out from the city of Ur Kaśdim on a line of flight, 'not knowing where he was to go' (Heb. 11.8). In contrast, the Greek hero, Odysseus (Ulysses), deterritorialized from Troy only to reterritorialize to familiarity of his homeland, Ithaca, after the war, and Abraham's reterritorialization was absolute (Chalier 2002: 106): he had no thematizable destination. When God commanded Abraham to 'go forth' (Gen. 12.1), there was no possibility of reterritorialization but only the uncertainty of an unknown future.

The Gospels portray Jesus as an outlandish figure: he was an itinerate preacher, who wandered from village to village, connecting with people on the margins of territories, men with leprosy, a woman with chronic bleeding (§ 15.1), demoniacs (§ 15.2), gluttons, drunkards and tax collectors (Mt. 11.19). At the end of his life, his body was deterritorialized diagrammatically on a cross (§ 17.1). What could be more outlandish than the Son of God nailed up high on a cross? Christ's resurrection constitutes another diagrammatic deterritorialization: heavenly messengers at the empty tomb declared to the woman who came to prepare Christ's body for burial, 'Why do you look for the living in the territory of dead? He is not here'. *He has deterritorialized diagrammatically!* (Lk. 24.5). He has become *outlandish*! He has now entered into 'becoming-imperceptible' (§ 17).

3.4. The machinic function

Machinic deterritorialization entails the interplay of knowledge and power through the coordination of an 'abstract machine' or power/knowledge 'diagram' (§ 8.4). Through the coordinating function of this 'abstract machine', the production of Christian discourse was '*machinically*' *deterritorialized* by coordinating the production of discourse with a group's iterative practices.

Through such machinic deterritorialization, 'literary machines' were 'materialized' within power/knowledge diagrams of power, while diagrams of power were 'semiotized' within regimes of signs (§§ 8, 11).

Mixtures of these four deterritorializing functions introduce elements of contingency, transformation, discontinuity and rupture into discursive and nondiscursive territories. As I shall discuss in the following chapters, this fourfold typology provides a set of tools for mapping the territorializations, deterritorializations and reterritorializations of Christ groups and their discourses.

Conclusion

The Graeco-Roman world was heavily territorialized, and the Christ groups that emerged within it *were territorialized by it*. Therefore, the interpretation of the Christ groups requires an understanding of the principles of territorialization. The territory of any Christ group entailed more than a physical space. First and foremost, a 'territory' is a set of *structural relations* that controlled, regulated and represses flows of desiring production. Every aspect of early Christianities was territorialized. The territories of Christ groups entailed a complex set of structural relations between their places of assembly, iterative practices, discourses and the individual bodies of Christ followers. Such territories were coded in terms of gender, ethnicity, wealth, legal and social status – codings that overlapped with the territorialization of human bodies in Graeco-Roman society at large.

However, the primary focus of Deleuzo-Guattarian philosophy is not territorialization but processes of *deterritorialization*. To be deterritorialized is to become abstracted from a set of structural relations and the flows they regulate. Deterritorialization is often followed by *reterritorialization*, whereby one exits one territory by entering another. Hence, territorialization, deterritorialization and reterritorialization are relative and interdependent processes. Every aspect of territorialized 'Christianity' was subject to territorialization, deterritorialization and reterritorialization.

D&G's typology of deterritorialization entails four semiotic (asignifying) functions: namely, a generative, transformational, diagrammatic and machinic function. Each of these functions was virtually available within *every* territory of the Graeco-Roman world, including Christ groups and their discourses. This fourfold typology of deterritorialization provides a set of conceptual tools for mapping the transformation of Christ groups in the first four centuries of the Common Era. Mixtures of these deterritorializing functions introduced elements of contingency, transformation and rupture into territories of Christ groups. Owing to the operation of these functions, Christ groups were not static structures with essential characteristics but were highly changeable formations continuously at risk of change, alteration and transformation.

6

Deterritorialization in the Gospels: A typology of lines

As Jesus walked by the Sea of Galilee, he saw two brothers, Simon, ... and Andrew his brother, casting a net into the sea, for they were fishermen. And he said to them, 'Follow me, and I will make you fish for people'. Immediately they left their nets and followed him.

Mt. 4.18-20

The lives of Simon and Andrew were characterized by rigid territoriality. Afterall, they were fishermen who worked, day in and day out, by the Sea of Galilee, performing the same repetitive tasks: loading nets into the boat, casting nets into the sea, gathering the nets back into the boat and separating out the fish, and, finally, mending the torn nets. All this is to say, the lives of Simon and Andrew were *territorialized*. And they would have remained territorialized, if Jesus hadn't appeared out of nowhere and shouted out to them, 'Come, follow me' (Mt. 4.19). In effect, Jesus bid them to *deterritorialize diagrammatically* – to leave their territory – to follow an 'outlandish' teacher and healer (Mt. 8.20). In the very moment they dropped their nets, they too became outlandish. At this point in the narrative, the reader is left to wonder, what happened? How could the rigid territoriality of the lives of two ordinary fishermen be so dramatically deterritorialized? And, we, the readers, ask what is going to happen next?

1. Lines in literature

One of the most remarkable features of Deleuzian philosophy is its intense encounters with literature (§§ 14–15). Deleuzo-Guattarian philosophy is premised on *an intrinsic connection* between philosophy, literature, music, art and life. Literature is an expression of life, and writing literature sometimes involves thinking through the philosophical questions which life poses. Indeed, in Deleuze's view, literature and philosophy share a common problematic, which is that of temporality and transformation. In their analysis of literature in *A Thousand Plateaus*, D&G reformulate the problem of territorialization and deterritorialization in terms of 'lines of writing' (*lignes d'écriture*). They argue that literature in general is defined less by its genres, themes, characters and motifs than it is by the 'lines of writing' that run through it (TP 4).

Their analysis of these 'lines of writing' draws inspiration from F. Scott Fitzgerald's novella, 'The Crack-up', in which Fitzgerald distinguishes three types of lines that compose a human life: 'breaks', 'cracks' and 'ruptures'.[1] These lines can be arranged on a spectrum that ranges from 'break' lines to lines of 'rupture'. Break lines are forces, sometimes taking the form of 'sudden blows', that territorialize life into rigid segments (Fitzgerald 1945: 69).[2] In contrast, 'rupture' lines explode break lines, causing significant deterritorializations in life; they may take the form of outbursts of emotion, transgressions of law, contraventions of social norms and conflicts that take life in a new direction. Located somewhere at the medial point of this spectrum of break lines and rupture lines are 'crack' lines, or 'crack-ups'. These crack lines generally go undetected when life is going well but take life in unexpected directions. Based on Fitzgerald's three types of lines, D&G devise a threefold typology of lines consisting of lines of 'rigid segmentarity', lines of 'supple segmentarity' and 'lines of flight'. In life and literature these three types of lines are intertwined. What is more, the literary characters in the Gospels are positioned at the convergence of these three types of lines. They are 'caught where the machine and structure meet' (PT 322).

1.1. Molarity and molecularity

The three types of lines can be arranged on a spectrum from 'molar' (*molaire*) to 'molecular'. The difference between molar and molecular lines primarily entails modes of bodily composition. As Brian Massumi explains, whereas 'in a molecular population (mass) there are only local connections' between bodies, 'molarity implies the creation or prior existence of a well-defined boundary enabling the population of particles to be grasped as a whole' (1992: 55). A molecular body constitutes a field of molecular forces, which interacts with other such bodies, as fields of forces (§ 14). Molecular forces differentiate themselves immanently, without reference to molar bodies. In contrast, molar formations repress difference through the organization of molecular forces by the application of exterior forces. They incorporate molecular bodies into systems of redundancy. As I shall explain in later chapters, molar bodies code (territorialized) and overcode (stratified) molecular bodies through acts of forceful capture into arborescent structures (§§ 4, 7, 10).

Lines of rigid segmentarity are *molar* in nature; these are rigid, clear-cut lines that divide life into predetermined segments. In contrast, lines of supple segmentarity are *somewhat* molecular in character; they serve to destabilize lines of rigid segmentarity. Lines of supple segmentarity can precipitate various types of deterritorialization over the course of time. Lines of flight are 'abstract' in the sense that they do not distinguish between molar subjects and objects, signifieds and signifiers, and content and expression (§ 8.3). These lines introduce contingency and transformation into the rigid segmentation of human lives. These three types of lines are similar in the sense that they are all *semiotic*, which is to say, they are asignifying in character. Despite the fact that they are embedded in the signifying structures of literature, *they are devoid of linguistic meaning*. Indeed, these three types of lines do not signify anything: they are 'nothing but forces' (C2 139).

1.2. Lines of rigid segmentarity

The lives of literary characters are 'segmented' by lines of rigid segmentarity (*lignes de segmentarité dure*) in every direction. These lines often intrude on life from the outside as acts of territorialization and stratification (§ 7.2). They impose forms and structures onto life that imprison bodily intensities, locking them into rigid blocs of redundancy. These rigid lines are relatively easy to identify. In Gal. 3.28, Paul specifies, with remarkable precision, the rigid lines that segmented human bodies in the Graeco-Roman world: Jewish versus Greek, freeman versus slave and male versus female (Gal. 3.28). Such rigid lines determined how people were territorialized in the ancient world. Deleuze speaks of signs of 'universal alteration' (*l'universelle alteration*) such as signs of aging, illness and the anticipation of death (PS^f 179, PS 132). Indeed, such rigid lines are inescapable: in life and literature, human lives are segmented in terms of forms of conjugality, types of employment, growing old, growing poor, periods of illness and the encroachments of death. When viewed from the perspective of these rigid lines, everything in life 'seems calculable and foreseen, the beginning and end of a segment, the passage from one segment to another' (TP 195). From the perspective of these rigid lines, living seems to entail little more than moving from one rigid segment to another, moving ever closer to the grave.

Rigid lines of segmentarity comprise the dominant type of line in Graeco-Roman biography, including the canonical Gospels, where literary characters are generally *molar* in nature (§ 1.3). For example, the Gospel of Mark describes the segmentation of the life of a woman who suffered from a chronic haemorrhage of blood for twelve years (Mk 5.25-26) (§ 15.2). Similarly, the Gospel of John describes the rigid segmentation of the life of a man who was unable to walk for thirty-eight years (Jn 5.5). When viewed from the perspective of these rigid segments of illness, the lives of this woman and man seemed to be predetermined and unalterable. Likewise, the life of the rich man, who approached Jesus and asked him how to be saved, was also characterized by lines of rigid segmentarity, which imposed a repressive determinism on his life (Lk. 18.18-23). In the case of the so-called 'Canaanite' woman in the Gospel of Matthew, who implored Jesus to heal her daughter, the rigid lines were based on gender and ethnicity (Mt. 15.21-28). These lines prevented Jesus from responding to her – 'He did not answer her at all' (Mt. 15.23) – until these lines were subsequently disrupted by supple lines.

Rigid segments also take the form of domesticated and stereotyped cultural behaviours. Through the endless cycles of performing stereotyped behaviours, human bodies are organized into territorialized systems. In ancient Israel, social customs relating to benefaction and hospitality (Gen. 18.4), marriages and dowry (Gen. 24.57-58, 29), mourning (2 Sam. 1.11-12), dealing with ritual impurity, oaths, sacrifices and punishment (Acts 7.54-60, 14.19-20, 16.20-24, Jn 8.1-11) all depended on lines of rigid segmentarity. In the case of Simon and Andrew, their lives were segmented by the trade of fishing. The rich man's inability to give away his wealth is a 'sign' (to the reader) of lines of rigid segmentarity that determined his life (§ 14.2); his life was segmented by the management of wealth. Hence, when Jesus invited him to reterritorialize absolutely – to give away his wealth and follow him – what happened? Nothing. The lines of rigid segmentarity prevailed, 'for he was very rich' (Lk. 18.23). His life remained rigidly segmented.

1.3. Lines of supple segmentarity

Human lives, characterized by rigid lines of segmentarity, are predictable in the short term but *unpredictable* in the long term because human lives are also cross-cut by lines of supple segmentarity (*lignes de segmentation souple*) that dismantle them. These quasi-molecular lines can be compared to the 'micro-cracks' – termed 'crazing' – in an old piece of glazed pottery. They appear unexpectantly and enlarge over time, resulting in severe breakage (TP 198–201).

Lines of supple segmentarity are always present in life, even when they are not expressed as deterritorializing events. These lines arise when *molecular* forces, ambiguous intensities, cause very fine micro-cracks (*micro-fêlures*). Over the course of time, aleatory events can amplify these micro-cracks and precipitate transformational deterritorializations, by which one exits a territory by entering a new territory (§ 5.3). Such lines introduce elements of chance and contingency, which may, at some time in the future, precipitate slippages of functions, mutations and unexpected redistributions of desire (TP 44). Lines of supple segmentarity gradually dismantle molar formations at their most vulnerable points. In comparison with lines of flight, they provide 'a kind of compromise' between rigid lines and lines of flight (TP 205). They are 'supple', or flexible, in the sense that they tolerate regressions, and they elude the rigid segmentations of gender, class, race, status and so forth.

For example, the unexpected death of a loved one may result in changes in the virtual/actual interface that trigger new behaviours. Likewise, a tryst may function as an aleatory event that triggers a new block of conjugality as in the case of David and Bathsheba (2 Sam. 11). All this is to say that micro-cracks can become magnified over time and precipitate life changes at a later point in time. As a result of the presence of supple lines, inadvertent, chance events can result in serious unexpected consequences: 'You don't deviate from the majority unless there is a little detail that starts to swell and carries you off' (TP 292). To identify the lines of supple segmentarity, one must be attentive to unexpected behaviours, contraventions of social etiquette, unexpected signs of emotion, unanticipated social conflict, microaggressions, transgressive acts and so forth.

The story of Mary and Martha is cross-cut by rigid and supple lines (Lk. 10.38-42). These women lived in a house segmented by lines of rigid segmentarity, with well-determined territories for men and women. But these territories were also cross-cut by ambiguous, supple lines of segmentarity that afforded Mary the chance to deterritorialize from the territory of women, where Martha was 'distracted by many tasks' (Lk. 10.40), to the territory of men, where she sat at Jesus' feet and was praised for having 'chosen the better part'. The lines of supple segmentarity in Mary's life bestowed on her body the capacity to reterritorialization by transgressing gender-based rules of behaviour; she thereby escaped the rigid segmentarity of social convention (Lk. 10.38-42). In contrast, Martha's life remained territorialized by lines of rigid segmentarity (Lk. 10.42).

The reader is left to wonder why the micro-cracks that introduced contingency in Mary's life did not have the same effect on Martha.

Lines of supple segmentarity are also present in conversations. Nathalie Sarraute discusses how, within the clear-cut segmentarity of conversations, one can always detect, what she terms, 'subconversations', which act like 'supple' lines (1963: 92). These lines deterritorialize rigidly segmented conversations by introducing intense micro-movements. To identify these 'subconversations' in literature we must look for instabilities, variabilities and uncertainties in conversations. These instabilities may take the form of gestures, emotions, allusions and even silences. For example, in the case of the so-called 'Canaanite' woman's conversation with Jesus, we can discern two types of segmentations: rigid lines of gender and ethnicity which, at the outset, prevented a conversation between a Gentile woman and a Jewish man, and less localizable supple lines, which criss-crossed the disciples and other witnesses (Mt. 15.21-28). At the outset of the story, Jesus' behaviour is determined by rigid lines of segmentarity with respect to gender and ethnicity. These lines prevented Jesus from answering her. Hence, *silence* follows her first entreaty; Jesus refuses to converse with her. But when she persists, 'shouting' and begging, we, the readers, can detect the workings of lines of supple segmentarity which gradually opened an unexpected *micropolitics of conversation*. Jesus seems to sense that ignoring her in silence is no longer an option, despite the rigid lines of segmentarity. However, he still refuses to engage directly with her in conversation: instead, he commands his disciples to 'send her away, for she keeps shouting after us' (Mt. 15.23). Jesus' irritation and command is yet another sign of the operation of supple lines. But when these supple lines become magnified crack lines, Jesus feels compelled, albeit begrudgingly, to enter into conversation with her directly: 'I was sent only to the lost sheep of the house of Israel' (Mt. 15.24). What happens next? More micro-cracks become evident, in the form of gestures and emotion: the woman *kneels* at Jesus' feet and she *passionately* beseeches him, 'Lord, help me!' (Mt. 15.25). The conversation continues! Jesus, whose behaviour is still determined by rigid lines, replies to her, 'It is not fair to take the children's food and throw it to the dogs' (Mt. 15.26). At this point, it seems that the conversation has come to an end; the rigid lines seem to have prevailed. But, with supple lines, it is always difficult to know if something new is about to happen. And something unexpected *does* happen: the woman retorts, 'Sir, even the dogs under the table eat the children's crumbs' (Mk 7.28). At this point, the semiotic force of her retort amplifies the micro-cracks. By accepting Jesus' insult – 'yes, indeed, we are dogs!' – the remaining lines of rigid segmentarity *disintegrate*. Both Jesus and the woman are swept along by these enlarged crack lines towards an unexpected outcome. Jesus praises her: 'Woman, great is your faith! Let it be done for you as you wish' (Mt. 15.28). Her daughter experiences a line of flight; she escaped the demon that had possessed her body. We, as readers, are left to ask, how could this have happened? How could a subconversation of molecular intensities destabilize Jesus' conversation with this Gentile woman? This story illustrates how supple lines, which cannot be identified at the moment they occur, can precipitate unexpected deterritorializations in conversations over time.

1.4. Lines of flight

Lines of flight (*lignes de fuite*) introduce major ruptures into lives which have been segmented by rigid and supple lines. Lines of flight are signs of molecular events that involve asignifying particles (§ 1, n. 5). Even though territories are *molar* formations, an escape from such formations is always possible because *all bodies, including human bodies, are located at the interface of machinic processes and structural formations*, at the interface of the virtual and the actual (§ 1). The desiring production of the plane of immanence undermines all rigid segmentation by ceaselessly giving birth to intensities, whose aggregate value may later subvert molar boundaries we may experience as chance events (§ 2). Consequently, molar individuals, in both life and literature, are always encompassed by what D&G term a variable 'quanta of relative deterritorialization' (TP 88), which is to say, a virtual exposure to deterritorialization.

Lines of flight are perhaps the easiest to identify because they tend to be accompanied by dramatic signs: in effect, one's new way of living announces to the world, 'Goodbye, I'm leaving and I won't look back' (TP 327). When Simon and Andrew dropped their nets and abandoned their trade to follow Christ, they followed a line of flight. In Phil. 3.4-7 Paul catalogues the molar boundaries that had once segmented *his* subjectivity: he was a Hebrew, not a Gentile, a Pharisee, not a mere Jew, he was blameless under the Torah, not a transgressor; but clearly his encounter with the resurrected Christ – however one understands this event – introduced fresh intensities into his body that triggered a line of flight from this molar (territorialized) Jewish subjectivity to a life oriented around 'proclaiming the faith he once tried to destroy' (Gal. 1.15, 23).

D&G's threefold typology of lines does not imply that rigid lines of segmentarity are always harmful and dangerous, and that lines of flight are always beneficial and desirable. There are dangers that are associated with both types of line, even in literature. While it is true that lines of rigid segmentarity are often harmful because they overcode, or 'stratify' (§ 7), desiring production and impose a repressive determinism onto life, it is equally true that many of the conditions for a happy life depend, at least to some extent, on the continuation of rigid lines. Lines of flight entail even greater risk. While it is also true that lines of supple segmentation can open up possible ways of escape from an overdetermined life, a positive outcome is never assured owing to the ambiguity and unpredictability of lines of flight. Lines of flight may also plunge a life into chaos; they can lead to black holes, to an abyss, from which one can never recuperate (TP 506). Thus, all three types of lines – rigid, supple and lines of flight – can be beneficial or harmful, depending on the circumstances. Hence, when analysing the three types of lines in the Gospel narratives, the interpreter must always ask, at what personal risk and at what price do the characters follow these lines? What might have happened if the characters had responded differently? For instance, what kind of life would the rich man have had, if he did give away all his wealth and joined a movement, led by an 'outlandish' teacher and healer named Jesus? What might have been the consequences if both Mary *and* Martha had reterritorialized together at the feet of Jesus in an act of solidarity? Would Jesus, whose behaviour was also determined by rigid lines of segmentarity, have welcomed both Mary and Martha? Thus, one must always consider the characteristic risks and dangers of each line, as well as their potential life-giving benefits.

Conclusion

Every aspect of early Christianity was subject to territorialization and deterritorialization including its narratives. In their analysis of narrative, D&G theorize the functions of territorialization and deterritorialization on the basis of a threefold typology of lines: lines of rigid segmentarity, lines of supple segmentarity and lines of flight. These lines can be arranged on a spectrum ranging from *molar* lines of rigid segmentarity to *molecular* lines of flight, with lines of supple segmentarity occupying a medial position between these two poles. The difference between molecular and molar lines primarily concerns modes of composition: in a molecular body there are only local connections between bodies; when molecular bodies interact, forces differentiate themselves immanently *without reference to molar formations*, such as literary characters. In contrast, molar bodies are formed through the imposition of force on molecular bodies *from the outside*. All literary characters in the Gospels are positioned at the point of convergence of these three types of lines.

The three types of lines in literature do not pose a problem of meaning, for these lines are asignifying in character. They have functions, not meanings, and these functions *produce affects on human bodies* (§ 14). This typology of lines provides a set of analytic concepts for the analysis of early Christian literature, one that does not depend on the signifying structures of language. When the familiar signifying plane of the canonical Gospels is recentred onto this plane of asignifying lines, the analytic task shifts from that of deciphering Greek words and phrases to the mapping of the different types of asignifying lines that are operative in narrative blocs. This analysis requires one to be sensitive to both the deterministic structures that stabilize and overdetermine the lives of literary characters, as well as to the machinic processes that destabilize and transform these lives. When viewed from the vantage point of these lines, the lives of characters narrated in the Gospels are defined less by their linguistic meanings than they are by the types of lines that traverse them.

7

The stratification of Christ groups in the Roman despotic socius

Let every person be subject to the governing authorities; for there is no authority except from God, and those authorities that exist have been instituted by God. Therefore, whoever resists authority resists what God has appointed, and those who resists will incur judgment.

Rom. 13.1-2

The apostle Paul asserts that the authority of the Roman bureaucratic assemblage, which is to say, the authority of its emperor, governors, prefects and magistrates, was guaranteed by the Christian Father God (Rom. 13.1-4). He argues that whoever 'resists' these authorities also resists the Father God who appointed them. However shocking Paul's terrifying logic may be from a contemporary theological perspective, when considered in *structural* terms, nothing about Paul's assertion is surprising: for this 'Father God' fulfils the *same* structural function in Paul's imaginary Roman Empire as did the pagan god Jupiter in *actual* Roman Empire. Indeed, little is at stake as to whether we conceptualize the 'despotic signifier' of the Roman Empire in terms of the pagan god, Jupiter, or assign this despotic signifier the identity of Christianity's God.[1] In both scenarios, a despotic signifier grounds the authority of the emperor, and all the officials whom he invests with civil authority. On the basis of this rationale, Paul argues that 'there is no authority except from God, and those authorities that exist have been instituted by God': therefore, Christ followers should obey Roman authorities in all matters: 'Whoever resists authority resists what God has appointed, and those who resists will incur judgment' (Rom. 13.1-2). Thus, through the linking of the authority of civil officials to Father God, Paul subordinated the Christ group in Rome to the despotic signifier of the Roman Empire, warning its members that the Father God would punish those who resist civil authority.

In this chapter I will argue that this assimilation of early Christianity's Father God to the 'despotic signifier' of the Roman Empire reflects a general tendency in Paul's thought towards 'stratification'. The process of stratification is characteristic of the despotic socius, which overcodes human bodies on the basis of the vertical alliance of a despot-god (as surplus value) to despotic signifier (a chief God as idealized transcendental).[2] In the case of the Roman Empire, this surplus value took the form of a 'despot-god' (emperor) who was vertically affiliated to a 'despotic signifier' (Jupiter). Of course, the plane of immanence is devoid of fixed points, including despotic signifiers (§ 2.3); every point on the plane of immanence is an in-between, a set of transitory connections between multiple machines. But through stratification, the State apparatus constructs a historical 'plane of organization' that 'stratifies' rhizomatic formations into 'arborific' structures. Hence, D&G also term the process of 'stratification' as 'state overcoding' (AO 199).

> Overcoding is the operation that constitutes the essence of the State, and that measures both its continuity and its break with previous formations: the dread of flows of desire that would resist coding, but also the establishment of a new inscription that overcodes, and that makes desire into the property of the sovereign. (AO 199)

All stratifications presuppose prior territorializations (§§ 5.1, 7.2). But strata and territories have different orientations: territories entail *lateral* alliances and entail filiations between extended kinship groupings and clans, at the centre of which is a tribal chief as a surplus value (AO 145–53). In contrast, stratification is a process that overcodes these lateral, territorial alliances and filiations of territories through a *vertical* relation to a fictive transcendental, such as the vertical filiation of 'despot' (king or emperor) to a chief god as a 'despotic signifier'. In the process of stratification, former lateral tribal and filial alliances remain intact, but they are forced to converge upon the despot, who is fetishized as a 'despot-god' (*dieu-despote*) on the basis of his filiation to a chief deity (§ 12.2.2). In short, through stratification, older territorial alliances are subordinated to a supra-terrestrial 'imperial state in the sky' (WP 43).

1. The three great strata

Stratification is a process that overcodes lateral territorial alliances by imposing a *vertical* alliance to an idealized transcendental. Through stratification so-called 'strata' formed, which are overcoded, low-intensity, molar formations that integrate individuals and groups into a dominant set of structures. Stratification produces 'phenomena of centering, unification, totalization, integration, hierarchization, and finalization' (TP 41). Three strata in particular lie before us, whose specificities and interrelations must be examined. For in *A Thousand Plateaus*, D&G single out three strata, in particular, which they term the 'three great strata' (*trois grandes strates*), owing to their harmful effects on the human body: namely, the stratum of organism (*organisme*), the stratum of signification (*signifiance*)[3] and the stratum of subjectification (*subjectivation*) (MP 197, TP 159). An 'organism' is formed through the idealization of the laws of the fathers; signification is connected to the idealization of language, and the subject is formed through the idealization of lack (§§ 10.1.1, 2.1). Taken together, the three great strata constitute a delusional system of thought that organizes human desire with respect to the dominant historical form of social production (§§ 7.2, 10). Through the superimposition of one stratum upon another, the strata resonate, reinforcing each other by means of *stratigraphic resonance*: the 'organism' reinforces 'signification', which reinforces the 'subject' which, in turn, reinforces the stratum of the 'organism'. Through the process of stratification, human bodies become indistinguishable from the system social production that formed them. D&G marvel at how, through the external overcoding of desire in terms of law, an ideal signifier and lack, human 'desire can be made to desire its own repression' (AO 115).

When these strata are superimposed upon one another, and resonate together, they produce a *system of judgment*. D&G playfully term the 'artist' that creates this system of judgment the 'Lobster God': they declare that 'God is a Lobster, or a double pincer, a double bind. ... Each stratum exhibits phenomena constitutive of double articulation' (TP 40). This 'Lobster God' employs his pincers to compress the strata, from above and below, into a system of stratigraphic resonance, which constitutes the 'judgment of God'. As previously discussed, Antonin Artaud yearned 'to have done with the judgment of God', to be rid of his 'badly constructed' overcoded body – the body of an 'organism' – and have his 'true freedom' restored him (§ 4.1). Artaud attempted to enact a kind of ontological revolt against this Lobster God.

1.1. The organism and idealized transcendental law

The 'organism' is only possible through a betrayal of the 'body without organs'. The stratum of the 'organism' is produced through the overcoding of a full 'body without organs' on the basis of a transcendental – variously termed 'Law', 'Morality' or the 'God' – produced through an *idealization* of the laws of biological fathers (§§ 4, 11.1.2). D&G observe how '*Organisms are the enemies of the body*' (TP 158, original emphasis). As I shall discuss below, the 'despotic socius' revolved around an economy structured around transcendental law, transgression and the accumulation of spiritual debt, through which the bodies of men and women were stratified into reproductively, economically and militarily useful 'organisms'. When human desire is repressed, an 'organism' is formed that experiences lack in relation to Law, that is, as a Subject that is denied by Law what it desires. Hence, the starting point of the 'organism' is prohibition (§ 10.1.2). In the specific case of the Roman Empire, law (or the gods) collectively supplied a set of despotic signifiers for the construction of a sociopolitical hierarchy. But idealized law is essentially unknowable because it is empty. It is without content. Idealized law is a *pure form that produces forms of empty repetition: connections, repetitions and repressions*. But this idealized Law, as an empty form, had the power to set in motion the pervasive judgment of all aspects of life (SPP 26). The law, being unknowable, makes itself known only through the guilt and punishments that it induces with respect to human bodies. As Claudia Landolfi observes, 'judgement is the main expression of the Law' (Landolfi 2019: 546, 547). Thus, the purpose of transcendental law is not to prevent transgression but the opposite: to make transgression, judgment and the accumulation of guilt possible (AO 194–5).[4] Thus, within the despotic socius, transgression and obedience are structurally equivalent moves that reinforce the structure of the despotic socius (§ 10.1.3).

The apostle Paul knew all about the purpose of transcendental law: he describes the purpose of the Jewish law in the plainest possible terms in Gal. 3.19a: 'Therefore why the law? It was added to bring about transgressions' (Gal. 3.19a). Likewise, in Romans, Paul explains that the law served to 'multiply sin' in that grace may abound (Rom. 5.20, 4.15). Paul depicts the law as that which *provokes* transgression by inciting humanity's rebellious nature; by so doing, it serves to 'enclose everything under sin' (Gal. 3.22).[5] Thus, obedience and transgression, which are both 'moves' that are provided by the law (as an empty structure) have the same function: they both reinforce law as a fictive transcendental.[6] Both moves testify to a transcendental law, as a 'despotic signifier', to which all earthly laws ultimately refer. However, in this socius, disobedience has greater value than obedience because the ultimate function of this stratifying structure is not providing a means of forgiveness but the *accumulation of spiritual debt*. Indeed, as Deleuze observes, the 'very principle of imperial overcoding' is that debt must *never* be repaid because debt functions in connection with apparatuses of social control (Neg. 21). Thus, ultimately, *it is the accumulation of debt, not law, that holds the despotic socius together* (§ 7.2). For through the accumulation of debt, the 'body without organs' is imprisoned as an 'organism', under the control of the dominant social order.

2. Social production and surplus value of the despotic socius

D&G's concept of 'stratification' was inspired by Lacan's symbolic (*symbolique*) register, just as their concept of 'territorialization' was inspired by Lacan's imaginary (*imaginaire*) register (§ 5, n. 2). But whereas Lacan's imaginary and symbolic registers are ahistorical and ontological in nature, D&G's *Anti-Oedipus* historicizes these complementary registers as *historical* configurations within *successive* stages of social production (AO 385). Starting with the premise that '*social production is purely and simply desiring-production under determinate conditions*' (AO 38, emphasis original), D&G adapt Lacan's imaginary and symbolic registers on the basis of Frederick Engel's three stages of economic production, arguing that throughout history, social production has been produced by three types of 'socius' or 'abstract machine' (§ 8.4): namely, a 'primitive territorial socius', a 'despotic or imperial socius' and a 'modern capitalistic socius'.[7] All three socii entail the creation of surplus value (*plus-value*). In each stage of social production, the socius of society establishes fixed pathways for social production on the basis of a *specific form* of surplus value: a tribal chief, a despot-god and capital, respectively. This overcoding process, termed 'stratification', is a distinctive feature of the 'despotic socius' (AO 200-16).[8] Once formed, this surplus value organizes society into a productive whole through the repression and organization of flows of desire.

2.1. Surplus value

As previously discussed, in the second passive synthesis, termed a 'disjunctive synthesis', the 'body without organs' develops boundaries through the formation of a surplus value (§ 4.2.2). Society can be mapped as one such 'body without organs'. In the case of the 'primitive territorial socius', this surplus value took the form of a tribal chief; in the case of the 'despotic socius', the surplus value takes the form of a despot (king, pharaoh, emperor), who becomes a 'despot-god' (surplus value) through his vertical filiation to a chief deity (§§ 4.2, 12.2).[9] For example, as noted above, in Rom. 13.1-2 Paul describes the structure of the Roman socius, in which all relations converge, through civil magistrates, upon the Roman emperor, who functions as a despot-god (surplus value) through his vertical filiation to the Christian Father God (despotic signifier). In the case of all three socii, the surplus value (chief/despot/capital) seems to have an autonomous existence, apart from the society that forms it. It thereby attains the status of society's quasi-cause (§ 4.2).[10] The State apparatuses of the Ptolemaic, Seleucid and Hasmonean dynasties, as well as the Roman Empire, were all established through stratification, which imposed an 'alliance system' on territories, one in which a king, pharaoh or emperor is established 'in direct filiation with the deity' as such a surplus value (despotic signifier) (AO 192).[11]

2.2. The surplus value of voluntary religious associations

In the Hellenistic and Roman periods, voluntary associations are well attested. Such associations included professional associations or guilds, funerary societies and voluntary religious societies. Many of these associations prescribed sacred laws concerning many aspects of their communal cultic life and membership. Not surprisingly, the structure of these religious associations often mirrored the structure of the despotic Roman socius. For in many such associations, the founder of the association acquired the status of surplus value through his linkage to the association's titular deity (despotic signifier).

In the case of the association dedicated to Zeus Saviour in Asia Minor (Philadelphia), the founder of the association, Dionysios, was vertically linked to Zeus Saviour who 'chose' him (Barton and Horsley 1981). As a 'despot-god' (surplus value), Dionysios was effectively the face of Zeus within the association: he spoke on behalf of Zeus, declared the laws of Zeus and received portions of sacrifices offered to Zeus (§ 12.2.2). Zeus, as the despotic signifier of the association, determined how the individual members ('organisms') functioned in relation to Dionysios: obedience to Zeus Saviour took the form of *obedience to Dionysios*. For only he alone was vested by Zeus with authority to oversee adherence to the groups sacred laws with respect to such practices as the taking of oaths, offering of sacrifices and the performance of purifications and cleansings. *Through the repetition of such practices, the status of Dionysios as surplus value was continuously strengthened.*

Likewise, in the case of the aforementioned association dedicated to Mēn Tyrannos, its founder, Xanthos, also functioned as despot-god (surplus value) through his vertical filiation to Mēn Tyrannos (§ 4.2.2.3). The sacred laws of this association confirm that the god Mēn Tyrannos 'chose' Xanthos while he slept and charged him with the authority to establish a cultic association, to engrave his sacred laws on a stone stele and to oversee all aspects of the association including ritual purifications and regular sacrifices, followed by the consumption of sacrificial meat and wine in honour of Xanthos. Xanthos was the face of Mēn Tyrannos, and he spoke on Mēn's behalf. The very presence of Xanthos, as surplus value, stood as a witness to the authority and power of the Mēn Tyrannos, the despotic signifier of the association. Hence, obedience to Mēn Tyrannos took the form of obedience to Xanthos as surplus value.

3. The stratification of Christ groups

There is evidence that the structure of the Christ group in Corinth, like the associations dedicated to Zeus Saviour and Mēn Tyrannos, mirrored the stratification of the Roman despotic socius. As discussed above, Paul situates Christ groups within the structure of the Roman Empire as a despotic socius (Rom. 13.1-4). He stratifies the bodies of Christ followers into 'organisms' by compelling them to obey Roman authorities, who have been appointed by a 'despot-god' (the emperor), who is vertically linked to the Christian Father God, as a despotic signifier. In Paul's mind, this Father God exercised judgment and punishment *through* the Roman authorities appointed by the emperor. As I shall argue below, this assimilation of Christianity's Father God to the structure of the Roman despotic socius reflects a general tendency in Paul's thought towards 'stratification'.

3.1. The stratification of Christ groups (1 Cor. 11.3, Col. 3.22, 4.1, *Did.* 4.10-11)

Paul's statement, 'Christ is the head of every husband, and the husband is the head of wife, and God is the head of Christ' (1 Cor. 11.3), assimilates the Father God to the surplus value of the Roman despotic socius. For this statement structures the Corinthian Christ group as a hierarchy, culminating in Christ as surplus value (despot-god).[12]

In this hierarchical structure, husbands were elevated to a position of power and authority over their wives, while simultaneously being organized *under* Christ, as a despot-god (surplus value) who is, in turn, vertically filiated to God as a despotic signifier (§ 4.2.2).[13] Thus, all relations in the Christ group converge upon Christ, as surplus value. It is striking how Paul's logic in 1 Cor. 11.3 mirrors

Rom. 13.1-4: just as Christ followers in society are said to be subject to the authority of the Roman emperor, as 'despot-god', so also are Christ followers in a Christ group subject to the authority of *Christ*, as despot-god, on the basis of the *same* despotic signifier, the Father God! Thus, in both scenarios, the bodies of Christ followers are *stratified* into 'organisms' on the basis of the same idealized transcendental, the Father God.

We find the same stratified structure in the (possibly pseudonymous) Letter to the Colossians: the author states that the bodies of domestic slaves are stratified in relation to their 'earthly masters' or 'lords' (σάρκα κυρίοις)' by linking these masters, as surplus value, to a 'heavenly Master', the 'Lord' above (κύριον ἐν οὐρανῷ), as a despotic signifier (Col. 3.22, 4.1).[14] Slaves are instructed to *obey* their earthly masters (as surplus value) on the basis of their relation to a despotic signifier, the Father God (cf. Eph. 6.5-9). Thus, the parallelism between citizens in Rom. 13.1-2, husbands and wives in 1 Cor. 11.3 and slaves in Col. 3.22, 4.1 is exact.

The status of masters as surplus value (despot-god) is made explicit in *Did.* 4.10–11, which instructs slaves to obey their earthly masters *as if they* were a 'replica of God' himself. Thus, just as the authority of Dionysios and Xanthos as despot-gods over the cult members was guaranteed by the gods, Zeus Saviour and Mēn Tyrannos respectively, so also is the authority of Christian masters guaranteed on the basis of the same logic, that every master is a veritable 'replica of God'. Thus, the logic of overcoding is the same: obedience to the despotic signifier (Jupiter, Zeus, Mēn, Father God) always takes the form of obedience to earthly surplus value (emperor, founder of an association, Christ, slave master); in each case, the 'body without organs' of each citizen, husband, wife and slaves, is *stratified* into an 'organism', and an individual desiring production is overcoded by social production.

3.2. Destratification

To destratify is to 'open up to a new function, a diagrammatic function' (TP 134). Destratification begins with this overcoded, Oedipalized 'organism', and traces such a body back to a hyperdifferentiated 'body without organism'. After the non-stratified 'body without organs' of individual Christ followers was stratified into an 'organism', was it possible for their bodies to become destratified again? Was stratification an irrevocable condition? I shall argue that by following their own cartographies of productive desire, every Christ 'organism' retained the virtual capacity to disrupt its own stratification by entering into new experimental assemblages: a virtual 'body without organs' is always present within an actual 'organism'. Hence, stratification and destratification are concurrent processes. Indeed, D&G remind us that, while 'stratification in general is the entire system of the judgment of God', it is equally true that 'the body without organs, constantly eludes that judgment, flees and becomes destratified, decoded, deterritorialized' (TP 40). Indeed, as I shall discuss in Chapter 9, while the abstract machine of the Roman Empire (termed the 'ecumenon') was constantly stratifying the bodies of its citizens, the abstract machine of the plane of immanence (termed the 'planomenon') was simultaneously uprooting the same bodies from the three great strata by destratifying them. For there is no hiding from abstract machines, even in the strata of the Roman socius. Small groups, such as Christ groups, which were characterized by repressive determinism, still preserved the virtual degrees of freedom, owing to the virtual dimension of the plane of immanence. Despite the fact that life in the Roman Empire was largely governed by a closed determinism owing to ubiquitous stratification processes, the potential always remained for 'destratification'. Hence, the primary theme of D&G's *Anti-Oedipus* is a call for subjectivity – whether the subjectivity of individuals or groups – to destratify, to cease functioning as an organism by constructing new cartographies of self-reference.

Conclusion

D&G enunciate two primary principles that govern the entire social field: first, that the entire social field is invested by desiring production: '*There is only desire and the social, and nothing else*' (AO 29, original emphasis). The second principle is that, in historical, anthropological terms, all desiring production is co-opted by social production: '*social production is purely and simply desiring production itself under determinate conditions*' (AO 29, original emphasis). This chapter has discussed the ways in which the desiring production of first Christ groups and individual Christ followers was 'stratified' under the determinate conditions of the social production of the Roman Empire, considered as a despotic socius.

The process of stratification is characteristic of the despotic socius, which overcodes human bodies on the basis of the vertical alliance of a despot-god (as surplus value) to despotic signifier (such as a chief god as idealized transcendental). In the specific case of the Roman despotic socius, human bodies were overcoded through the vertical filiation of the Roman emperor, as surplus value, to the god Jupiter, as a despotic signifier. Through vertical filiation, the despotic emperor became a 'despot-god'. In *A Thousand Plateaus*, D&G single out three 'great strata' in particular, owing to their detrimental effects on the human body: 'the stratum of organism, signifiance, and subjectification'. Through the idealization of law, language and the subject, the State apparatus 'stratifies' human desiring production for the purposes of social production. While each of these strata has its own distinct characteristics, through stratigraphic resonance they reinforce one another for the purposes of the regulation, discipline and normalization of human bodies.

This chapter has demonstrated a tendency in the writings of the apostle Paul towards stratification. In Rom. 13.1-4 Paul assimilates early Christianity's Father God to the structure of the Roman despotic socius by his assertion that the authority of the emperor, and all the officials whom he invests with civil authority, was guaranteed by the Father God, as a despotic signifier. However shocking Paul's terrifying logic may be from a contemporary theological perspective, when considered in *structural* terms, nothing about Paul's assertion is surprising: for this 'Father God' fulfils the *same* structural function in Paul's imaginary Roman Empire as did the pagan god Jupiter in *actual* Roman Empire. Through the linking of the authority of pagan authorities to this Father God, as a despotic signifier, the bodies (without organs) of Christ followers were stratified into Christ 'organisms'.

We find the same tendency towards stratification in 1 Cor. 11.3, where Paul stratifies the bodies of husbands and wives, by organizing them hierarchically under Christ, as a surplus value, who is vertically filiated to the Father God as despotic signifier. In this stratified formation, the structural function of God, as despotic signifier, is to ground the authority of Christ, as despot-god, over men, and by extension, the authority of men over women. Similarly, in the Letter to the Colossians, the structural relation of Christian citizens to the Roman emperor (Rom. 13.1-2), and men and women to Christ (1 Cor. 11.3), is paralleled in the relation of slaves to masters, as surplus value: the author instructs slaves to obey their Christian masters based on the structural relation of these masters, as surplus value, to a despotic signifier, who is 'Master' of all (Col. 3.22, 4.1, cf. Eph. 6.5-9). While examples could be multiplied, the pattern of stratification is unmistakable. The logic of stratification is *always the same*: obedience to the despotic signifier (whether Jupiter, Zeus Saviour, Mēn Tyrannos or the Father God) must take the form of obedience to an earthly surplus value (emperor, the founder of an association, Christ, masters of slaves). Through stratification, the 'body without organs' of citizens, husbands, wives and slaves was overcoded into 'organisms', just as their desiring production was overcoded for the purposes of social production. Clearly, early Christian discourse sometimes played a role in the stratification of the bodies of Christ followers. But D&G remind us that, every Christ 'organism' retained the virtual capacity to disrupt its own stratification by entering into new experimental assemblages: a virtual 'body without organs' is always present within an actual 'organism'. While 'stratification in general is the entire system of the judgment of God', it is equally true that 'the body without organs, constantly eludes that judgment, flees and becomes destratified, decoded, deterritorialized' (TP 40). Destratification begins with this overcoded, Oedipalized 'organism', and traces such a body back to a hyperdifferentiated 'body without organism'. Hence, the primary theme of D&G's *Anti-Oedipus* is a call for subjectivity – whether the subjectivity of individuals or groups – to destratify, to cease functioning as an organism by constructing new cartographies of self-reference.

8

Christ groups as social assemblages and abstract machines: Discourse and power

All scripture is inspired by God and is useful for instruction, for discipline and punishment, for correction, for discipline in righteousness, so that everyone who belongs to God may be proficient, equipped for every good work.

2 Tim. 3.16-17

Discourse does much more than communicate ideas and information. By virtue of being a 'little nonsignifying machine', discourse is always embedded in nondiscursive practices (§ 1.3). The author of 2 Timothy instinctively knew this. For he draws an explicit connection between discourse (scripture) and various nondiscursive practices that shape the human body: he states that scripture is useful (ὠφέλιμος) because of its *productive capacity* for the instruction, punishment, correction and discipline of human bodies. From this author's vantage point scripture, as discourse, is 'useful', not because it communicates important ideas and information but because it is *effective for the moulding of human bodies.*

My elaboration on the relation of the discursive and nondiscursive in this chapter will begin with a discussion of the Deleuzo-Guattarian 'assemblage' in general, followed by an exposition of a particular type of assemblage, biform social assemblages. Specifically, I shall discuss how discursive and nondiscursive planes are organized in biform social assemblages, such as Christ groups, to enhance the functional capacities of the 'assemblage' as a whole (§ 8.1-2). Based on this exposition, I will then turn my attention to the discursive and nondiscursive components of a social assemblage (§ 8.3). Finally, I shall discuss the 'abstract machine' of bifold social assemblages that coordinates these nondiscursive and discursive components within a shared power/knowledge diagram (§ 8.4). On the basis of this excursus on abstract machines, I will demonstrate how, in the case of the Christ group addressed by 2 Timothy, discourse was made effective through the coordination of scripture (discourse) with (nondiscursive) practices.

1. What is an assemblage?

The concept of an *agencement* was first introduced in D&G's *Kafka – Pour une littérature mineure* (1975), and was subsequently developed in *Mille plateaux* (1980).[1] The English translators of these works rendered the French term *agencement* as 'assemblage', a gloss which is potentially misleading because the English term 'assemblage' falsely implies a derivation from the French verb, *assembler*, meaning 'to join together', when the noun *agencement* is clearly derived from the verb, *agencer*, meaning 'to organize', 'arrange' or 'fit together'.

This thought, which at first glance may seem like a minor quibble, is in point of fact quite important because one of the primary attributes of an *agencement* is that it does *not* 'join together' its component parts but only *arranges them*, or *fits them together*, into a loose cluster. Hence, Tano Posteraro suggests that the French term *agencement* should more precisely be translated by the term 'arrangement' (2020: 3), while Mario Perniola proposes the term 'concatenation' (2019: 486). While these are both excellent suggestions, I shall continue to employ the term 'assemblage' owing to the cumulative weight of contemporary academic usage.

The component parts of a Deleuzo-Guattarian 'assemblage' (*agencement*) can be compared to the stones making up a traditional dry-stone wall, in which irregularly shaped stones are *arranged, or fitted together*, without being physically joined together with mortar. In such a wall, stones are in *direct* contact with other stones through their points of contact. Collectively, these points of contact constitute a network or 'diagram' of power that holds the wall together, a point to which I shall return later (§ 8.4.1). The key point is, by virtue of *not* being joined together, any individual stone can be removed from the wall and integrated into another structure (such as a house, bridge or barn). Like a traditional dry-stone wall, the parts of a Deleuzo-Guattarian assemblage are simply arranged, or clustered, together, and are held in place through their relations of force between them. But nothing prevents these parts from being removed and incorporated into other assemblages.

This concept of an assemblage can be applied to almost anything. Two lovers form a human–human assemblage, which is not composed of two independent bodies but, rather, one body produced through *intra-action*.

For through the resolution of forces between two bodies, both identities are *produced* differentially *with reference to one another* (Barad 2007: 56). Within this assemblage of lovers, a single assemblage of a 'lover-and-the-beloved' is formed. The concept of an assemblage can also be applied to large-scale bodies such as Graeco-Roman cities, as well as to small-scale civic institutions such as gymnasia, temples, law courts, Asklepieia, civic mystery religions, not to mention a variety of voluntary associations such as immigrant associations, occupational guilds, burial associations, synagogues, religious associations (§§ 4.2.1.1, 7.1.2), including Christ groups. These diverse instantiations of an 'assemblage' can be arranged on spectrum ranging from hard, compact segments, such as found in civic institution, to assemblages characterized by a diffuse micro-segmentarity, such as first-century Jewish synagogues and Christ groups.

A Christ group can be mapped as an assemblage that is formed by 'organizing', 'arranging' or 'fitting together' various parts (μέλη), notably including the bodies of Christ followers, so that all parts co-functioned with other parts *for the benefit of the whole assemblage*. By way of example, the Christ group in Corinth, as an assemblage, was an arrangement of heterogeneous parts including *discursive* parts (scripture readings, homilies, ethical teachings) and *nondiscursive* parts (iterative practices, Christ followers). These parts were *not* joined together into an organic whole but rather, like a dry-stone wall, they were only loosely arranged together. But through their co-functioning, this Christ assemblage was able to maintain its *productive capacity*.

All assemblages, including Christ assemblages, can be said to be 'passional' in the sense they are always *coupling* with other assemblages. What is more, the individual parts of the Corinthian assemblage routinely departed from the assemblage, on a temporary basis, to be constituted as parts of *other* assemblages. For example, Paul, Prisca and Aquilla were also constituted as the 'parts' of a tentmaker assemblage.[2] Erastus functioned as a part (*quaestor*/treasurer) of a civic assemblage (Rom. 16.23). Certain wealthy members occasionally departed to become parts of banquet-assemblages where sacrificial meat was served (1 Cor. 10.27-18, Rom. 14.2). And, of course, most members functioned as the parts of kinship assemblages, such as the household of Stephanus (1 Cor. 1.14-16), just as low-status members were arranged as parts (slaves or dependent workers) of Chloë household-assemblage (1 Cor. 1.10-11). Thus, we can confidently say, without fear of contradiction, that *all* parts of the Corinthian Christ assemblage also functioned as parts of other assemblages. There were no celibate Christ assemblages! All Christ assemblages were *passional*. One of the remarkable characteristics of Christ assemblages in the Graeco-Roman world was their capacity to couple with a diversity of other assemblages, including civic assemblages composed of compact segments, as well as other assemblages characterized by a diffuse micro-segmentarity. Owing to their great combinatory power, every Christ assemblage can be analysed in terms of the *exteriority* of their intensive relations to other types of assemblages.

2. An assemblage as a co-functioning of parts

As a general principle, it must be emphasized *there is no assemblage without production*. The heterogeneous parts of an assemblage are always arranged and organized to enhance the productive capacity of the assemblage as a whole. By way of example, consider the sphinxes that were often set up outside the gates of Hellenistic cities to defend them from their enemies. A sphinx is an assemblage that is formed through the arranging of three parts: the head of a woman, the body of a lion and the wings of an eagle. Through the arrangement of these parts together, a 'woman-lion-eagle assemblage' is formed that possessed the productive capacity (at least theoretically) to defend a city from attack.

The same point can be made in the case of the 'man-chariot-horse assemblage' described in the story of the Ethiopian Eunuch, who drove his chariot from Jerusalem to Gaza (Acts 8.27-30). Individually, each part of this assemblage – the man, chariot and horse – could perform many different functions. But when these parts were arranged together, as parts of a single assemblage, the productive capacities of each were narrowed and co-opted for the productive capacity of *rapid velocity*. To accomplish this purpose the individual contributions of each part had to be restricted and regulated: the contributions of the horse had to be limited to inputs that were in response to the prods of the charioteer; the contribution of the charioteer likewise had to be limited to the range of the actions of his hands and feet, which signalled his intentions to the horse to gallop, speed up, turn and stop; similarly, the inputs of individual parts of the chariot – its platform, wheels, chariot-pole, yoke, bridle and breast-strap – had to be restricted to their intended functions. The cumulative result of assembling these parts was a 'man-chariot-horse assemblage' in which the arm of the rider was articulated with the chariot-harness and chariot platform, which was, in turn, articulated with the horse by the chariot-pole, whereby the whole assemblage possessed the productive capacity for rapid velocity.

As noted above, an assemblage is formed through an arranging (but not joining) of parts. In other words, an assemblage *lacks an organic unity*: it functions through a mere *sympathy*, or symbiosis, of parts (D 69). Indeed, the only essential characteristic of an assemblage is the co-functioning of its parts, each of which is defined by its *external relations* to other parts. In this respect, social assemblages, such as Christ assemblages, were not inherently different from nonhuman, or mixed type, assemblages such as the aforementioned 'woman-lion-eagle' sphinx assemblage and the 'man-chariot-horse' assemblage. As D&G observe, 'there is no such thing as either man or nature, but only an *intra-active* process that produces the one within the other and couples the machines together … the self and the non-self, outside and inside, no longer have any meaning whatsoever' (AO 2). Therefore, a second principle regarding associations must also be affirmed: the analysis of a 'Christ assemblage' must also include an elaboration of the *productive capacity* it achieves through the interrelation of its parts. If one can speak of the unity of such a Christ assemblage, the sign of such unity would be its *productive capacity*. For example, as previously discussed, the Corinthian Christ assemblage was composed of diverse parts including prophets, teachers, healers and miracle workers (1 Cor. 12.8-11, 28–29), whose productive capacity, according to Paul, functioned for the 'common good' of the whole Christ assemblage: 'To each part is given the manifestation of the Spirit for the common good' of the Christ assemblage, 'for the body [as assemblage] does not consist of one part but many' (1 Cor. 12.7, 14, §§ 1.2, 4.2.2).

3. Biform social assemblages

All social assemblages are *biform* in nature in the sense that every social assemblage entails a combination of nondiscursive and discursive components (F 39).[3] The Roman Empire consisted of countless biform social assemblages of varying complexities, each of which entailed a *nondiscursive* component such as iterative practices (e.g. awarding of honours, voting of crowns, erecting statues, sacrifices and dedications to the gods, interring the dead, manumitting slaves and banqueting) and a *discursive* component (e.g. decrees, laws, accounts, letters, biographies). For example, the Greeks and Romans engaged in many iterative practices including civic rituals, sacrifices to the gods as civic protectors, processions, games and festivals. Small associations, exhibiting a diffuse micro-segmentarity, such as the aforementioned associations dedicated to Mēn Tyrannos and Zeus Saviour (§§ 4.2.2.3, 7.1.2), were also biform social assemblages: they consisted of a *nondiscursive* component (sacrifices, purifications and cleansings, banquets) and a *discursive* component (sacred laws, oaths, prayers to the gods). Likewise, Christ assemblages can be analysed in terms of their nondiscursive component (e.g. places of assembly, meetings on the first day of the week for prayer, singing, the Lord's Supper, agape meals)[4] and a discursive component (e.g. readings from the Septuagint, ethical exhortations, catalogues of vices and virtues, moral maxims and household codes).

3.1. Louis Hjelmslev's form–substance complexes

In their analysis of biform social assemblages, D&G employ a modified form of the linguistic theory developed by Danish linguist Louis Hjelmslev.[5] For this reason, progress in this line of inquiry must proceed by way of a detour through Hjelmslevian linguistics.

Ferdinand de Saussure defined the 'sign' as the basic unit of linguistics (Saussure 1976); by definition, a 'sign' is formed from the union of a 'signifier' (the psychological impression or sound-image that a spoken sign makes) and a 'signified' (the abstract *concept* of a thing).[6] Saussurean semiology has several obvious weaknesses. First, as Jacques Derrida has observed, Saussure's sign function is problematic. A sign is composed of two different *forms*: the signifier has a *linguistic* (phonemic) form, while the signified has a *non-linguistic* form, the form of human thought. A *qualitative difference* exists between the form of a signifier and the form of a signified. Derrida likened Saussure's sign to a 'hinge' (*brisure*) that both *joins and breaks* two different forms (1974: 69). But Derrida's metaphor of a 'hinge' does not solve the problem of Saussure's sign function.

Louis Hjelmslev reconceived the interrelation of Ferdinand de Saussure's signifieds and signifiers in terms of two independent planes, a 'plane of content' and a 'plane of expression' respectively. His 'plane of content' is comparable to Saussure's signifieds, while the 'plane of expression' is more or less equivalent to Saussure's signifiers.[7] On the basis of this distinction between a plane of content and plane of expression, Hjelmslev developed a linguistic model comprised of two 'form–substance' complexes: namely a content complex consisting of a 'form of content' and 'substance of content', and a corresponding expression complex consisting of a 'form of expression' and 'substance of expression'. On the basis of these two form–substance complexes, Hjelmslev went further, by distinguishing between the form and substance of the plane of content, on the one hand, and the form and substance of the plane of expression.

1. Hjelmslev's *plane of content* is produced by the projection of a 'form of content' (*forme de contenu*) onto amorphous thought ('purport'), whereby amorphous thought is transformed into the 'substance of content' (*substance de contenu*), that is, structured thought.[8]
2. The *plane of expression* is produced by the projection of a linguistic 'form of expression' (*forme d'expression*), onto sound-chains of phonemes, transforming them into words and phrases, that is, into the substance of expression (*substance d'expression*), which is to say, into oral and written discourse.

Not only does Hjelmslevian linguistics distinguish between a nondiscursive 'plane of content' and a discursive 'plane of expression', but it also recognizes that these two planes are in a *non-relation* by virtue of the fact that they have *different forms*: for thought has a non-linguistic form, whereas discourse has a linguistic form. By virtue of having different forms, these planes *do not interact, and indeed cannot interact, directly*. Consequently, there can be no simple cause-and-effect relation between the plane of content and the plane of expression, an essential point to which I will return below. As D&G observe, it is 'precisely because content, like expression, has its own form, one can never assign the form of expression the function of simply representing, describing, or averring a corresponding content' (TP 95). Thus, in Hjelmslevian linguistics, the 'content' (plane) of thought and the 'expression' (plane) of language are not interdependent planes of language (as implied by Saussurean linguistics) but rather are *independent* planes, each of which functions according to a different set of rules.

3.2. The application of Hjelmslev's form–substance complexes to social assemblages

Whereas Hjelmslev's model dealt solely with discourse, D&G adapted Hjelmslev's two 'form–substance' complexes for the purposes of an analysis of biform social assemblages, which entail both a discursive and *nondiscursive* component. In D&G's modified version of Hjelmslev's 'form–substance' complexes, the plane of expression is discursive, whereas *the plane of content is nondiscursive*.[9]

3.2.1. The nondiscursive plane of content

In this modified version, the 'form of content' provides a *nondiscursive* form for the organization, regulation and discipline of human bodies, which collectively comprise the 'substance of content'.[10] For example, in the Graeco-Roman world, one can speak of a gymnasium form, a military fort form, a temple form and a workshop form, as instances of the form of content.[11] Notably, the form of content also includes iterative practices such as education (in the case of the gymnasium form), training (in the case of the military fort form) and sacrifice (in the case of the temple form). Hence, the gymnasium can be said to be an 'education machine' just as the temple is a 'sacrifice machine'. In the case of the religious association dedicated to the lunar god, Mēn Tyrannos, the form of nondiscursive content was jointly constituted by the association's sanctuary (ἱερόν) and its iterative practices including purifications and sacrifices, which were performed in this sanctuary (§ 4.2.2.3).

Through the 'form of content', a 'substance of content' is produced, namely, the *human bodies* of ephebes, soldiers, artisans and worshippers, which were variously educated, trained, disciplined for the purposes of citizenship, warfare, civic construction, sacrifice and so forth. Of course, many voluntary associations possessed no dedicated architectural form of content. In the case of the religious association dedicated to Zeus Saviour, the form of content consisted not of a temple but the household (οἶκος) of its founder, Dionysios, a place where members regularly gathered to perform a variety of cultic practices such as the taking of oaths, performing purification rituals and sacrifice (§ 7.1.2). Similarly, Christ groups of the first century of the Common Era possessed no architectural spaces dedicated solely for their assemblies. Like the association of Zeus Saviour, the form of content of Christ groups entailed the private homes of wealthy members such as Gaius, who hosted the whole church, and Stephanas, where members also assembled for prayers, hymns, teaching and communal meals (Rom. 16.23, 1 Cor. 1.16).

3.2.2. Discursive plane of expression

In the case of the plane of expression, the form of expression provided a form for production of various types of discourse. Such forms included literary forms (genres) and paradigmatic domains.[12] In the case of the associations dedicated to the gods, Mēn Tyrannos and Zeus Saviour (§§ 4.2.1.1, 7.1.2), the expression-form was comprised of the *discursive form* of sacred laws, which was instantiated as the association's *actual* laws, and the substance of expression, which were inscribed on stone stelae and set up for all to read and obey (McLean 2002: 189–92). Similarly, the discourses of Christ assemblages entailed a variety of forms of expression including the Graeco-Roman biography genre in the case of the canonical Gospels (§§ 1.3, 6.1.1), the ancient history genre in the case of the book of Acts, the epistolary genre in the case of Paul's letters, as well as a variety of other genres for apocalypses, ethical instructions, miracles, pronouncement stories and so forth. In each of these cases, the 'form of expression' provided a literary structure for the 'substance of expression', which is to say, actual discourses, notably including what 2 Tim. 3.16 terms 'scripture'. All this is to say that *every Christ group, as a bifold social assemblage, entailed a nondiscursive plane of content and a discursive plane of expression*. Since these two planes operated independently of each other, one essential question remains unanswered: by what means did these nondiscursive and discursive planes interrelate?

4. The abstract machine as a diagram of power

The most striking feature of Deleuzo-Guattarian biform social assemblages is that planes of content and expression *do not share a common form*. Owing to the fact that a qualitative difference exists between the *nondiscursive* form of content and the *discursive* form of expression, there can be no direct causality between content and expression (F^f 39, F 31).[13] For example, the 'form of content' of a Hellenistic Jewish synagogue was *nondiscursive* (entailing a physical place of meeting and various iterative practices), while its 'form of expression' was *discursive*, as actualized in the substance of expression – the Septuagint and Jewish midrashim – which were read in these synagogues (Mosser 2013). Therefore, owing to these different forms, the relation between synagogues, on the one hand, and Septuagint/midrashim could not have been cause-and-effect relationship.[14] By virtue of their independence, synagogues as a machine of content and scripture as a machine of expression, *each had their own distinctive histories*.

The independence of the 'plane of content' and the 'plane of expression' poses a profound problem, not only for the interpretation of 2 Tim. 3.16-17 but also for other texts such as Heb. 4.12: 'For the word of God is alive and active. Sharper than any double-edged sword, it penetrates even to dividing soul and spirit, joints and marrow; it judges the thoughts and attitudes of the heart'. Heb. 4.12 also presumes a connection between the discursive and nondiscursive; it presupposes that the 'word of God', as the substance of expression, intersects directly with human bodies, as the substance of content, by 'penetrating' the flesh like a 'two-edged sword, … divides soul from spirit, joints from marrow'. Once again, we must ask, by what mechanism could the discursive (word of God) 'penetrate' nondiscursive fleshy bodies, which possessed heterogeneous forms? How can the 'word of God' be more dangerous than a double-edged sword? In other words, how does the biform assemblage achieve its productive capacity? Since there is no direct causality between the nondiscursive plane of content and the discursive plane of expression, D&G theorize an immanent non-unifying cause that connects them *indirectly*. They term this immanent cause variously an 'abstract machine' (*machine abstraite*) and a power/knowledge 'diagram' (*diagramme*) (TP 110–11).

Abstract machines are 'abstract' in the sense that 'know nothing of forms and substances' (TP 511). Being semiotic in character, they cannot distinguish between *nondiscursive* and *discursive* forms, or between content and expression (F 54). An abstract machine 'operates via *matter,* not substance, and via *function* and not form' (TP 511). It effectuates a cybernetic feedback loop between content and expression through the flow of singularities, or 'particles-signs' (§ 3, n. 14), whereby these planes are accommodated to one another. These flows of singularities do not signify anything: being both matter *and* energy, particle *and* wave, virtual *and* real, singularities are in a non-relation to the distinction between signified and signifier, and between content and expression (§ 6, n. 3). They perform non-linguistic, asignifying transfers of force (Genosko 2008). Through the flow of singularities, the plane of content and plane of expression are *reciprocally determined*. As 'functives (*fonctifs*) of the same function (*fonction*)', the abstract machine *deterritorializes* both content and expression (Deleuze, Guattari and Stivale 1984: 15). Owing to this backchannel between the discursive and nondiscursive, 'there are no individual statements' but 'only statement-producing machinic assemblages' (TP 36). A Christ assemblage can be conceived as an arrangement of nondiscursive content and discursive expression, which are unified by a single abstract machine.

It must be stressed that the abstract machine is not a third part or component of a bifold social assemblage. The abstract machine is the *virtual* dimension of an actualized assemblage (§ 3.2). This is not to imply that the abstract machine is akin to 'a Platonic Idea, transcendent, universal, eternal' (TP 510). As previously discussed, D&G reject the ontological dualism of Plato (§ 2.3). They theorize *the virtual as fully real* (§ 3.2). Theirs is a philosophy that privileges the virtual over the actual, just as it privileges machinic processes over static structures. As an immanent network of interrelations, the abstract machine supplies the *virtual* conditions that are actualized as a social assemblage. While this abstract machine is imperceptible, its functioning is manifested by all that is given. The abstract machine is a diagram of the virtual relations of force (*puissance*) that are operative as power (*pouvoir*) within an assemblage at any given moment (F^f 48, F 41): 'The relations between forces (*puissances*) ... are *merely virtual*, potential, unstable, vanishing and molecular, and define only possibilities of interaction' (F 37).

The result of this coordination of the discursive and nondiscursive is a shared power/knowledge 'diagram' (*diagramme*). Each abstract machine composes a *historical* power/knowledge diagram. This diagram, being formless and highly changeable, optimizes the co-functioning of nondiscursive apparatuses of (nondiscursive) power, as a machine of content, and discursive knowledge, as a machine of expression, through which the social assemblage, as a whole, adapts to ever-changing needs and contexts. Through this diagram singularities (particles-signs) flow freely between the discursive and nondiscursive components. It can be imagined as a kind of 'electric circuit' that provided a power/knowledge diagram, that is, pathway for the flows on intensities.[15] This 'electric circuit' provides a non-unifying immanent set of pathways for the flow of intensities, which 'is coextensive with the whole social field' (F 37).

It must be stressed that an abstract machine, or diagram, is not an atemporal structure or function. Not only is an abstract machine characterized by its own temporality, it also has its own specific history, one which cannot be reduced to the history of a group or discourse. Not only does 'everything operates through abstract-real machines', but these abstract machines 'have names and dates' (TP 146). Consequently, no two abstract machines are identical.

Deleuze applies his theory of the abstract machine to historical social systems such as feudalism (TP 89–90), and to historical institutions such as Bentham's Panopticon, which allowed guards in a centrally located tower to maintain surveillance on all the prisoners in their cells without being seen (F 23–44). For example, he discusses Foucault's concept of 'panopticism' as one historical instantiation of an abstract machine. In 1975, Foucault published *Surveiller et Punir* (translated in 1977 as *Discipline and Punish*), in which Foucault demonstrated how the nineteenth-century incarceration system, known as Bentham's Panopticon, employed power to *produce new knowledge* through the close observation and study of prisoners. This new knowledge, in turn, was employed to *increase the power* of the prison system over the bodies of prisoners. On this basis, Foucault famously argued that *power and knowledge are not external to one another but rather operate in a mutually generative manner*. This insight is concisely captured in the Foucaultian neologism 'power/knowledge' (1977a: 27–8). The Deleuzo-Guattarian 'abstract machine' or 'diagram' restates this same insight concerning the interrelation of power and knowledge. As I shall discuss below, we even find evidence for the interrelation of power and knowledge in 2 Tim. 3.16-17 and Heb. 4.12.

4.1. Apparatuses of power and linguistic meanings

D&G's concept of an 'abstract machine' and 'diagram' has considerable consequences for the interpretation of early Christian discourse. A purely linguistic model entails *two* components, a plane of expression (signifiers) and a plane of content (signifieds). But, as noted above, D&G's revision of Hjelmslev's model has additional dimensions, namely a *nondiscursive* plane of content, and an 'abstract machine' or 'diagram', which is not an additional component but the *virtual* dimension of the assemblage as a whole. Owing to the functioning of this virtual abstract machine, signifying processes do not operate independently of the world, representing it from the outside: through the abstract machine, *signifying processes always function as extensions of nondiscursive processes within a shared power/knowledge diagram*. As a general principle, *all early Christian discourse was social in both its origin and destination*. By implication, texts such as 2 Tim. 3.16-17 and Heb. 4.12 entail more than linguistically encoded ideas or information. Through the effectuation of a power/knowledge diagram of a social assemblage, 2 Tim. 3.16-17 and Heb. 4.12 functioned within a power/knowledge 'diagram'. Once we become aware of the function of abstract machines as a power/knowledge diagram, the relation of discourse to the exercise of power over human bodies can no longer be ignored. We can no longer conceive of texts such as 2 Tim. 3.16-17 and Heb. 4.12 from a purely linguistic or informational perspective. Now, a whole new series of questions arise. Instead of asking, 'what do these texts mean?', we must ask 'how did they function?', 'what effects did they produce in human bodies?' and, more specifically, what role did they have in the discipline, punishment and correction of Christ followers?

Conclusion

The Deleuzo-Guattarian concept of an assemblage can be applied to both large-scale bodies such as Graeco-Roman cities and to small-scale voluntary associations such as Christ groups, and even to human beings. These diverse instantiations of an assemblage can be arranged on spectrum ranging from hard compact segments, such as found in civic institutions, to assemblages that were characterized by a diffuse micro-segmentarity, such as first-century synagogues and Christ groups.

A primary principle of assemblage theory is that *there is no assemblage without production*: the heterogeneous parts of an assemblage are always organized to enhance the *productive capacity of the assemblage as a whole*. Individual Christ followers were 'organized' as the working 'parts' of Christ assemblages, through which these assemblages attained their own productive capacity. Hence, the primary characteristic of these Christ assemblages was the *co-functioning* of their parts to achieve a productive capacity.

In specific terms, all Christ groups can be mapped as a special type of assemblage: a *biform* social assemblage, in which discourse (as a machine of expression) functioned in coordination with nondiscursive practices (as a machine of content). Perhaps the most striking feature of these biform assemblages is that the plane of expression and plane of content *did not share a common form*: a qualitative difference existed between the *discursive* form of expression and the *nondiscursive* form of the content. This qualitative difference prevented any direct causality between them. This observation raises a profound problem for traditional exegetical theory: if a qualitative difference existed between the discursive form of Christian texts and the nondiscursive form of Christian practices and bodies, *how were the discursive and nondiscursive components of a Christ assemblage coordinated?*

D&G theorize an immanent non-unifying cause of both expression and content, which they term an 'abstract machine' and 'diagram'. Every historical Christ assemblage can be traced back to a historical abstract machine as its immanent cause. The relation of this abstract machine to the assemblage, as a whole, was one of mutual presupposition: it was a relation of the virtual to the actual. The abstract machine of a Christ group supplied a set of virtual relations for a power/knowledge diagram, which functioned as a kind of cybernetic feedback loop through which content and expression were diagrammatically connected by flows of singularities. By virtue of this diagram, all Christian discourse was linked in a circular relation with the systems of power.

By virtue of the functioning of the abstract machine, signifying processes in Christ groups did not operate independently of the Graeco-Roman world: through the operation of abstract machines, signifying processes functioned in coordination with nondiscursive processes within a shared power/knowledge diagram. All early Christian discourse was social in both its origin and destination. As 2 Tim. 3.16-17 and Heb. 4.12 illustrate, Christian discourse did not function independently of the world, representing theological 'truths' from the outside: discourse was always coordinated with networks of power and iterative social practices. Every Christ social assemblage effectuated its own, historically specific virtual abstract machine, which coordinated its discursive production with its iterative practices.

9

The God of religion and the schizo God

Jesus said, 'Do not think that I have come to abolish the law or the prophets. I have not come to abolish them but to fulfil them. ... Therefore, anyone who sets aside one of the least of these commands and teaches others accordingly will be called least in the kingdom of heaven'.

Mt. 5.17, 19a

Therefore, why the law? It was added to bring about transgressions. ... The law was given through angels and entrusted to a mediator. ... The scripture has locked up everything under the control of sin, ... But now that faith has come, we are no longer under a guardian.

Gal. 3.19, 22, 25

The Christ assemblage addressed by the Gospel of Matthew claimed *continuity* with covenantal Judaism.[1] This Gospel portrays Jesus Christ as a Jew, who followed the Jewish law, and expected his followers to do likewise (Mt. 5.17-20). This Jewish Christ is even portrayed as the new Moses, one who came not to abolish the Law but to 'fulfil' it. This Christ stresses the importance of living a righteous life through faithful observance of the Jewish law (§ 18.1). In contrast, the apostle Paul declared to the Gentile Christ assemblages in Galatia a profound *rupture* from the Jewish law and, by extension, from normative Judaism. He goes so far as to contend that the Jewish law has been irrevocably abrogated, that the law does not lead to righteousness but only to a curse (Gal. 3.10). He describes the purpose of the law in the most negative possible terms: 'Therefore why the law? It was added to bring about transgressions' (Gal. 3.19a), to incite humanity's rebellious nature, and thereby to 'enclose everything under sin' (Gal. 3.22) (§ 7.1.1).[2] How is it possible that the Matthean Christ assemblage was characterized by a profound *continuity* with normative Hellenistic Judaism, while Christ assemblages identified with Pauline Christianity were characterized by a profound *rupture*?

My previous analysis of biform social assemblages in Chapter 8 accounts for the coordination of the discursive and nondiscursive components of Christ assemblages in a shared power/knowledge diagram to achieve a productive capacity. However, a complete theory of social assemblages must also be able to account for *historical phenomena of continuity* and *rupture*. In this chapter, I will explain how some Christ assemblages achieved structural stability, while others underwent structural rupture.

1. The polarization of social assemblages

An assemblage can be modelled as a co-functioning of two types of *structural* components – a territory (§ 5) and strata (§ 7) – through the coordination of a historically specific, abstract machine or power/knowledge diagram (§ 8.4). This model, which highlights the *structural* components of social assemblages, their territory and strata, seems to imply that social assemblages are relatively stable formations. But, as the aforementioned example of the Pauline Christ assemblages demonstrate, social assemblages were also capable of extraordinary structural transformations.

All assemblages are capable of structural transformation and rupture because the territory of an assemblage is arranged along a *polarized axis*, ranging from territorialization to deterritorialization. The strata are similarly arranged along a *polarized axis* ranging from stratification to destratification (TP 145). By virtue of the polarization of the territory and strata, Christ assemblages were *tetravalent* formations: they oscillated between territorialized and deterritorialized, and between stratified and destratified forms. By implication, the schizoanalysis of Christ assemblages must include an analysis of how they functioned at their tetravalent poles. It must elucidate why some Christ assemblages exhibit stability and continuity, while others exhibit instability and rupture.

2. The ecumenon and planomenon

All assemblages are 'passional' in the sense that they are always coupling with other assemblages. In the Graeco-Roman world, small assemblages are characterized by a diffuse micro-segmentarity, such as synagogues and

Christ assemblages, routinely coupled with progressively larger assemblages up to, and including, the level of the abstract machine of the entire Roman Empire, considered as a mega-social assemblage. D&G term this mega-abstract machine the 'ecumenon'. An ecumenon diagrammatically coordinates the entire field of social assemblages, as an architectonic unity of systems, within the State apparatus.[3] As a case in point, the Roman ecumenon was a low-intensity abstract machine that *constituted the unity of the entire State apparatus*. While this ecumenon was never completely actualized in any single civic institution, *every civic* institution participated as extensions of the ecumenon. Consequently, power, manifested at the level of the individual civic institutions, was coordinated by the Roman ecumenon, through which they were grafted into an expansive diagram of power which connected all aspects of society. At any given moment, this Roman ecumenon constituted a virtual power/knowledge diagram of Graeco-Roman society (§ 8.4). Through the ecumenon, relations were established between all forms of social production.

The abstract machine of every Christ assemblage functioned, from lesser to greater degrees, in relation to other assemblages by means of the Roman ecumenon, which was always operating in the background, *attracting all assemblages towards their territorialized and stratified poles*. One might ask, what effect did the Roman ecumenon have on functioning of Christ assemblages in particular? To the extent that Christ assemblages were integrated into the Roman ecumenon, its discourses and iterative practices would have been linked to other social assemblages within society. It would thereby have functioned as an extension of the Roman ecumenon. Heavily stratified texts such as that we find in Rom. 13.1-2, 1 Cor. 11.3, Col. 3.22, 4.1 and *Did.* 4.10-11 reflect the power of the Roman ecumenon to attract Christ assemblages towards structural stasis (§ 7).

In addition to the ecumenon, D&G also theorize a *second* mega-abstract machine, one that is co-extensive with the plane of immanence (§ 2.3). They term this abstract machine the 'planomenon'. This abstract machine has a different mode of existence. In contrast to the *low*-intensity ecumenon, the planomenon is a *high*-intensity molecular abstract machine that *attracts* the structural components of territories and strata *towards their deterritorialized and destratified poles* (TP 40). As previously discussed, abstract machines operate within concrete assemblages as the 'cutting edges' of deterritorialization and destratification. This planomenon was always operating in the background of the Graeco-Roman world, destabilizing its assemblages and triggering various types of deterritorializations and destratifications. By virtue of the functioning of planomenon, all Christ assemblages were perpetually at risk of undergoing various types of transformations.

The operation of ecumenon and planomenon has profound implications for understanding the discursive production of early Christian texts. For all ancient texts emerged at the intersection of these two mega-abstract machines. Consequently, the textual production of Christ assemblages had an *excess of exteriorities* (F^f 51, F 43). Not only did such textual production (*qua* expression) occur in relation to the nondiscursive content through the coordination of an abstract machine or diagram (§ 8.2), but Christian 'writing machines' were also synchronized with that which was *exterior to* the Christ assemblage, namely, the Roman ecumenon. Textual production thereby became an extension of social systems of normalization, prohibition and coercion (cf. 2 Tim. 3.16-17, Heb. 4.12). However, the Christian 'writing machine' was also synchronized with what was *exterior to* the Roman ecumenon, namely the planomenon of the plane of immanence, the great orchestrator of all becomings, where all kinds of machines, including 'writing machines', coupled in unregulated profusion. Hence, Christian 'writing machines' possessed a *surplus of exteriorities,* consisting of the abstract machine of Christ assemblages, the Roman ecumenon, *and* the planomenon, each of which pulled discursive production in a different direction.

3. The God of religion and the schizo God

On the basis of these two conflicting mega-abstract machines – the ecumenon and planomenon – D&G differentiate two types of God: a 'God of religion', which operates in the ecumenon, and a 'schizo God', which functions in the planomenon (AO 85). These Gods are neither semi-personal powers, archaic archetypes, supernatural agents, nor illusory transcendentals. Indeed, they belong to the same differential 'Idea'. Deleuzian essences or 'Ideas' are simultaneously transcendental *and* immanent; they are concrete universals (§ 3.2). Like so many Deleuzo-Guattarian concepts, the God of religion and the schizo God imply one another. They belong to the same Deleuzian Idea, which is a problematic field, or 'perplexion', that puts human thought into motion.[4]

Whereas 'monotheistic consciousness' of orthodox Christianity requires a unitary God on a transcendental plane, these two Gods occupy the same virtual plane (Hillman 1975: 158). Though they are not semi-personal powers, being virtual, these Gods are nonetheless 'fully real' (*pleine réalité*). As previously discussed, D&G theorize *the virtual as fully real* (§ 3.2). Events on the virtual plane of a multiplicity are continuously actualized, indeed 'incarnated', on the historical plane of organization. Hence, changes in the intensive relation between the God of religion and the schizo God on the virtual plane give rise to changes on the actual plane of organization.

By far, the most familiar of these Gods is the God of religion. This God functioned as an extension of the social production of the Roman ecumenon, reinforcing the striated space of the organism, signification and subjectification (§ 7). Through this God, the Roman Empire attained the power to elevate the historically particular to the level of a universal or absolute *imperium*. As I have previously discussed, some Christ assemblages functioned in tandem with the Roman State apparatus (§ 7). The apostle Paul assimilated the Christian Father God to a despotic signifier that grounded the authority of emperors, governors, prefects and magistrates in the 'despotic socius' (Rom. 13.1-2). Through this God of religion, the bodies of Christ followers were stratified into 'organisms' that made up the working parts of the Roman State mega-assemblage. The Christian discourse which was 'inspired' by the God of religion derived its coherence from its effectiveness in supporting the social production of the Roman Empire.

Notwithstanding the self-evident role of the God of religion in the last two thousand years of Christianity, we must not overlook the opposing, diagrammatic activity of the schizo God, which disrupted the social production and opened up virtual lines of flight (§§ 6, 10, 15). Indeed, this schizo God could even function as a 'war machine' that undermined the workings of the God of religion (§ 18). Owing to the functioning of this schizo God, Christ assemblages, which seem to be closed, deterministic structures, always retained the capacity to become deterritorialized and destratified, to enter 'a more indistinct zone' where they had the possibility of undergoing 'a singular mutation or adaptation' (TP 383).

Hence, there is no simple opposition between the actions of these two Gods in early Christianity: they were interconnected within the same syllogism (AO 85). Like all Deleuzo-Guattarian concepts, the God of religion and schizo God do not compose a dualism but a *spectrum* of possibilities for actualization. Since the relations between these Gods are virtual and ideal, we should *always expect mixtures of them in historical formations*. Consequently, the inner workings of Christ assemblages were always conflicted, being tied to the social production of the Roman Empire and, simultaneously, capable of improvising lines of escape from social production.

Conclusion

Deleuzo-Guattarian assemblage theory can account for phenomena of both continuity and rupture in Christ assemblages. All Christ assemblages were located at the intersection of two mega-abstract machines, a low-intensity, Roman 'ecumenon' and a high-intensity 'planomenon'. Christ assemblages were caught between two, conflicting mega-abstract machines, resulting in complex phenomena of continuity and rupture. These two mega-abstract machines had very different modes of existence. This ecumenon diagrammatically coordinates the entire field of social assemblages, as an architectonic unity of systems, within the State apparatus. It functioned as the non-unifying, immanent cause of all social assemblages in the Roman Empire. It facilitated the co-functioning of the parts of the Roman State apparatus by reinforcing the stratified space of the organism, signification and subjectification. The diverse historical phenomenon that scholars collectively term 'early Christianity' was embedded in this Roman ecumenon. It operated in the background of all Christ social assemblages, attracting them towards their territorialized and stratified poles. By virtue of the Roman ecumenon, all Christ groups functioned, to a lesser or greater degree, as extensions of the social production of the Roman Empire. Consequently, power manifested at the level of individual Christ groups was often an expression of this vast power/knowledge diagram, which was co-extensive with the Roman Empire. However, the planomenon also operated in the background of Christ assemblages, attracting them towards their deterritorialized and destratified poles. The planomenon triggered processes of deterritorialization and destratification in Christ groups, which were manifested historically as phenomena of transformation and rupture. By virtue of the planomenon, Christ assemblages retained the virtual capacity to function as open, nondeterministic systems.

The functioning of the ecumenon and planomenon has implications for the exegesis of early Christian texts. For Christ assemblages, as 'writing machines', were caught between these conflicting abstract machines. Not only did the textual production of Christ assemblages (*qua* expression) function in tandem with the nondiscursive plane of content through the coordination of an abstract machine (or diagram), but Christian 'writing machines' were also governed by the Roman ecumenon, which was *exterior* to the social assemblage, through which they functioned as an extension of social production. But this is not the whole story: Christian 'writing machines' were also conditioned by *second* mega-abstract machine, the planomenon, which was *exterior* to the Roman ecumenon: the planomenon functioned as the hidden force behind all manner of deterritorializations and destratifications of early Christian discourse.

Based on these opposing mega-abstract machines, D&G distinguish between two types of God, a God of religion, which operates in the ecumenon, and a corresponding schizo God, which functions in the planomenon. We are all too familiar with the stratifications wrought by the God of religion throughout the history of Christianity: in the first four centuries of the Common Era, the schizo God functioned as an extension of the social production of the Roman Empire, reinforcing the stratified space of the organism, signification and subjectification. However, as a survey of historical sources would demonstrate, the emergence of early 'Christianity' was not a unitary phenomenon. Therefore, scholars of early Christianity must take care not to overlook parallel diagrammatic workings of the schizo God in small Christ groups. Therefore, schizoanalysis of Christ groups must be two pronged, with due attention directed towards both the low-intensity Roman ecumenon and its God of religion, *and* towards the high-intensity planomenon and its schizo God.

10

The myth of Eve: Falling into, and out of, delusion

Let a woman learn in silence with full submission. I permit no woman to teach or to have authority over a man. She is to keep silent. For Adam was formed first, then Eve; and Adam was not deceived, but the woman was deceived, and became a transgressor. Yet she will be saved through childbearing.

1 Tim. 2.11-15

What must you do to be saved? The author of 1 Timothy does not prevaricate: if you are a woman, the answer is simple: be silent, submissive, sexually available to your husband and, above all, produce lots of children. This is the teaching of 1 Tim. 2.11-15, which is based, in part, on an interpretation of the myth of Eve (Gen. 3.1-13). This primeval myth memorializes Eve for having been deceived by a snake into transgressing the law of God. Not only did Eve transgress the command of God, but she also has the distinction of being the first human being to do so. Hence, the author of 1 Timothy argues that since Eve is the *prototype for all women*, all women, as Eve's descendants, are dangerous and must be subordinated to the authority of their husbands.

Given the importance of Eve in the early Christian imagination, it is surprising that she is never mentioned again in the Hebrew Bible after Gen. 4.1: 'Adam had sexual intercourse with his wife Eve, and she became pregnant and gave birth to Cain.' But the memory of Eve was revived in Hellenistic period in both Judaism and early Christianity, at a time when male anxiety over women was on the rise. Though we may be inclined to ignore the place of Eve in the early Christian imaginary, it is not a matter of indifference that no less a figure than the apostle Paul remembers Eve as the one who was deceived by the serpent, and then deceived her husband: 'But I fear, lest by any means, as the serpent deceived Eve in his craftiness, your minds should be corrupted from the simplicity and the purity that is toward Christ' (2 Cor. 11.2-3). In the Hellenistic period, the myth of Eve condensed the threat that *all* Christian wives posed to their husbands.

As I shall explain below, the myth of Eve can be mapped in terms of three interrelated errors of desire: namely, errors connected with lack, law and language. First, Eve's desire was organized by her experience of a *lack*, with respect to the fruit from the tree situated in the middle of the garden (Gen. 3.6a). Second, Eve's desire was organized with respect to God's *law* (Gen. 3.2-3). And third, her desire was *signified* by the serpent through language (Gen. 3.4). Judged on the basis of the themes of lack, law and language the myth of Eve bears a striking similarity to D&G's 'three errors of desire' in *Anti-Oedipus*, the errors of 'lack (*manque*), law (*loi*), and signifier (*signifiant*)' (AO^f 132, AO 111). Indeed, if one superimposes D&G's 'three errors of desire' onto the myth of Eve, it becomes evident that a complex relationship exists between them.[1] In making this observation, I am in no way implying that D&G employed this myth as a model for their analysis of desire. The myth of Eve is nonetheless evocative of D&G's 'errors of desire' in a very specific fashion. As I shall explain below, the explanation for the correspondences between the myth of Eve and D&G's three errors of desire is somewhat more convoluted.

The missing link between the myth of Eve and D&G's 'three errors of desire' is Jacques Lacan's structural analysis of desire, who, in turn, *was interacting with some of the key themes of theological anthropology*. Hence, even Lacan's notion of desire (§ 2) can be said to be 'theological', a point made by D&G, who humorously observe that Lacan's 'notions cannot be prevented from dragging their theological cortege behind: namely, the insufficiency of being, guilt, signification' (AO^f 132, AO 111). Lacan's so-called 'theological cortege' is connected with theological anthropology's 'grammar of God', which continues to be preoccupied with the themes of humanity's insufficiency, or *lack*, before God, humanity's guilt arising from the transgression of the *law* of God and the theologian's heavy task of *signifying* the true meaning of existence through language. Of course, the touchstone for this theological anthropology is Augustine's doctrine of original sin, which maintains that, through Eve's transgression of God's law, and Adam's transgression through Eve, human nature has been irrevocably corrupted, and all human beings are thereby born into a state of original sin.[2] The legacy of this tradition of theological anthropology is a 'grammar of God' that has survived to the present day, a point to which I shall return below.[3]

In his psychoanalytic theory Jacques Lacan translated this theological 'grammar of God' into a set of *structural* operations within the symbolic register. He employed this 'grammar of God' as a structure – albeit an *empty* structure

– for his psychoanalytic theory.[4] Thus, D&G's 'three errors of desire' are *directly connected* to Lacan's symbolic register and, through it, they are indirectly *connected to theological anthropology and the myth of Eve*. Based on this somewhat complex set of interconnections, this chapter will discuss the myth of the 'fall' of Eve in relation to D&G's three errors of desire. I will argue that Eve's 'fall' was not a fall into primordial sin, as Augustine supposed, but rather hers was a *fall into a delusional system of thought* that can be traced back to the three errors of desire, namely, the errors of lack, the law and the signifier.

1. Falling into delusion

According to D&G the three errors of desire – the errors of lack, law and the signifier – stem from one and the same error, which is the error of idealization (AO[f] 132, AO 111). As previously discussed, stratification is a process that overcodes human bodies on the basis of a vertical alliance of a surplus value to an idealized transcendental (§ 7). D&G single out three strata in particular – 'three great strata' – owing to their harmful effects on the human body: the strata of subjectification, the organism and signification (§ 7.1). As I shall discuss below, and the 'subject' is formed through the idealization of lack, the 'organism' is produced through the idealization of law, and signification through the idealization of language. Thus, the three errors of desire are also connected with the three great strata.

1.1. The idealization of lack: The subject

Eve's desire was organized on the basis of the idealization of her experience of 'lack' (*manque*). Theological anthropology argues that Eve experienced the lack an empirical object – the fruit of the tree – which she believed was 'desirable as a source of wisdom' (Gen. 3.6). As previously discussed, Lacanian structural analysis defines desire in terms of *lack* but, contrary to theological anthropology, not in terms of the lack of an empirical object (§ 2.1). In Lacanian analysis lack is an *empty* position because the object-cause (*objet a*) of desire, being a fantasy, is always missing. The fruit upon which Eve gazed functioned as a kind of screen upon which she projected her idealized object of desire, *objet a*, namely, a fruit that would make her 'like divine beings' – like gods – 'knowing good and evil' (Gen. 3.4). This delusional object of Eve's desire, being a phantasmatic object, was unobtainable. At a deeper level, that which is lacking is not just the object of desire but the very 'being' of the subject: 'The lack is the lack of being (*manque à être*) properly' (Lacan 1988: 223). In truth, an ontological subject of lack is missing. But Eve mistakenly idealized her experience of lack back to a unified *subject* of this experience: through her idealization of lack, a 'subject' of lack is produced (§ 2). The ontological subjecthood of Eve was created through a positivization of an absence.

1.2. The idealization of the law: The organism

Eve's desire was also organized through the idealization of law. Theological anthropology idealizes the prohibition directed at Eve as a divine commandment: '*God* said, "You shall not eat of the fruit of the tree in the middle of the garden or touch it, lest you die"' (Gen. 3.2-3). On this basis, Augustine interpreted Eve's transgression of this divine law as her 'fall into' sin. However, when viewed from a Lacanian perspective, Eve's desire was organized, *in advance*, by the prohibition of law. Indeed, her desire to transgress God's law was a function of the prohibition itself: 'Desire is essentially the desire to transgress, and for there to be transgression it is first necessary for there to be prohibition' (Lacan 1992: 83–4, § 7.1.1). According to Lacan, the law is the same as repressed desire (1966: 765–90). Eve could only desire what the law prohibited (Lacan 1966: 787). Hence, the object of the law and desire are the same: the imposition of law and acts of transgression are complementary structural operations. For without law, transgression is impossible. The law itself is nothing. It is an empty, pure form that makes transgression possible. Through idealization, human laws are transformed into divine Law, a despotic signifier (*signifiant despotique*), characterized by *lack*.[5] But from a structural perspective, the idealization of laws as Law is nothing but a kind of positivization of the structural *absence* of a despotic signifier in language. The endless syntagmatic process of words pointing to other words (*signifiance*) cannot be halted owing to the absence of a master signifier. As Lacan observes, language as 'Other' (*Autre*) has no Other (*A̶u̶t̶r̶e̶*) (Lacan 2002: 300–2).[6] But with the idealization of laws as Law, Law functions as the final reference point or master signifier, for all signifying processes. D&G observe that there is little to say about this idealized Law because it is 'a pure abstraction, … it is nothing. Lack or excess it hardly matters' (TP 115). Thus, Law is a master signifier of *absence*. Hence, such Law is intrinsically unknowable because it is nothing but an *empty pure form*, devoid of content, that produces guilt and punishment. The Law, being unknowable, *makes itself known only by the guilt and punishments that it induces*, that is, as it applies to human bodies.

This Law produces the 'organism' which is always already guilty before the law (§ 7.1.1).[7] Hence, Eve's transgression, which may seem so rebellious and transgressive to us, was determined in advance by law. Just as the idealization of lack produces Eve as a subject who experiences lack, so also does *the idealization of law as transcendental Law produces Eve as an 'organism', who is always already guilty before the law.*

1.3. The idealization of language: The master signifier

Eve's desire was organized, not only by the idealization of lack and law but by the idealization of language. Indeed, language is *the* dominant component of the symbolic register (§ 12.1). Language as Other (*Autre*) supplies a symbolic framework for the construction of the 'object-cause' of desire (*objet a*) (§ 2.1). Language as a signifying system binds human beings tightly to the strata of the organism and subjectification.

Through language, the serpent interpreted Eve's desire to her, and likewise through language that Eve, in turn, interpreted the 'object-cause' of her desire to Adam (Gen. 3.4, 6b). Lacan would argue that through language, Eve became a 'divided subject': she became a 'subject of the statement' (*sujet d'énoncé*) that was *subjectified by* language, and simultaneously a 'subject of enunciation' (*sujet d'énonciation*) that was *subjected to* language (§ 13.1.2). In other words, Eve's subjecthood was *divided* by the formal structure of language into an 'I' who speaks, and an 'I' that reveals its unconscious through speaking.[8] But prior to Eve's entry into language, there was no subject to divide. For it is language that establishes the very grounds of possibility for subjectification (§§ 7, 12). Hence, the divided subjecthood of Eve does not mask a prior ontological Subject. Like the idealization and lack and law, *the idealization of language* produces a Subject that is nothing, a mere divided subject produced by the structure of language.

When considered on the basis of the themes of lack, law and language, the myth of Eve bears a striking similarity to D&G's three errors of desire, the errors of lack, law and the signifier. What is more, when considered the vantage point of Lacanian structural analysis, we can conclude that Eve's 'fall' was not a fall into primordial sin, as Augustine supposed, but rather was a fall in a primordial *delusion founded on lack*. Eve, having fallen into this delusion, was ignorant of the ways in which she inhabited the symbolic world, and especially of the ways in which this symbolic world had stratified her desire and overcoded her into an organism.

However, Augustine was correct on one point: Eve's 'fall' was *primordial* in the sense that the myth of Eve condenses the delusional state of *all* human beings, including the community of Christ followers addressed by 1 Timothy. For the three errors of desire, which underlie the myth of Eve, also inform the interpretation of this myth in 1 Tim. 2.11-15. Through Christian interpretation of this myth, God's curse on Eve (Gen. 3.16) was transformed into a *curse on all female Christ followers*. Consequently, women, as offspring of Eve, were forced to submit to the authority of their husbands for their sexual pleasure and the production of children.

If Eve is the paradigmatic model of transgression, then Mary, the mother of Jesus, is the corresponding model of obedience (§ 15.2.1). By virtue of her obedience to the Father God, in the form of her sexual submission – 'Let it happen to me as you have said' (Lk. 1.38) – Mary functioned as the model for all women to imitate. Upon first inspection, it may seem that Eve is the anti-type of Mary, for Eve disobeyed God, and brought a divine curse upon humanity, whereas Mary obeyed God, and brought humanity blessing. But from a structural point of view, Eve's transgression and Mary's obedience are equivocal moves: transgression and obedience are both structure operations that reinforce in almost equal measure the Law as a despotic signifier.

As 1 Timothy's interpretation of Eve demonstrates, the myth of Eve also had a role to play in the maintenance of male subjectivity. Luce Irigaray has observed that, despite woman's liminal, 'not-fully-man' status, she still functions as the *necessary* 'other', the 'backside' against which man has affirmed his own delusional subjectivity (1985: 135). As Eve's descendants, all women supply the necessary backside of the male delusional ego: woman – as copies of Eve – had to be abjected to the periphery of the 'despotic socius' (§ 7.2) to define its centre, where the male delusional ego took its final meaning and authority.

Lacan argues that there is no escape from the ontological and ahistorical delusions generated by the symbolic order: 'desire-as-lack', and the errors connected with lack, law and language are an inescapable human condition. At the point when a child enters the symbolic register of lack, law and language, it becomes an 'oedipal' subject for whom the 'real' becomes the 'impossible real' (*réel impossible*). With the disappearance of the 'real', there is no way to escape from the illusion of 'reality'. However, D&G are not so pessimistic: they argue that there is an *exteriority* to human 'desire-as-lack' in which desire lacks *nothing*. As previously discussed, the plane of immanence is always working in the background of society, destabilizing the symbolic register and delusions produced through the errors of desire (§§ 2.3, 9.1). Therefore, the stratification of human desire *can be reversed* by disrupting the processes of social production that overcoded desire in the first place (§§ 7, 10). Hence, the narrative of *Anti-Oedipus* takes the form of a *felix culpa*, a 'happy fall'.

Of course, *Anti-Oedipus* traces the gradual transformation of an intense, germinal 'body without organs' into an overcoded 'organism'. This is a history of the increasing contraction of relations from 'primitive' connections within tribes, in relation to a chief as surplus value, to a 'despotic' form of organization based on the vertical filiation of a king ('despot-god'), as surplus value, to a deity (despotic signifier) (§ 12.2.2); it then traces the transformation of this 'organism' into a privatized subjectivity, as the ultimate point of contraction, based on capital as surplus value (§ 7.2). But the narrative of *Anti-Oedipus*, considered in epic terms, actually takes the form of a *felix culpa*, for it anticipates the possible 'eschatological' re-emergence of the 'body without organs' in a 'kairotic' moment. Indeed, the primary theme *Anti-Oedipus* is a call for subjectivity of both subjected individuals and groups *to cease functioning as a closed system* (organism), and instead to construct new cartographies of self-reference as a 'body without organs'. Through involution, the 'body without organs' can actualize possibilities that are *virtually* available to it.[9] Owing to the virtual presence of this 'body without organs' in every human body and group, nothing is predetermined or inevitable about our 'fallen' human condition. On this basis, we can even dare to interpret Eve's 'fall' into delusion as a 'happy fall' because it points towards the virtual, unrealized possibilities of the 'body without organs' of an individual or group. When viewed from this vantage point, Eve's 'fall' serves as the *starting point* for new ways of desiring, one that is disengaged from lack.

2. Falling out of delusion

Is there evidence that Christ groups of the first three centuries of the Common Era managed, at least in limited ways, to escape from a delusional system of thought as old as Eve? In theoretical terms, this scenario seems likely because every Christ group was positioned at the boundary between the Roman ecumenon and the planomenon, between the God of religion and the schizo God (§ 9), which conferred on it virtual points of deterritorialization and destratification. Minimally, the incitement of such a 'schiz' or bifurcation could provide the means for it to reach a less repressive, less neurotic equilibrium.

Félix Guattari is particularly interested in investigating how a 'subjected group' (*groupe assujetti*), characterized by societal repression, can become deterritorialized and transform into a 'subject group' (*groupe-sujet*), which is capable of constructing its own cartographies of self-reference (Guattari 2015: 39–51, 102–20, 206–34, 318–29). Guattari theorized that, through forms of experimentation, such subjected groups could escape from determinism and societal repression and liberate new potentials for living. Caught between stratified 'desire-as-lack' of social production and the desiring production of the planomenon, Christ groups would have had the sensation of living in two places simultaneously: as a 'subjected group', they would have had the sensation of being 'at home' in their delusions and self-repression; but as a 'subject group', they would also have the feeling of being called into an 'elsewhere', a virtual 'kingdom of the schizo God' exterior to it. Is there any evidence to support this theoretical conjecture? Did subjected Christ groups, characterized by the delusions of desire, ever actualize their virtual capacity as subject groups to fall out of this same delusion? By way of answering this question, let us consider the stories of two female Christ followers, Thecla and Maximilla, as narrated in the Acts of Paul and Thecla and in The Acts of Andrew, respectively.[10]

3. Falling out of delusion in the Apocryphal Acts

The Apocryphal Acts, considered as discursive components of various historical Christ assemblages, functioned as 'expression', which was coordinated with (nondiscursive) 'content' (§ 8.3). In the Apocryphal Acts, women are consistently portrayed as being superior to men (except for the apostles) and models of self-control, faith and endurance in the face of adversity. In this chapter, I will focus on the lives of two such women, Thecla, a follower of the apostle Paul, and Maximilla, a follower of the apostle Andrew who through her choice to remain chaste was transformed into the new Eve. I will argue that in different ways, both Thecla and Maximilla disrupted the delusion of desire-as-lack.

3.1. The case of Thecla 'falling out' of delusion

In terms of the 'form of expression' (§ 8.3.2.2), the Acts of Paul and Thecla is a hagiographic romance.[11] The hero of this narrative, Thecla, is a young virgin who is attracted to Paul's preaching on 'the word of God about sexual abstinence and the resurrection' (Acts Th. 5). In many respects, this ethics of sexual abstinence constitutes the opposite to the morality advanced in 1 Timothy, which defines women's bodies in terms of sin, sex and childbearing.

The subject matter of Paul's preaching in the Acts of Paul and Thecla is based on an amalgamation of texts, including the advice Paul gives in 1 Cor. 7.29, and select Matthean beatitudes (Acts Th. 5.1–6.7). In 1 Cor. 7.29, Paul advised the Corinthians that, in view of the nearness of Christ's return (parousia), 'those who have wives be as though they had none'. In the Acts of Paul and Thecla, this piece of informal pastoral advice is converted into an ethical imperative: Paul commands, 'Fear only one God and to live in sexual abstinence' (Acts Th. 9).

This purported preaching of Paul on sexual abstinence anticipates the remarkable story of Thecla that follows. For the author holds up Thecla as a hero of virginity for all women to follow (McLean 2017: 78–9). Next, the author quotes a Matthean beatitude (Mt. 5.8), 'Blessed are the pure in heart, for they shall see God' (Acts Th. 5.1). But he strategically modifies this beatitude with the addition of new beatitude, 'Blessed are they that have kept the flesh chaste (ἀγνή), for they shall become a temple of God; blessed are those who are sexually abstinent (ἐγκρατεῖς), for God shall speak to them' (Acts Th. 5.2-3). By means of this supplementary beatitude, the author transforms Mt. 5.8 into 'the word of God concerning sexual abstinence (ἐγρατεία)' (Acts Th. 5).

Paul's preaching, considered in the literary context of the Acts of Paul and Thecla, is directed to women. But, as I have argued elsewhere, a close reading of these beatitudes suggests that the intended audience of these beatitudes may have been married *men* (McLean 2017: 75–8). Acts Th. 5.5 declares that 'Blessed are they that *have wives as not having them* (quoting 1 Cor. 7.29), for they shall inherit God.'[12] Perhaps, these beatitudes served as a reminder to husbands that the renunciation of the world included the renunciation of sexual pleasure, even with their own wives. And that which applies to wives also applies to daughters, for every virgin is a man's daughter, and potentially another man's fiancé. Hence, the beatitudes also praise female virginity with great extravagance: 'Blessed are the bodies of the virgins (τὸ σώματα τῶν παρθένων), for they shall be well-pleasing unto God and shall not lose the reward of their chastity' (Acts Th. 6.7). Even if the intended audience of these beatitudes may have been men, this does not exclude the possibility that female Christ followers also reflected on these stories, perhaps in terms of their own vulnerability to their husbands and would-be suitors. By illustrating strategies of resistance, Thecla, a hero of sexual abstinence, may also have provided a role model for women to follow.

As previously discussed, every Christ group can be mapped as a biform social assemblage in which discourse, as expression, functioned in coordination with nondiscursive practices, as content (§ 8.3.2.1). What impact might this discourse on the life of Thecla (*qua* expression) have had on the social assemblage to which it belonged? Did the Christ assemblage, whose substance of expression included the Acts of Paul and Thecla, discover a way to *fall out of* the delusions of desire? Through the abstract machine, as a shared power/knowledge diagram, male and female bodies would have been organized in relation to discourse (§ 8.4). The Acts of Paul and Thecla (*qua* expression) may have played a role, through the mediation of this power/knowledge diagram, in dismantling the stratification of women's bodies, as modelled by the life of Thecla herself, and thereby opened up ways of 'falling out' of the delusions of desire.

3.2. The case of Maximilla 'falling out' of delusion

The story of Maximilla may also have played a role in the destratification of Christian desire. In contrast to the unmarried virgin, Thecla, the female hero of the Acts of Andrew is a *married* woman, Maximilla. When the apostle Andrew arrived in Patras, Andrew met her husband, Aegeates, who was distraught because Maximilla was dying.[13] Andrew miraculously healed Maximilla and, from that day forward, her life was changed; she invited Andrew to visit her daily and teach her the new faith. Andrew's instruction on sexual abstinence led her to adopt a life of sexual abstinence, much to the dismay of her husband, Aegeates (McLean 2017: 79–80). Aegeates became so enraged that he had Andrew thrown into prison in the hope of compelling Maximilla to resume sexual relations with him. When Maximilla visited Andrew in prison and explained her dilemma to him, the apostle exhorted her to remain chaste, and to not submit to Aegeates' demands. Andrew's speech, which follows this advice, relocates the life of Maximilla, and his own life, in terms of the myth of Adam and Eve: Maximilla, he declares, is the 'second Eve', and he proclaims himself to be the 'second Adam' (cf. Rom. 5.6-21). He explains that, just as Eve brought sin into the world, Maximilla has the power to repair the effects of Eve's sin in her own life through her own decision to remain chaste, and thereby *undo the harm done to women by Eve*:

> Surely in you I see Eve repenting and in myself Adam returning; for that which she suffered in ignorance, you now (for whose soul I strive) set right by returning. … For her defect you have remedied by not suffering like her; and (Adam's) imperfection I have perfected by taking refuge with God; that which she disobeyed you have obeyed. … For it is ordained that everyone should correct (and raise up again) his own fall. (Acts And. 5)

Through her decision to remain constant in her life of chastity, Maximilla absolved all women of Eve's transgression. She thereby restored women to their prelapsarian condition. Just as women were deformed by the 'fall' of Eve, so also is an escape from the 'fall' miraculously afforded to all women through the life of the *second Eve*, Maximilla. Considered from the vantage point of assemblage theory, this discourse on the life of Maximilla, as the second Eve, functioned as the 'substance of expression' in relation to the nondiscursive 'substance of content' of a Christ assemblage. Did this discourse introduce fresh intensities into the 'subjected group' to which it belonged? Did this 'subjected group' manage to escape the delusions of desire, at least in some measure, and become a 'subject group'? Before attempting to answer this question, it is important to bear in mind that a full destratification of a 'subjected group' is neither achievable nor desirable. As D&G advise,

> You have to keep enough of the organism for it to reform each dawn; and you have to keep small supplies of significance and subjectification, if only to turn them against their own systems when the circumstances demand it, when things, persons, even situations, force you to; and you have to keep small rations of subjectivity in sufficient quantity to enable you to respond to the dominant reality. Mimic the strata. You don't reach the BwO, and its plane of consistency, by wildly destratifying. (TP 160)

D&G advise that subjected groups should carefully and cautiously dismantle their strata. Care and caution are required because 'Staying stratified – organized, signified, subjected – is not the worst that can happen; the worst that can happen is if you throw the strata into demented or suicidal collapse' (TP 161). It is only through careful attention to the strata that one succeeds in finding a 'line of flight'. Evidence for the destratification of a subjected group would not take the form of 'wild' destratifications but of small experiments in living, such as we find in the stories of Thecla and Maximilla. Perhaps the lives of Thecla and Maximilla did inspire such experiments in living outside of the delusions of desire.

Conclusion

In strong contrast to the desiring production on the plane of immanence, human desire is organized through the idealization of lack, law and language. The ensuing stratification of desire results in three 'errors of desire', which collectively constitute a delusional system of thought. So widespread is this delusional system of thought that it is evident even in the myth of the 'fall' of Eve. For if one superimposes the three errors of desire on the myth of Eve, it is evident that a complex relationship exists between them. The law that prohibited Eve from eating the fruit was the same as repressed desire, for one can only desire what the law prohibits.

The Christian interpretation of the myth of Eve in 1 Tim. 2.11-15 illustrates how the desire of Christ followers was also stratified on the basis of the myth of the 'fall' of Eve. While theological anthropology remains preoccupied with the themes of humanity's insufficiency before God, guilt and questions of meaning, this chapter has argued that Eve's 'fall' was not a fall into primordial sin, as Augustine supposed, but rather a 'fall' into a primordial *delusion* founded on the idealization of lack, law and language.

The narrative of *Anti-Oedipus* traces the gradual transformation of the intense germinal 'body without organs' to the overcoded 'organism'. The primary thrust of *Anti-Oedipus* is a call for subjectivity – both subjected individuals and groups – to cease functioning as a *closed system* (as an 'organism'), and to construct new cartographies of self-reference as a 'body without organs'. Thus, the overarching narrative of *Anti-Oedipus* takes the form of a *felix culpa*, a 'happy fall', by anticipating the re-emergence of the eventual 'body without organs'. Drawing inspiration from this insight, this chapter has argued that Eve's 'fall' into delusion may also have been a *felix culpa*. For this myth implies that if humanity has 'fallen into' such a delusional system of thought, it is also possible to 'fall out' of it again. From this vantage point, Eve's fall is *instructive* to us, at least insofar as it provides the de facto starting point – the overcoded 'organism' – for a schizoanalytic practice that is aimed at disengaging human desire from its fixation on idealized lack, law and signifiers.

Is it possible that some Christ followers managed to escape from a delusional system as old as Eve? This chapter has discussed two female heroes of the Apostolic Acts, Thecla and Maximilla, who promoted an ethic of desire that was diametrically opposed to the morality promoted in 1 Timothy. It seems that, between the Apostolic Acts and 1 Timothy, a war was being waged between the 'body without organs' and the 'organism'. Thecla is held up as a hero of virginity for all women to follow. Maximilla, who commits herself to a life of sexual asceticism, even within marriage, is accorded the *status of the new Eve*. Her actions eradicated the negative effects of Eve's 'fall' for all women.

If we map Christ groups as biform social assemblages, then discourses such as the lives of Thecla and Maximilla would have functioned (as expression) in coordination with nondiscursive practices through the mediation of a power/knowledge diagram (§ 8.3-4). What impact might these discourses have had on Christ groups, as 'subjected groups', within the Roman ecumenon? Could these discourses have introduced fresh intensities into these subjected groups, whereby they transformed into 'subject groups'?

While these questions are ultimately unanswerable, we must bear in mind that the existential territories of human beings are impregnated with virtual potentials. Through practical experimentation, subjected groups can trigger a 'schiz' or bifurcation that actualizes previously unrealized potentialities (§ 4.2.3, n. 11). In this way, the lives of Thecla and Maximilla could have had a role in helping Christ followers 'fall out' of this delusional system of thought. Considered in light of the heroic lives of Thecla and Maximilla, the ancient myth of Eve's 'fall' into delusion anticipates the possibility of 'falling' out of the delusions of 'desire-as-lack' and awakening to the possibilities of life disengaged from idealization.

11

On several regimes of signs and several Christs

As Christ was setting out on a journey, a man ran up to him and knelt before him, and asked, 'Good teacher, what must I do to inherit eternal life?' Christ answered, 'Why do you call me good? No one is good but God alone'.

Mk 10.17-18

Was Jesus a good man? Beginning with the prologue, the Gospel of Mark repeatedly tells the reader that Jesus is the Son of God (Mk 1.1). At his baptism, Jesus is informed by God, 'You are my Son, the beloved, with you I am well pleased' (Mk 1.11), and even the demons recognize that Jesus is the Son of God (Mk 1.1, 3.11). If we accept that Jesus is the Son of God, then common sense would dictate that Jesus was also, at the very least, a *good* man. So why then does Mark's narrative seem to change gears in Mk 10.18? When a man addresses Jesus as '*good* teacher' (διδάσκαλε ἀγαθέ), why does Jesus reprimand him, asking, 'Why do you call me good? Why does he declare, 'No one is good but God alone.'[1] Why does Jesus take offense at this modest compliment? In this transformation from Jesus, the Son of God, to Jesus, the 'not-so-good-teacher', we seem to have crossed over a threshold from one Christology to another or, more precisely, from one 'regime of signs' to another.

Jesus' reprimand in Mk 10.18 poses a problem to traditional exegetical practice, which (as I have previously argued) is structured on a communicational model. Exegesis views early Christian texts as linguistic containers for the storage and retrieval of ideas and information communicated by their authors (§ 1.3). Thus, for Friedrich Schleiermacher, authorial intent constituted the truth of the text (though this truth may not be true in terms of 'correspondence'). In effect, 'ex-egesis' (ἐξ-ήγησις) attempts to retrieve, or bring 'out' (ἐξ), these hidden ideas and information, and render them in contemporary language. Such exegetical practice is so thickly overlaid with undeclared and untested assumptions that the ideas and information it retrieves is often of dubious value.

Another such assumption is the belief that every occurrence of the name 'Christ' in the texts of the New Testament designates the *same* referent. Even at the level of redaction criticism, this assumption is highly problematic: for we are accustomed to speak of Mark's Christ, as suffering Son of God, and Matthew's Christ, as Jewish messiah, and Luke's Christ, as prophet from God (§ 12), and John's Christ, as Son sent by the Father God (§ 13) – and indeed many other Christs besides – but we cannot speak of a single, unequivocal referent that is 'Christ'. Indeed, the proliferation of Christs in early Christian writings fragments the term 'Christ' to such an extent that it loses any essential *truth*. The multiplication of Christs in early Christian discourse exposes the *untruth* of any purported unified referent. However, the problematic assumptions associated with traditional exegetical practice go well beyond the multiplication of discursive constructions of Christ: the greatest failing of exegesis is its lack of awareness of the operation of regimes of signs. For, as Foucault observes, truth is always part of a 'regime of truth' (1980: 133). Hence, we must not harbour the empty dream of articulating in the human signifying systems non-contextual truth statements.

1. What is a regime of signs?

D&G describe a 'regime of signs' (*régime de signes*) as a 'specific formalization of *expression*' in relation to nondiscursive 'content' (TP 111, § 8.3.2.1). By virtue of regimes of signs, every Christian discourse functioned *as expression* within a biform social assemblage in relation to 'content' (nondiscursive formations), including iterative group practices and human bodies, through the coordination of a power/knowledge 'diagram' or 'abstract machine' (§ 8.4). As previously discussed, this 'diagram' functioned as a kind of virtual 'electric circuit' that coordinated expression and content in relation to the ecumenon (§ 9). Just as structures in general are subordinate to machinic processes (§ 1.1), so also are *linguistic* structures subordinate to regimes of signs (§ 1.3). As Ronald Bogue observes,

> Language has an important function within the anthropomorphic stratum, but only as a component of a semiotic machine, i.e., a collective arrangement of enunciation or regime of signs. Yet an abstract machine … is also immanent within every regime of signs, and hence within language as well. (1989: 149)

Language and linguistic signifying processes – including the Hellenistic Greek of the New Testament – are primarily a *linguistic codification of a power/knowledge diagram*. Only secondarily is language a vehicle for the storage and retrieval of ideas, theologies and information. In short, *language is a semiotic flow before it is a linguistic code*. D&G give the example of the linguistic statement, 'I love you'. The analysis of this statement depends on the regime of signs in which it is embedded, and what nonlinguistic elements give it consistency.

> There is a presignifying 'I love you' of the collective type in which, … a dance weds all the women of the tribe; there is a counter-signifying 'I love you' of the distributive and polemical type that has to do with war and relations of force …; there is an 'I love you' that is addressed to a center of significance and uses interpretation to make a whole series of signifieds correspond to the signifying chain; and there is a postsignifying or passional 'I love you' that constitutes a proceeding beginning from a point of subjectification, then another, and yet another. (TP 147)

Likewise, the diverse linguistic statements concerning Christ in early Christian writings are all operationalizations of specific regimes of signs. For discourses such as the canonical Gospels to emerge on the historical 'plane of organization' – which we term the Graeco-Roman world – they first had to fulfil a set of complex rules or conditions, which were *predetermined* by a specific regime of signs. In other words, the very possibility of writing a 'life' of Christ was *supplied in advance* by a specific regime of signs. As previously discussed, these rules determine *in advance* what is thinkable in any age; they determine, in advance, what discursive 'statements' can be 'caught in the true' (§ 0.4). Discursive 'truth' is always part of a 'regime of truth' (Foucault 1980: 133).

In point of fact, no discursive (or redactional) construction of 'Christ' operated purely on the level of language and linguistic signification: every discursive 'Christ' entailed a regime of signs, which participated in a historically specific power/knowledge 'diagram' or 'abstract machine' (§§ 1.3, 8.4). By virtue of this power/knowledge diagram, discursive constructions of Christ functioned in ways that cannot be reduced to a set of authorial ideas and information, *much less to theological concepts*. What is more, every power/knowledge diagram functioned in coordination with progressively larger abstract machines up to the level of Roman ecumenon and its 'God of religion', through which it was connected with the relations of power at work in the Graeco-Roman 'despotic socius' as a whole (§ 9). *In sum, all early Christian texts were formed by regimes of signs, and all regimes of signs functioned within power/knowledge diagrams.* When we recognize the complex interrelation between discourse, regimes of signs and diagrams of power a new set of questions present themselves. Instead of asking, 'Who was Christ?', the interpreter would ask, Within what Christ assemblages and diagrams of power were various discursive 'Christs' produced?

2. Mapping regimes of signs

In *A Thousand Plateaus*, D&G map out what they describe as an 'arbitrarily limited' typology of four regimes of signs: namely, a 'presignifying regime', which is associated with the 'primitive territorial socius',[2] a 'signifying despotic regime', which is associated with the 'despotic or imperial' socius (§§ 7.2, 12), a postsignifying 'passional subjective regime' (§ 13) and a 'countersignifying' regime.

To explicate these regimes of signs, D&G employ 'mapping' as an analytical tool (§ 0.4). Hence, these four regimes of signs are really four maps, not four representations or 'tracings'. To explicate these regimes of signs, D&G employ 'mapping' as an analytical tool (§ 0.4). Hence, these four regimes of signs are really four maps, not four representations or 'tracings'. A map is not a representation. As D&G themselves observe, their philosophy 'has to do with surveying, mapping, even realms that are yet to come', not with 'signifying' or representing (TP 5). A Deleuzo-Guattarian 'map' is rhizomatic in the sense that it is an *open* system with multiple entryways and exits (§ 0.3). D&G employ 'mapping' as a means of exploring the *exteriority* of systems in relation to other systems. For every map is connectable to other maps.

For we must always bear in mind that the four regimes of signs, which constitute D&G's typology, *imply one another*. Like a Deleuzian 'Idea', their typology of four regimes of signs composes a *single* set of interrelations. For example, whereas the 'signifying despotic regime' is an *impersonal* regime that converges on the *face* of a 'despot-god', located at the centre of a system of interrelated discursive circles (§ 12), the 'passional subjective regime' is a *subjective* regime, in which a passional figure (such as a prophet) *betrays the face* of the 'despot-god' (§ 13). Thus, the relation of the former to the latter regime of signs can be formulated in terms of the opposition between signifying versus postsignifying, the impersonal versus subjective, and faciality versus the betrayal of faciality. All this is to say that these are abstract opposition relations. D&G are more interested in the *interrelation* regimes of signs, and how regimes dismantle (deterritorialization) one another, than they are in defining the regimes themselves in their separateness.

It must be stressed again that D&G's four maps of regimes of signs are *not* representations, or 'tracings', of historical regimes of signs. The concept of a map, like all Deleuzo-Guattarian concepts, is a nonrepresentational concept (§ 0.4). Mapping is an experimental process, which has to do with performance, not competence. Maps are 'entirely oriented toward an experimentation in contact with the real' (TP 12–13). In other words, the exercise of mapping is not external to the object of analysis: mapping is a process that *contributes* to the theorization of an object. But despite their nonrepresentational status, maps are useful for the study of early Christian discourse because they provide a set of virtual coordinates by which early Christian discourse can be plotted and theorized.

When applying these maps to historical discourses, such as we find in the New Testament, we must always bear in mind that these regimes of signs are manifested as *only mixtures of regimes of signs*. Indeed, D&G consider Christian discourse to be 'a particularly important case of a *mixed semiotic*', which, as I shall demonstrate in Chapters 12–13, is dominated by the 'signifying despotic regime' and the postsignifying 'passional subjective regime' respectively (TP 125). I shall argue that the dominant figures of Christ in the Gospel of John and Gospel of Luke are a product of these two regimes of signs (§§ 12–13). Hence, D&G, following the analysis of Jean Paris, distinguish between a 'despotic' Christ and the 'passional' Christ (TP 184).³

3. The scapegoat machine

D&G's fourfold typology of regimes of signs does not signal a turn towards structuralism: D&G are more interested in the deterritorialization of regimes of signs than they are in the structure of the regimes themselves. For theirs is a philosophy that privileges the virtual over the actual, and machinic transformations over static structures. Like all structures, regimes of signs are *open* systems that retain the capacity for transformation. While it is true that regimes of signs manifest predictable, stable behaviours over short periods of time, over extended periods of time they possess the virtual capacity to self-organization on a molecular level when an influx of intensity triggers a bifurcation point or 'schiz'.

The virtual dimension of every regime of signs entails four deterritorializing functions: a generative, transformative, diagrammatic and machinic function, which endow them the capacity for transformation (§§ 3.2, 5.3, 11.2). Of particular importance in their analysis of the transformation of regimes of signs is the 'scapegoat' mechanism, which is a *machinic function*. In literal terms, the term 'scapegoat' designates the goat, described in the book of Leviticus, that carried away the sins of the Israelites on the Day of Atonement (Lev. 16.7-10, 20-22).[4] Following the act of transfer, a messenger would lead the 'the faceless, depressive scapegoat' away from Jerusalem 'in its headlong flight into the desert' (TP 116, cf. Lev. 16.21). But Western scholarship has abstracted the scapegoat concept from its Levitical roots and employed it in diverse ways, particularly in the context of the study of violence in religion. The practice of using animals and humans in apotropaic rituals was a very ancient practice and was by no means restricted to the Levitical cult. This modern usage of the scapegoat concept can be traced back to the third volume of James Frazer's *Golden Bough*, entitled *The Scapegoat* (1915), which chronicled countless instances of mass violence against individuals. In the century following the publication of Frazer's *The Scapegoat*, the 'scapegoat concept' has been applied in such diverse fields as Greek myth (Bremmer 1983; Burkert 1979: 59–77, 1985: 82–4; Hughes 1991: 139–65), violence and religion (Girard 1986: 39–41, 1987: 26–7) and Jungian psychology (Sylvia Perera). All this is to say that the term 'scapegoat' has connotations in scholarship that go well beyond its Levitical origins, including ritual sacrifice, orgiastic violence, symbolic representations of primitive violence, the victimization of minorities, evasive defence mechanisms, misplaced guilt and violent political tactics. Hence, it comes as no surprise that the scapegoat concept is employed in Deleuzo-Guattarian philosophy as well.

What then is a Deleuzo-Guattarian scapegoat? In general terms any human being or animal that is deterritorialized from a regime of signs or social assemblage is a 'scapegoat'. In other words, the Deleuzo-Guattarian scapegoat is a *machine* that acts on the exteriority of structures (§ 1). The effect of a scapegoat on such structures may be generative, transformation, diagrammatic or machinic (§ 5.3). If the historical emergence and growth of early Christianity is a machinic history of desiring production, as I have argued (§§ 1–2), then it is also a *history of the scapegoat mechanism*, which is a machinic process. Viewed from this perspective, the 'despotic Christ' of the Gospel of John and the 'passional Christ' of the Gospel of Luke represent little more than temporary monuments within a succession of deterritorialized Christs.

From this Deleuzo-Guattarian perspective, the Levitical scapegoat represents the paradigmatic instance of a deterritorialized victim: following the transfer of the transgressions of the Israelites to the goat (Lev. 16.21), it *turned away* from the Jerusalem Temple and deterritorialized into the wilderness (TP 116–18, 121–2, 135).[5] In the case of the Levitical scapegoat ritual, this deterritorialization was 'generative' in the sense that the scapegoat's expulsion served to stabilize the signifying despotic regime, allowing it to thereby reproduce itself (§§ 5.2,

12.1.4). As I shall explain in Chapter 12, Christ as scapegoat in the Gospel of John fulfils this generative function (§ 12.2.4).

The deterritorialization of a scapegoat does not necessarily entail movement: the 'turning away' of a scapegoat victim can take the form of movement 'in place' (*sur place*),[6] which is to say, an interior movement of a *turning away* of one's spirit from a regime of signs. By way of example, Deleuze cite the lives of Jewish prophets, and particularly the life of Christ (L 266–75). In the case of the passional subjective regime, violence against a prophet, as scapegoat, fulfils a *transformational* function in which the prophet remains 'in place' (§ 13). Through his betrayal of a 'despot-god' of the signifying despotic regime, and by suffering violence and cruelty at his hand (as in the case of Christ in his crucifixion), the prophet as scapegoat is *deterritorialized* from the signifying despotic regime and *reterritorialized* in the passional subjective regime. Likewise, the prophetic Christ as scapegoat in the Gospel of Luke 'betrays' the signifying despotic regime, while being simultaneously betrayed by it. In his cry of dereliction, this Christ screams out this double betrayal to the whole world (§ 13.2).

How is one to be sure that violence against the scapegoat will have a consistent result? In point of fact, one can never know. The violence against a scapegoat can spontaneously trigger other deterritorializations besides the generative and transformational functions. Consequently, the passional subjective regime of signs represents only one of many possible outcomes of the scapegoat mechanism. The possibility of more radical deterritorializations – veritable 'becomings' – can never be ruled out. As I shall demonstrate, this diagrammatic scapegoat function also facilitated numerous unheard of 'becomings' of Christ including his 'becoming-woman' (§ 15), 'becoming-animal' (§ 16) and 'becoming-imperceptible' (§ 17). Viewed from this diagrammatic perspective, the Johannine 'despotic Christ' and Lukan 'passional Christ' are little more than temporary monuments within a succession of deterritorialized Christs.

The practice of mapping regimes of signs also provides a means to theorize not only the interrelation of regimes of signs in early Christian discourse but also how such regimes functioned within Christ groups, considered as biform social assemblages (§ 8). The best evidence for the multiplication of Christs within such assemblages is the *history of early Christianity itself*. Christological controversies of the first four centuries, and the endless branding of this or that group as 'heretical', provides abundant evidence for a *history of the deterritorialization of regimes of signs*.[7] Owing to this surplus of non-potentiated, diagrammatic deterritorializations, the proliferation of Christs in the first three centuries of the Common Era was inexorable. Constructions of Christ were repeatedly deterritorialized and reterritorialized within different social assemblages, such as those connected with the Ebionites, Marcionites and so-called 'gnostics' and 'proto-orthodox' groups. Within these social assemblages lay the *silent potential for the emergence of countless new Christs*, as well as the disappearance of old ones. Hence, thanks to D&G's concept of a regime of signs, now, for the first time, something like a history of the transformation of Christs within regimes of signs is possible. When we recognize the interrelation between constructions of Christ and regimes of signs, new questions present themselves. Instead of asking, who was Christ?, and, what was the theological meaning of his life?, schizoanalysis asks, on the basis of which regimes of signs were different Christs produced?, and within which Christ assemblages and power/knowledge diagrams did they function?

Conclusion

Every linguistic construction of Christ entailed a regime of signs, which was connected, in turn, to a historically specific power/knowledge 'diagram' or 'abstract machine'. Over the first four centuries of the Common Era, different regimes of signs produced different discursive constructions of Christ, within a diversity of Christ assemblages. None of these Christs operated solely on the level of linguistic signification or theology. For *before* a discursive Christ could be 'caught in the true' of Christian belief or theology, it had to fulfil a complex set of discursive conditions, which were predetermined by a specific regime of signs. Different regimes of signs produced different constructions of Christ in different Christ assemblages. Hence, every linguistic representation of Christ and every theological *truth* about Christ belonged to a *regime of truth*. Hence, all early Christian texts were formed by regimes of signs, and all regimes of signs functioned within power/knowledge diagrams.

When we recognize the complex interrelation between constructions of Christ, regimes of signs and power/knowledge diagrams, a new set of questions present themselves. Instead of asking, 'Who was Christ?', and 'What was the theological meaning of Christ's life and death?', schizoanalysis asks, 'On the basis of which specific regimes of signs were different Christs produced?', and 'Within which Christ assemblages and power/knowledge diagrams did they function?' While every Christian discourse entails a *mixture* of regimes of signs, we, as readers, often encounter a relative dominance of one regime over another in any given discourse. As I shall demonstrate in Chapters 12–13, the dominant figures of Christ in the Gospel of John and Gospel of Luke were produced by a relative dominance of the 'signifying despotic' regime of signs and the 'passional subjective' regime of signs respectively. This observation allows us to distinguish between the Johannine 'despotic Christ' and the Lukan 'passional Christ'.

D&G's primary interest lies not in mapping regimes of signs but in analysing their diverse forms of deterritorialization. For every regime of signs possessed a virtual capacity for deterritorialization, which can be theorized in terms of four destabilizing functions: a generative, transformative, diagrammatic and machinic function respectively. The profound points of divergence between this passional Christ and the Johannine despotic Christ illustrate not only the oppositional relationship between two regimes of signs but more generally the fundamental principle that every regime of signs is susceptible to multiple types of deterritorialization. When viewed from the perspective of these four destabilizing functions, the Johannine 'despotic Christ' and Lukan 'passional Christ' represent little more than transitory monuments within an almost limitless diversity of possible Christs.

Of particular importance in such deterritorializing processes is the scapegoat mechanism, which is a *machinic* function. In general terms, any human being or animal that is deterritorialized from a regime of signs (or social assemblage) is a 'scapegoat'. In the Gospel of John, Christ-as-scapegoat performs a generative deterritorialization (§ 12), whereas in the Gospel of Luke, Christ-as-scapegoat performs a transformational deterritorialization (§ 13). Over the first four centuries of the Common Era, different regimes of signs produced different Christs, and through successive deterritorializations, one Christ morphed into another. We can conclude that the history of the multiplication of Christs throughout early Christian history of the first six centuries of the Common Era was, in part, a *history of the scapegoat mechanism*. What unified these many Christs was not their historical facticity, much less their theological truth, but the expression of the scapegoat mechanism, and the virtual dimension of the plane of immanence (planomenon) that facilitated it. The best evidence for the multiplication of Christs is the history of early Christianity itself: Christological controversies, and the arbitrary branding of this or that group as 'heretical', provide rich evidence for a *history of the deterritorialization of regimes of signs*. Thus, the recognition of this scapegoat function opens for us a new field of academic inquiry. For the first time, something like a history of the transformation of Christs within regimes of signs is now possible. Writing such a history will entail mapping of regimes of signs and scapegoat functions, and an analysis of the dynamic interplay and precarious balance between a diversity of Christs. So let us tentatively begin by exploring two interrelated regimes of signs, the 'signifying despotic regime of signs' (§ 12) and the 'passional subjective regime of signs' (§ 13).

12

The despotic Christ and the signifying despotic regime of signs

Christ said, 'Whoever has seen me has seen the Father. So how can you say, "Show us the Father?"… Believe me that I am in the Father, and the Father is in me'.

Jn 14.9, 11

In the Gospel of John, Christ not only claims that he has been sent by God but also that he *is* God: 'I and the Father are one' (Jn 10.30). As the heavenly Word (λόγος), Christ was with God 'in the beginning' (Jn 1.1, cf. Gen. 1.1). He uniquely possessed the glory of the Father even 'before the world was made' (Jn 17.5). And as the heavenly 'Word', he 'became flesh and lived among us, as we have seen his glory, the glory as of the Father's only Son' (Jn 1.14). Christ performed 'signs' with the expressed purpose of demonstrating his *vertical filiation* to this Father God (Jn 20.30-1). Christ even claims that *he* alone provides a way of access to the Father God: 'No one can come to the Father except through me' (Jn 14.6, cf. 1 Jn 4.14-15). This Christ, who was uniquely the Son of God, was the very *face* of God on earth (Jn 1.18). Hence, he declares, 'whoever has seen me has seen the Father' (Jn 14.9). This chapter will argue that this Johannine Christ, who was *vertically filiated* to God and, indeed, the *very face of God* on earth, operationalized the 'signifying despotic' regime of signs, which is an 'abstract faciality machine'. For in the Gospel of John, the truth of God is always accompanied by the *faciality* of the Son of God.

1. The linguistic despotism of traditional exegesis

At first glance, the use of the term 'signifying' in connection with the 'signifying despotic regime' may seem like a redundancy. How could it be otherwise? Are not all regimes of signs signifying? The answer to this question is no. While it is true that all regimes of signs are *semiotic*, only a very small subset are signifying. For language, as a signifying structure, is only found in anthropomorphic formations. For only in the case of language, considered as a signifying system, do content and expression function independently (§ 8.3). While birds and animals may communicate through sounds and gestures, such communication does not rely on signifiers connected with signifieds. In natural, physicochemical and organic formations, non-linguistic semiotic forces are expressed independently of linguistic expression. Indeed, in point of fact, most regimes of signs are non-linguistic (§ 14): 'For nonsignifying language, anything will do … no flow is privileged', including chemical and biological signals, and genetic codes (AO 240). After all, natural, organic and animalistic signs do not wait in patient silence for the advent of human beings to be translated into human languages! Hence, *linguistic* signs constitute a very limited subset of the set of the semiotic systems that constitute our lifeworld. As Deleuze observes,

> Writing is one flow among others, with no special place in relation to the others, that comes into relations of current, counter current, and eddy with other flows – flows of shit, sperm, words, action, eroticism, money, politics, and so on. (Neg. 8)

Thus, if we temporarily suspend our human-centred view of our lifeworld, it immediately becomes obvious that language, as a *signifying* system – with signifiers (expression) and signifieds (content) – is limited to anthropocentric strata.[1] And indeed, even prehistorical human settlements functioned primarily through natural codings such as through wordless gestures, rhythms and dance, rather than through signifying systems. Even in language, as a signifying system, we can attune our senses to the semiotic forces that operate through language. Nondiscursive 'unsaid' semiotic flows function through the discursive 'said'. Of course, traditional exegetical practice ignores the semiotic dimension of language. To borrow a phrase from Guattari, traditional exegesis could be accused of 'linguistic despotism' in the sense that it 'despotically' imposes signification on us 'over all other modes of semiotization' (1995: 49). Arguing against the practice of linguistic despotism, Guattari states that 'there is no reason to grant any title of nobility to productions which depend upon language rather than those concerning other systems of encoding or signs' (2011: 199). Hence, as we now turn our attention to the '*signifying* despotic regime', let us bear in mind that signification represents only one of many semiotic systems and, furthermore, that semiotic flows are operative even in the signifying despotic regime. Every regime of signs, including the signifying despotic regime, composes a set of relations of force.

2. The signifying despotic regime: A regime of faciality

The relations of force in the 'signifying despotic' regime of signs can be mapped in terms of four interrelated coordinates. First, a chief deity functions as the 'despotic signifier' for the entire signifying system (§ 7). Second, a 'despot' (such as a king, emperor or Pharaoh) acquires the surplus value of a 'despot-god' (*dieu-despote*) through his vertical filiation to the chief deity, and is thereby installed at the centre of the signifying system; henceforth, the radiating *face* of the despot substitutes for the face of the deity, making this regime an 'abstract faciality machine'. Third, the signifying despotic regime is 'interpretive' in character in the sense that the continuous interpretation of the despot-god's utterances by bureaucrats ('priests') is required to connect the utterances issuing from the face of the despot-god to a discursive circular system of signs. Finally, this 'despot-god' has a counter-body, which is a scapegoat victim, that *turns its face away from the face* of the despot-god to perform a generative deterritorializing function, thereby taking away all that exceeds the discursive circularity of signs (§§ 11.2, 12.4).

2.1. A deity as despotic signifier

In the signifying despotic regime, a deity functions as the despotic signifier (*signifiant despotique*), which is to say, the final reference point or master signifier, for all signifying processes. Language (*langage*), as a general system of signification, *lacks* a master signifier.[2] By implication, the determination of the semantic value of any sign is indefinitely 'disseminated' or deferred. Gilles Deleuze explains semantic value as follows:

> Every sign refers to another sign, and only to another sign, *ad infinitum*. That is why, at the limit, one can forgo that notion of the sign, for what is retained is not principally the sign's relation to a state of things it designates, or to an entity it signifies, but only the formal relation of sign to sign insofar as it defines a so-called signifying chain. The limitlessness of signifiance replaces the sign. … All signs are signs of signs. The question is not yet what a given sign signifies but to what other signs it refers, or which signs add themselves to it to form a network without beginning or end. (TP 112)

In Lacanian terminology, we would say that language as 'Other' (*Autre*) has no Other (*A̶u̶t̶r̶e̶*).[3] In the absence of a master signifier (or despotic signifier), the syntagmatic and paradigmatic processes of language (*signifiance et interprétation*) continue unabated, resulting in the *infinite* deterritorialization of meaning.[4] But with the addition of a deity as a despotic (or master) signifier – as the 'Other' of language – the limitless deferral of meaning is *greatly reduced*. By anchoring chains of signifiers to a deity, as an ultimate reference point for all signifying processes, the endless deterritorialization of signs is halted.

As D&G observe, from a structural perspective, there is little to say about this despotic signifier: it is 'a pure abstraction, … it is nothing. Lack or excess it hardly matters' (TP 115). This despotic signifier can be said to be characterized by *excess* in the sense that, as the final reference point for all signification, nothing else in the signifying system can be substituted in its place. But it is equally characterized by *lack* in the sense that it is 'a pure abstraction' (TP 115). It is nothing. It a pure abstraction. It is an empty point that makes signification possible. Thus, from a structural point of view, it matters little whether we give this despotic signifier the name of a chief deity, such as Jupiter, Zeus, Athena or the Father God, or imagine it as idealized Law or Morality. In each of these scenarios, the despotic signifier functions structurally as a 'despotic' signifier – a zero symbol in a linguistic sense – that stabilizes the entire signifying system. But as 'lack', this despotic signifier *introduces lack into the entire signifying system*.[5]

2.2. The faciality of the despot-god

Since the despotic signifier is a pure abstraction, it requires *substance* to function within a despotic socius. This substance was furnished by the material body of a 'despot' (a king, emperor or Pharaoh). Through the vertical filiation of this despot to a deity (as despotic signifier), the despot acquires the 'surplus value' (*plus-value*) of a 'despot-god' (*dieu-despote*) (§ 7).[6] Indeed, his face becomes the *very face of god*. He is a 'Son of god', a metaphysical incarnation of the deity's face, voice and authority.

The Hellenistic age abounded in despot-gods: the Seleucid, Ptolemaic and Hasmonean dynasties, not to mention the Julio-Claudian, Flavian and Nerva-Antonine dynasties of the Roman Empire, all entailed a succession of kings and emperors who were deified in their own lifetimes as gods and sons of gods. The Hasmoneans, who ruled Judaea from 152 to 165 BCE, were theocratic rulers, appointed as both king and high priest. In the case of the Roman Empire, the deification of Julius Caesar formally constituted the beginning of the cult of the emperor (Price 1984; Small 1996). Augustus (Gaius Octavius), being Julius

Caesar's adopted son, was hailed *divi filius*, a title that could only be translated into Greek as the 'son of god' (θεοῦ υἱός). For logically speaking, if Julius Caesar was a 'god' (θεοῦ), then Augustus must be the 'son of (a) god' (McLean 2015: 59–61). Epigraphical evidence also attests to the relationship of Octavius to Julius Caesar being defined as 'god from god'. In the years that followed the death of Octavius, the deification of Julius Caesar and Octavius served as the paradigm for the deification of subsequent emperors of the *gens Julii*. Each, in turn, claimed descent from the gods through Julius Caesar, often employing the phrase 'son of god' (θεοῦ υἱός) to indicate that they were sons of the *deified* Julius Caesar and Augustus: for they *too* were 'despot-gods'.

By virtue of the fact that the 'despot-god' supplied the substance for an abstract despotic signifier, D&G term the signifying despotic regime an 'abstract faciality machine' (*machine abstraite de visagéité*). In contrast, the face lacked a privileged role in the primitive presignifying regime; in this regime, signs were connected to many parts of the body, as well as to plants, places and masks. Only in the signifying despotic regime did the *face*, and specifically the face of the despot-god, substitute for the lack of presence of the chief deity. Indeed, it is the radiating face of the despot-god that *gives the despotic signifier substance* (TP 115). And since speech proceeds from the face, good sense dictates that the speech of the despot-god, proceeding from his face, also *substitutes for the voice of God*. Hence, D&G observe that such signification is 'characterized by face-language relations' (TP 63). As a further consequence of faciality, the voice of the despot-god also *triggers the redundancy of the deity's voice*: the speech of the despot-god reduced the chief god to silence (AO^f 243, AO 206).

2.3. An interpretive regime

The centrality of the speech of the despot-god rendered the signifying despotic regime as an *interpretive* regime. The divine utterances proceeding from the face of the despot-god, located at the centre of the signifying system, radiated out in ever-widening discursive circles. These utterances also required interpretation. D&G suggest that it may have been this event that first gave rise to the practice of exegesis:

> It is perhaps at this juncture that the question, the exegetical question, 'What does this mean?' begins to be heard, and the problems of exegesis prevail over the problems of use and efficiency. The emperor, the god – what did he mean? (AO 206)

Every discursive circle required an interpretation of the utterances that proceeded from the face of the despot-god in accommodating them to the requirements of different contexts and circumstances. Bureaucrats were tasked with interpreting the utterances of the despot-god to discursive 'circles' associated with such diverse activities as farming, viticulture, mining, warfare, medicine and justice, and even to the private houses of citizens (TP 115). That which unified all these discursive circles in the kingdom was the *infinite* practice of interpretation, a process which had to be 'carried to infinity' by the bureaucrats ('priests') of the despot-god: for 'the priest administers the face of the god' (TP 115). This task of interpretation of *infinity* was because the bureaucrats never encountered 'anything to interpret that is not already itself an interpretation' (TP 114). *There was nothing primary to interpret.* As Foucault observed, everything was already interpretation, every sign was an interpretation of another sign (Foucault 1990: 64–6).

Through infinite interpretation all these discursive circles were interconnected within a single, *closed, self-referential* signifying system. All citizens were bound by a universal obligation of confinement within this system: they were prohibited from approaching the 'innermost circle' where these utterances were pronounced, and they were equally prohibited from going beyond 'the outermost circles' where this signifying system ended (TP 113). Hence, for the entirety of their lives, citizens were confined within this amorphous continuum of interconnected discursive circles. However, there was one notable exception to this universal obligation to confinement: the scapegoat victim.

2.4. The scapegoat victim as the counter-body to the despot-god

Not even the despot-god had the power to prevent all deterritorializations of the signifying despotic regime. For the planomenon of the plane of immanence was always operating invisibly in the background, inducing deterritorializations (§ 9.2). In order to keep such deterritorializations within tolerable limits, the signifying despotic regime required a mechanism by which to *take away* 'everything that resisted signifying signs, everything that eluded the referral from sign to sign through the different circles, ... everything that was unable to recharge the signifier' (TP 116). In short, this regime required a 'scapegoat', which is a deterritorializing machine, that could be 'laden with all the dangers threatening the [despotic] signifier' (TP 122). Hence, the body of the scapegoat is the *counter-body* to the despot-god within the signifying structure (TP 115). Fundamentally, this scapegoat is a *faceless* victim that turns away from the *face* of the despot-god and deterritorializes into the wilderness. The expulsion of the scapegoat accomplished a generative deterritorialization: by taking away all that resisted the despotic signifier, all that escaped the circularity of signs, the scapegoat stabilized the signifying regime, enabling it thereby to regenerate itself.

3. The despotic Christ

While each of the canonical Gospels entails a mixture of regime of signs, one or two regimes may establish a relative dominance over others in a particular Gospel. In the case of the Gospel of John, a relative dominance of the signifying despotic regime produces a relatively stable construction of a 'despotic' Christ.

3.1. Father God as despotic signifier

In the Gospel of John, the Father God functions as the despotic signifier of the entire Johannine signifying system. While functioning as the final symbolic reference point for all signifying processes, this Father God could not be signified, nor could anything else in the signifying system be substituted in his place. For the Father God was not signifiable.

Very little can be said about this despotic signifier. On the one hand, it is characterized by *excess*, for it was the Father God who sent his Son into the world, and all the words and deeds of the Son point back to the plenitude of the Father God. However, this Father God was equally characterized by *lack*, for by sending his Son into the world, he was reduced to silence. The incarnate Son displaced the divine voice (cf. Jn 1.14, 17, 6.35, 8.12, 24, 28, 58, 14.6). Thereafter, it was the Son who 'speaks the words of God', with the Father God being reduced to the status of a passive witness of the Son's words and deeds (Jn 3.34, 7.16, 14.9-11). Not only is this Father God rendered silent, he was also invisible: only his Son could see him (Jn 1.18). On the basis of the silence and invisibility of the Father God, the Fourth Gospel affirms the *lack* that characterizes this despotic signifier: 'No one has ever seen God. It is the "unique" Son, who is close to the Father's heart, who has made him known' (Jn 1.18).

3.2. The faciality of Christ as despot-god

In the Gospel of John, Christ, the Son of God, acquires the surplus value of a 'despot-god' through his vertical filiation to the Father God. Here is thereby installed at the centre of the signifying system.⁷ The disciple Nathanael witnessed to Christ's despotic status with his awestruck confession, 'You are the Son of God! You are the *king* of Israel!' (Jn 1.49, cf. 19.19).

The silent and invisible Father God *acquired substance* through the incarnation of his Son: 'And the Word became flesh and lived among us, and *we have seen his glory, the glory as of a Father's only Son*' (Jn 1.1-3, 14). Everything the incarnate Son did and said could be traced back to the Father God. The Son was the very *face of the Father God*. Hence, when Christ's face becomes machined, it becomes an abstract faciality machine: 'Whoever has seen me', whoever has seen my face, 'has seen [the face of] the Father. ... Believe me when I say that I am in the Father, and the Father is in me' (Jn 14.9, 11). As the very face of God on earth, as the one who is vertically filiated to this Father God, this Son of God acquired the surplus value of 'despot-god'.

3.3. An interpretive regime

In the Gospel of John, totalizing truth emanates from the radiating face of the Son of God in ever-widening discursive circles. These circles take the form of interfolded narratives and discourses, including the stories of the seven miraculous 'signs'⁸ and repeated 'I am' sayings,⁹ interspersed with lengthy discourses (Jn 13–17), followed by the account of Christ's passion (Jn 18–20). Thus, in this gospel, every miracle and discourse have a relational coexistence to other discourses.

Through Johannine interpretation, all narratives and discourses are unified via their connection to the Johannine Christ, who is the Son of God, the despot-god, and indeed the very face and voice of God. Johannine interpretation is an inexhaustible task because the interpreters never encounter anything that is not already an interpretation: Christ's symbolic reference to himself as the 'bread of life' (Jn 6.35, 51), anticipates the interpretation of Christ as the 'light of the world' (Jn 8.2), which is theologically connected to Christ as 'the gate for the sheep' (Jn 10.7-9), which points to Christ as 'the resurrection and the life' (Jn 11.25), which is connected with the interpretation of Christ as the 'true vine' (Jn 15.1), which in turn points to Christ as 'the way, the truth, and the life' (Jn 14.6), which is connected back to Christ as the 'bread of life'. Indeed, all these 'I am' sayings point to other Johannine signs and discourses within a self-referential signifying system, making the task of interpretation truly inexhaustible.

3.4. Christ as scapegoat as the counter-body of despot-god

In the Gospel of John, the structure language supplies an extended series of dualisms for the structuration of all its discursive circles: these dualisms include righteousness versus sin, truth versus falsehood, spirit versus flesh, life versus death, the world above versus this world below, freedom versus servitude and so forth. This comprehensive dualistic structure tolerates no ambiguities: it is a totalizing set of truths, at the centre of which is located Christ, the incarnate Truth. The entirety of this Gospel's 'life' of Christ is bound together by this underlying dualistic structure. All that does not fit into this dualistic structure is consigned to the category of the 'sin of the world' (Jn 1.29).

This dualistic structure functioned according to a set of structural rules, like the rules of chess (§§ 7.1.1, n. 9, 18.1.2). While acts of righteousness and sinful acts have negative and positive consequences for the lives of (molar) characters in the narratives, *both* righteousness and sinful acts contribute to the stability of the structure of the despotic socius. For these are structurally equivalent moves. Hence, it is not the negative pole of the Johannine dualisms – the pole of darkness, falsehood, flesh, death – that destabilized the despotic socius.

That which destabilized the Johannine signifying structure was not negative pole of the Johannine dualisms but unclassifiable pure difference. In short, the signifying despotic regime was continuously in danger of being dismantled by the plane of immanence, the great orchestrator of pure difference. On this plane, every point is an 'in-between,' which is not a place but rather is a set of connections that can be established between desiring-machines, for 'everything grows from the middle' (D 12). The Johannine signifying system could be deterritorialized by anything that could not be *catalogued, anything that could not be accounted for*, in the structural of Johannine dualisms. To stabilize itself against these incursions of pure difference, the Gospel of John required a scapegoat to *take away* all that it consigned to the category of 'sin' (Jn 1.29, 36). It required a scapegoat to take away 'everything that resisted signifying signs, … everything that was unable to recharge the signifier' (TP 116).[10]

As previously discussed, the scapegoat is a *machinic function*. It must be emphasized that this function is not tied to molar subjects (§§ 6.1.1, 14). As D&G observe, *even a despot or king can function as a scapegoat*: 'the body of the despot is sometimes subjected to trials of humiliation or even torture, or of exile and exclusion' (TP 115). In this scenario, the king and scapegoat *share the same body*. For example, in Sophocles' tragedy, *Oedipus Tyrannus*, King Oedipus functions as both king and scapegoat victim. In the first part of the tragedy, he consults the Delphic oracle to determine the cause of a plague that afflicted Thebes, and he prays that the curse may be transferred to the guilty party. But, in the second part of the tragedy, when it comes to light that it was Oedipus himself who had killed King Laius, *King Oedipus is transformed into a scapegoat*. He becomes deterritorialized, 'bearing the curse' to save the city of Thebes (Oedipus Rex 1290–93).[11] Thus, neither the structural function of despot-god (king) nor of scapegoat was tied to King Oedipus, as a molar subject. In point of fact, he did not truly know himself. He believed himself to be a true king, but his body was transformed into the *counter-body* of a king, a scapegoat, who was deterritorialized 'bearing the curse' to save the city of Thebes. Through a generative deterritorialization, this king-turned-scapegoat took away that which threatened the city of Thebes.

Like Oedipus, the Johannine Christ was both a king and a scapegoat. This Christ could function structurally as both a despot-god *and* a scapegoat victim because *structural functions are not tied to molar subjectivities*. A scapegoat is a molecular machine. Molecular processes do not correlate with molar subjects (§§ 6.2, 14.1). At the outset of his passion, Christ entered Jerusalem to the accolades of a crowd praising him as a king, 'Hosana! Blessed be the king of Israel' (Jn 12.13). Even at his crucifixion the Jewish high priest tried to finalize the meaning of Christ's identity as a Jewish king with a placard inscribed, 'Jesus the Nazarene, king of the Jews' (Jn 19.19). But Christ's kingship in the Gospel of John remains equivocal: for Christ is *both* a king (a despot-god) and a scapegoat 'who takes away the sin of the world' (Jn 1.29). Through his torture of the Cross, Christ lost his despotic *faciality* and was transformed into a *faceless* scapegoat. He became the 'inverted figure of a king' (TP 116).[12] For 'the one who is tortured is fundamentally one who loses his or her face' (TP 116). Even in moment of his extreme torture, Christ is hailed the '*king* of the Jews' (Jn 19.19). Somehow those who witnessed his crucifixion recognized the 'inverted figure' of a *king* in this scapegoat victim (TP 116). He became a Galilean Oedipus. Hence, Christ was both a despot-god, the very *face* of the Father God, who is located at the centre of the signifying system, *and* the counter-body of a king, a *faceless* scapegoat, located at the periphery of the Johannine regime of signs.

By taking away all that escaped the Johannine circularity of signs, Christ as scapegoat stabilized the signifying despotic regime, allowing it to perpetuate itself. In faithful obedience to the Father God, Christ took away the 'sin of the world', all that exceeded the signifying despotic regime of signs. He thereby saved the Johannine Christ group, which continued for decades thereafter, and subsequently produced the Johannine epistles. As these epistles attest, the

Johannine signifying system was disrupted again, this time by so-called 'false teachers', 'liars' and 'anti-Christs' (1 Jn 2.18-19).

Conclusion

The relations of force in the 'signifying despotic' regime of signs can be mapped in terms of four coordinates. First, a chief deity functions as the ultimate reference point, as the 'despotic signifier', for the entire signifying system. Second, through the vertical filiation of a despot (king) to this 'despotic signifier', the despot acquires the surplus value of a 'despot-god' which is at the centre of the entire signifying system. At the point when the radiating face of this despot-god displaces the face of the deity, the signifying despotic regime becomes an abstract faciality machine. Third, the signifying despotic regime is an 'interpretive' regime in the sense that the interpretation of countless bureaucrats ('priests') is required to accommodate the revelation issuing from the face of the despot-god to the diverse requirements of a circular system of discourses. Finally, the despot-god has a counter-body, which is the body of a scapegoat victim: the scapegoat that *turns away from the face* of the despot-god in a solemn act of betrayal and takes away all that threatens the signifying despotic regime. The scapegoat thereby performs a *generative* deterritorialization.

The Gospel of John exhibits a relative dominance of the signifying despotic regime, which, in turn, produces a relatively stable 'despotic Christ'. In this Gospel, the Father God, functioning as a 'despotic signifier', provides the ultimate reference point for the entire Johannine signifying system. Nothing else in this signifying system can be substituted in place of this Father God. Through the vertical filiation of Christ to this Father God, Christ becomes the Son of God, and thereby acquires the surplus value of a 'despot-god'. Christ's status as the incarnate face and voice of God simultaneously displaces the face and voice of the Father God, who is thereby reduced to silence. Henceforth, Christ speaks on behalf of the Father God: truth emanates from his radiating face, which is located at the centre of the Johannine system of signification, and spreads out in every widening discursive circles. Underlying all these discursive circles is an extended series of dualisms. All these discursive circles are interconnected by Johannine interpretation, which is an inexhaustible task because interpreters never encounter anything that is not already an interpretation. Interpreters consign all that exceeded this signifying structure to the category of 'sin'. The Johannine signifying regime required a scapegoat to 'take away' this sin (Jn

1.29), which is to say, all that disrupted this regime of signs. To this end, Christ, the very *face* of God, became a *faceless* scapegoat, who took away the 'sin of the world' in a solemn act of betrayal. Thus, in the Gospel of John, Christ functions simultaneously as the face of God *and* a faceless scapegoat, both the cause and solution of the same structural crisis.

13

The passional Christ and the passional subjective regime of signs

When Christ came to Nazareth, ... he went to the synagogue on the sabbath day. ... And he stood up to read, and the scroll of the prophet Isaiah was given to him. ... And (when he had finished reading from the scroll) he said to them, 'Today this scripture has been fulfilled in your hearing. ... Truly I tell you, no prophet is accepted in the prophet's hometown.'

Lk. 4.16-17, 21, 24

The Gospel of Luke often presents Christ as a prophet sent by God. At the outset of his public ministry, Christ explicitly claims to have been anointed as a prophet of God. On the day that Christ visited the synagogue in his hometown of Nazareth, he read from Isa. 61.1-2,[1] where the prophet Isaiah states that he was anointed with the spirit of God to 'bring good news to the poor … to proclaim release to the captives and recovering of sight to the blind, to let the oppressed go free to proclaim the year of the Lord's favour' (Lk. 4.18-19). When he had finished reading, Christ proclaims that Isaiah's prophecy had its fulfilment in his own ministry. Understandably, those in attendance reacted with shock, which provoked Christ to launch into a sermon – unique to the Gospel of Luke – on the subject of two other prophets, Elijah and Elisha, who were likewise sent by God to pronounce judgment against the Israelites (Lk. 4.24-27). His point was clear: like the prophets of old, he is a prophet sent by God, and he too will be rejected by his own people. This chapter argues that at many points in the Gospel of Luke, the figure of Christ is constructed as a prophet on the basis of the postsignifying 'passional subjective regime'. In contrast to the *impersonal* signifying despotic regime, this is a *personal* regime in the sense that it is a *subjective* regime based on an enunciating subject.

First and foremost, the passional subjective regime is a regime of *betrayal*. Such betrayal is in no way limited to the phenomenon of biblical prophetism.

For all passional fixations entail some type of betrayal. The passional anorexic saves herself by *betraying* food. Passional celibates – like Thecla and Maximilla – saved themselves by *betraying* sex (§ 10.2). Likewise, passional prophets save themselves by *betraying* the 'despot-god' of the signifying despotic regime. Like these other passional betrayals, it is the prophet's act of betrayal that opens up a line of escape, a 'line of flight'. D&G's paradigmatic example of a passional prophet is Moses, who *betrayed* the Egyptian Pharaoh, the 'despot-god' of the Egyptian *signifying* regime of signs, an act that opened up a way of escape from the signifying, Egyptian despotic regime to a *postsignifying*, passional subjective regime of signs.

1. The postsignifying passional subjective regime

The signifying despotic regime is a regime of faciality centred on the *face* of a despot-god (§ 12.2.2). The passional subjective regime can be said to be the inverse of this regime, for it is based on the *betrayal of the face* of the despot-god. The Jewish prophet *turns away from the face* of the king, and *turns towards* his own passional point of subjectification, namely, a *faceless* Hebrew God (§ 13.1.2). Thus, despot-gods have no regard for prophets because prophets have no respect for despot-gods.

1.1. Betrayal and the prophet as scapegoat

As previously discussed, the signifying despotic regime was continuously in danger of being dismantled by the plane of immanence, the great orchestrator of pure difference and new becomings. Hence, it required a scapegoat victim to perform a *generative* deterritorialization that would take away all that threatened this regime (§ 12.2.4). However, the outcome of the scapegoat mechanism, which is a machinic process, is in no way restricted to the generative function. As a case in point, the prophet as scapegoat victim performs a *transformational* deterritorialization through his betrayal of the despot-god. Indeed, his point of obsessive subjectification – the Jewish God – actually *necessitates* his betrayal of the despot-god and, by extension, the despotic signifier to which the despotic-god is vertically filiated. Through this act of betrayal, the prophet becomes *reterritorialized* in a new regime of signs, which is the 'passional subjective' regime.

Moses is the paradigmatic example of transformational deterritorialization: when he betrayed the Pharaoh, as despot-god, and

Amun-Ra, the chief Egyptian god (despotic signifier), Moses betrayed the entire Egyptian signifying regime. He was thereby reterritorialized in a new regime of signs, one based on his passional obsession with his point of subjectification, a faceless Hebrew God. Moses' betrayal was the first in a long line of prophetic betrayals: during the reigns of the kings of Judah and Israel, the lives of prophets and despots were repeatedly entangled in this same dynamic of betrayal and reterritorialization: Elijah betrayed King Ahab, Elisha betrayed King Jehu, Isaiah betrayed King Hezekiah, and the list of ranting, passional prophets betraying despots continued thereafter.

However, in contrast to the scapegoat victim, which was deterritorialized to *protect* the signifying despotic regime (§ 12.2.4), the prophet as scapegoat – as 'escape-goat' – is deterritorialized to *escape* from the signifying despotic regime altogether. In the case of Moses' deterritorialization, he led the Hebrew people in their escape from slavery and the temples of Egypt. He led them into the wilderness, taking with them a portable tabernacle and the Ark of the Covenant, 'a little packet of signs detached from the irradiating circular network' of the despotic signifying regime (TP 121). Thus, this deterritorialization, this Exodus, was relative in scope: for Moses and the Hebrews were both *reterritorialized* within a new regime of signs, namely, the passional subjective regime.

1.2. A point of subjectification and the prophet as divided subject

The prophet's point of subjectification – the Hebrew God – makes his betrayal of the despot-god imperative. In the absence of this point of subjectification, there would be no betrayal, and indeed there would be no prophet. In general terms the nature of this point of subjectification can be almost anything, such as a father or mother, certain foods, sexualized body, human body parts or symbolic objects connected with primitive or ritual violence. In the case of the Hebrew prophet, the point of subjectification is a faceless Jewish God, who cannot be seen. From the perspective of the 'despot god', this passional prophet is a social deviant in the grips of a delirium, one whose privatized point of subjectification has caused him to alienate himself from society, truth and morality. The fetishizing of his obsessional object has reduced the prophet to a solitary voice of unreason, a reprobate against the law and common sense alike, an enemy of the good order of the signifying despotic regime.

The prophet's passional attachment to his point of subjectification is *exterior* to language. While it is true that the prophet continues to employ language to speak, his speech has entered into *asignifying* relations, which are unprecedented in the signifying despotic regime. Yes, admittedly, it is true that the prophet does speak, but his delirium is forged at the slender point of contact between his passion and language, between his soul and syntax. He does not employ language to speak truth, so much as to express his passional commitment. His speech is monologic, imperatival and even offensive: he screams the Lord's 'order-words' (§ 1.3). Such 'order-words' are always haunted by the *unsaid* of his passional obsession, by his delirium. Thus, the signifying modality of his words conceals the asignifying forces that fuel his outrage. His prophetic oracles crystallize these forces, while simultaneously concealing them. But perhaps we are moving too quickly.

1.2.1. The subject of enunciation

We must slow down and take care not to give the impression that the speech of the obsessional prophet arises out of a unified ontological 'I' or self. For the prophet, as a 'subject of enunciation' (*sujet d'énonciation*), has no ontological essence or unity. He occupies the position of 'subject of enunciation' only by virtue of his subjection (*assujettissement*) to the structure of language. He merely *inhabits* an enunciative position that is *predetermined* by a linguistic structure, a position that allows him to employ the first personal pronoun 'I': 'The I, as subject of enunciation, designating the person that utters and reflects its own use in the statement … is the "I" appearing in propositions of the type "I believe, I assume, I think"' (MP 163, TP 130). This 'I', which is spoken *by language*, has a passion for love. It reveals the prophet's interior passional obsession. Consequently, the prophet, as a subject of enunciation, is not the agent of what he says, so much as he *is spoken by* what he says. His impassioned words always convey something *beyond* their determined linguistic meaning.

1.2.2. The subject of the statement

In point of fact, there are *two* subjects in prophetic discourse. The prophet is divided between being a 'subject of enunciation' and the 'subject of the statement' (*sujet d'énoncé*). Indeed, it is the 'subject of the statement' that *proceeds from* the subject of enunciation. In contrast to the 'I' that *is spoken*, this 'I' of 'subject of the statement' *speaks*. This 'I' has a passion for reason. This subject is 'bound to statements in conformity with' the dominant delusion or 'reality' of society (TP 129). This 'I' as subject of the statement indicates 'a state for which (the pronoun) "he" could always be substituted ("I suffer, I walk, I breathe, I feel …")' (MP 163, TP 130).

Thus, the prophet's point of subjectification distributes *two subjects and two forms of passion*, an 'I' that *is spoken* through speech, with a passion for love, and an 'I' which *speaks*, with a passion for reason. The result of these conflicting subjects and 'I's' is a *divided subject* (§ 10.1.3, n. 12). Hence, 'subjectification' is a *process that produces a divided subject*, a set of opposing subject-positions. It must be emphasized that in the case of neither the subject of enunciation, nor the subject of the statement, does the subject perform a linguistic operation: 'for a subject is never the condition of possibility of language or the cause of the statement: there is no subject, only collective assemblages of enunciation (*agencements collectifs d'énonciation*)' (MP 163, TP 130).

The primary point is that the passional prophet, being divided subject – an 'I' that is spoken, and an 'I' that speaks – is always part of collective assemblages. The prophet simply occupies a vacant place, a set of conflicting *relations*, between the unsaid and the said, within a collective assemblage of enunciation.

1.3. The end of faciality

As previously discussed, the signifying despotic regime is a regime of *faciality*. In this regime the radiating *face* of the 'despot-god' substitutes for the face of the chief deity, making it an 'abstract faciality machine'. The prophet, being obsessed with his own point of subjectification, has no choice to *betray* the face of the despot-god. As D&G observe, 'when the face is effaced, when the faciality traits disappear, we can be sure that we have entered another regime' (TP 587). Indeed, through his act of betrayal, the prophet is reterritorialized in a new regime, one that lacks faciality. For in the passional subjective regime, a *faceless* Hebrew God replaces *the radiating face of a despot-god*. Moses is the paradigmatic case of the prophet: in betraying, in his turning away, from the face of the Pharaoh, he did not turn towards the *face* of the Hebrew God. Moses was reterritorialized on the basis of his passional attachment of a *faceless* Hebrew God, a God whose face could not ever be seen (Exod. 33.20). In the passional subjective regime,

> God withdraws his face, becoming a point of subjectification for the drawing of a line of flight or deterritorialization; Moses is the subject of enunciation, constituted on the basis of the tablets of God that replace the face. (TP 128)

When the Lord called out to Moses from the midst of the burning bush, Moses was 'stricken with veritable fear of God' (TP 123). He *averted his face* (Exod. 3.6b). And when Moses subsequently entered the portable tabernacle, the so-called 'Tent of Meeting', this same faceless God warned him, 'You cannot see my face; for no man can see me and live', ... 'My face must not be seen' (Exod. 33.20, 23, cf. Isa. 6.5, 45.15, Acts 7.32).

1.4. Non-interpretive discourse

The passional subjective regime is non-interpretive. In contrast to the despotic signifying regime, the prophet delivers the Lord's words *without interpretation* (§ 12.2.3). Moses pleaded with the Lord on this very point (Exod. 4.10) and the Lord assured him that he would not require the gift of eloquence for the Lord would *stuff* his words into Moses' mouth. Hence, the prophet suffers from chronic 'word-ingestion' (TP 124). Countless prophets after Moses were given the same directive: 'do not interpret my words'. For the Lord stuffs his words into the mouth of the prophet, and the prophet is required to deliver them *without interpretation*. The Lord declared to Jeremiah, 'Herewith I put my words into your mouth' (Jer. 1.9, cf. 30.2, 36.2). Hence, countless prophets have announced that they have been commanded to deliver the words of the Lord: 'Thus says the Lord.'[2]

2. The passional Christ and his spectacle of betrayal

While all Christian texts exhibit mixed types of regimes, the figure of Christ in the Gospel of Luke often coincides with the coordinates of the passional subjective regime, which is the regime of 'universal betrayal' (TP 123). As previously discussed, the Gospel of Luke presents Christ as a passional prophet, as one in a long line of prophets who were sent to Israel, and were subsequently persecuted and killed (Lk. 11.49-51, cf. 18.31).[3] According to D&G, the betrayal of prophets, narrated in the Hebrew scriptures, culminates in the life of Christ, a saintly 'traitor', whose death 'universalizes the system of betrayal' (TP 124). In contrast to the 'despotic Christ', located at the centre of the Johannine signifying system, this saintly traitor *betrays* the Jewish signifying despotic regime and, in turn, is *betrayed* by it (TP 184). Christ repeatedly rebelled against the Jewish religious authorities who were directly or indirectly connected with the Jerusalem Temple; he even set out to 'cleanse' this Temple, which was located at the centre of the signifying despotic regime, and went so far as to prophesy its destruction.[4] Indeed, this prophet announced the end of all *earthly* despotic signifying regimes and all despot-gods, foreseeing the advent of a New Jerusalem that would replace them (Lk. 21.5-7).

Christ's passional attachment to the Hebrew God as his point of subjectification made the betrayal of the signifying despotic regime inevitable. In his inaugural sermon in the Gospel of Luke, Christ announced his passional attachment to the God of Moses, Isaiah, Elijah and Elisha as *his own* point of subjectification (Lk. 4.16-21). As in the case of prophets of old, the subjectification of Christ produced a *divided* subject: a 'subject of enunciation', with a passion for love, from which proceeded a 'subject of the statement', with a passion for reason. Christ's passional attachment to the Jewish God was conditioned by these divided subject-positions. Having entered into a lonely and obsessional relation with his point of subjectification, Christ cut himself off from all religious officials associated with the Jerusalem temple-state. In faithful obedience to the Jewish God, he became a saintly traitor who betrayed the high priest of the Jewish Temple, the Sanhedrin, chief priests, elders, scribes and Pharisees.

Indeed, the story of the crucifixion narrates a *double* betrayal: having *betrayed* the signifying despotic regime, Christ foretold that he must also *be betrayed by this regime*. In effect, he prophesied his role as a scapegoat that he 'must be rejected' – deterritorialized – by the religious officials of the Jewish temple-state (Mk 8.31–9.1), and 'be betrayed into human hands and killed' (Mk 9.30-31, 10.33-34). Why must he be betrayed in Jerusalem? Because Jerusalem was the centre of the Jewish signifying despotic regime (Lk. 13.31-35, 11.48, 18.31, Acts 7.52). Having been betrayed by Judas (22.1-6, 47-48), then betrayed by Peter (Lk. 22.54-62) and betrayed a third time by the Jewish people who chose Barabbas over him (Lk. 23.13-25), he was betrayed a fourth time by Caiaphas, the high priest of the Jerusalem Temple and president of the Sanhedrin, who charged him with blasphemy (Mt. 26.63-66). Finally, at the extreme point of his torture of the Cross, Christ is even *betrayed by the despotic signifier* of the entire signifying despotic regime: for even this God averts his face from the sight of the tortured Christ. Having betrayed the God of the signifying despotic regime, and having been betrayed by God, the crucified Christ proclaims this *double betrayal* in his cry of dereliction, accusing God of betrayal in the words of the psalmist: 'My God, my God, why have you forsaken me?' (Mk 15.34, Mt. 27.46, cf. Ps. 22.1). Christ's cry of dereliction transforms his crucifixion into a great *spectacle of betrayal*. At that very moment, Christ was transformed into the perfect scapegoat, who deterritorialized the signifying despotic regime in his own body. He thereby established in perpetuity double betrayal at the heart of early Christian thought.

Conclusion

The passional subjective regime is a *postsignifying* regime in the sense that it exhibits profound points of divergence with the *signifying* despotic regime. Whereas the signifying regime is despotic, signifying and interpretive, this postsignifying regime is passional, subjective and authoritative. The relations of force in this regime can be mapped in terms of four coordinates. First, the prophet functions as a scapegoat victim through his betrayal of the signifying despotic regime; the passional prophet *betrays* the 'despot-god' through his subjective attachment to his own point of subjectification, the Hebrew God. If Moses is the iconic passional prophet, then the Egyptian Pharaoh is the iconic 'despot-god' (TP 121–2). The despotic signifying regime has no place for passional prophets because passional prophets have no regard for despot-gods. Second, the prophet's point of subjectification, the Hebrew God, constitutes the prophet as a 'subject', *divided* between a 'subject of enunciation', who is *spoken by* language, and a 'subject of the statement', who *speaks through* language. This prophet, divided by these conflicting subject-positions, has no ontological essence: he occupies a vacant place, which is a set of virtual relations between the unsaid and the said, between passion and reason. Third, the betrayal of the prophet triggers the end of faciality: for, by betraying the face of the 'despot-god', the prophet is reterritorialized in a new regime, one *without faciality*, a regime in which a *faceless* God replaces the radiating face of a despot-god. Fourth, the resulting prophetic discourse is non-interpretive: the prophet, obsessed with the Hebrew God as his passional point of subjectification, delivers this God's order-words without interpretation. Nonetheless, the 'said' of the prophet's pronouncements is always haunted by the *unsaid* of his undeclared delirium.

The Gospel of Luke exhibits a relative dominance of the passional subjective regime, which, in turn, produces a relatively stable 'passional' prophetic Christ. This Christ is easily recognized, so closely does he resemble the Jewish prophets of old. In many ways, this passional Christ is the inverse figure of the despotic Christ of the Gospel of John. His passional attachment to his point of subjectification makes his betrayal of the Jewish signifying despotic regime compulsory. By entering into a lonely and obsessional relation with his point of subjectification, Christ cut himself off from the religious officials aligned with the Jerusalem Temple.

The life of this passional prophet is the story of a *double betrayal*. For having betrayed the Jewish signifying despotic regime, Christ, in turn, was betrayed by it. He was betrayed by the despotic signifier of the signifying regime: the God of this regime averted his face from the sight of the tortured passional Christ. In his cry of dereliction Christ accused this God of *betrayal*: 'My God, my God, why have you forsaken me?' Having betrayed the signifying despotic regime, and having been betrayed by it, Christ's cry of dereliction transforms his death into a *spectacle of universal betrayal*. For it was at this point that Christ was transformed into the perfect scapegoat victim. He thereby established in perpetuity the spectacle of double betrayal in early Christian belief.

14

What can Christ's body do?

The Lord himself will come down from heaven, with a loud command, with the voice of the archangel, and with the trumpet call of God, and the dead in Christ will rise first. After that, we who are still alive and are left will be suddenly seized and caught up together with them in the clouds to meet the Lord in the air.

1 Thess. 4.16-17

What can a body do? This was Benedictus de Spinoza's famous question: 'For indeed, no one has yet determined what the body can do' (1985: 71). One of the most striking aspects of Paul's exhortation to the Thessalonians is what the bodies he describes can do. He narrates an extraordinary scene of bodies in motion, affecting and being affected by other bodies within a vast bloc of becoming. Some bodies fly downwards, while others fly upwards to meet them – heavenly bodies, resurrected bodies, living bodies – all flying about high up 'in the clouds … in the air' (1 Thess. 4.17).

You may object that many things are possible in the literature, especially apocalyptic writings, which are not possible in real life. While this observation is true of literature in general terms and is especially true in the case of the New Testament, this objection misses the point of D&G's analysis of literature. For their philosophy is premised on the principle that there is *an intrinsic connection between literature, life and philosophy*. Literature is an expression of life and writing and interpreting literature is a means of thinking through the philosophical questions which life poses. D&G's philosophical method entails *forming assemblages with literature* that can result in a 'philosophy-becoming-literature'.[1] In Deleuze's view, literature 'is inseparable from "becoming": in writing, one becomes-woman, becomes-animal or vegetable, becomes molecule to the point of becoming-imperceptible' (ECC 1).[2]

Before we can proceed in further detail on the subject of what Christ's body can do, there is a negative work to be carried out: we must rid ourselves of two misunderstandings, the first of which is the concept of the molar subjectivity (*subjectivité molaire*). While Descartes contended that thinking individuals are individual substances, Spinoza turned the individual into a 'body' (a structured entity), as a mode of power, which has the capacity to affect, and be affected by, other bodies (Hardt 2015). This body is not an ontological subject but a structured entity that undergoes processes of becoming. In other words, the qualities of a body are not the qualities of a stable individual substance but rather are produced by the *differential interplay of forces between bodies* (§§ 7, 10).[3]

A second and closely related misunderstanding is the concept of the autonomous human body: we must disconnect Spinoza's concept of a body from any connotation of it functioning independently of other bodies. There is no 'body' that is a self-enclosed entity: every 'body' is a machine composed within a multiplicity (§§ 1–3). For example, in the scene described by Paul in 1 Thess. 4.16-17, the bodies of the Lord and the archangel, and the bodies of the living and the dead, descend and ascend *in relation to one another*, as machines composing the same multiplicity or bloc of becoming. After all, how could these human bodies be 'suddenly seized and caught up (ἁρπαγησόμεθα) … in the air', if not through the affect or attraction of the heavenly bodies? By bracketing out these erroneous concepts, that of molar subjectivity and the autonomous human body, D&G restore to the concept of a 'body' its spatiotemporal dimensions.

1. A body as a mode of power

What difference does 'in-betweenness' make to individual bodies? Spinoza conceived of a body as a 'mode of power', arguing that, by virtue of its spatiotemporal extension in relation to other bodies, a body is capable of two functions. First, a body has a *capacity for motion*. In his *Ethics*, Spinoza states that 'bodies are distinguished from one another by reason of motion and rest, speed, and slowness and not by reason of substance' (1985: I, 458). Perhaps the most notable feature of the bodies described in 1 Thess. 4.16-17 is that they are all in motion in relation to each other. Deleuze redefines Spinoza's theory of bodily movement as a 'set of relations of speed and slowness, of motion and rest' between singularities (particles-signs), which 'compose it' (SPP 127). In other words, 'movement' is primarily semiotic, and therefore it is *imperceptible*:

> Movement has an essential relation to the imperceptible; it is by nature imperceptible. Perception can grasp movement only as the displacement of a moving body or the development of a form. Movements, becomings, in other words, pure relations of speed and slowness, pure affects, are below and above the threshold of perception. (TP 280–1)

Returning to the case of 1 Thess. 4.16-17, one would say that the visible movement of heavenly and earthly bodies is an outward 'sign' of the interior movement of asignifying particles, or forces, between bodies (TP 262). Second, Spinoza argued that a body, as a mode of power, has the capacity to affect, and be affected by, other bodies. For a force only exists *in conflict with* other forces in a struggle for the augmentation of power: every force is a quantity, being active or reactive. Spinoza employs the Latin terms *affectio* and *affectus* to describe this event, which Deleuze glosses as 'affection' and 'affect' respectively. The term 'affection' (*affectio*) entails the interaction *between* bodies, while the term 'affect' (*affectus*) designates the resulting outcome of such interaction. In his lecture entitled 'Spinoza's Concept of Affect', Deleuze defines 'affection' as

> a state of a body insofar as it is subject to the action of another body. ... In other words, an effect, or the action that one body produces on another. ... *Affectio* is a mixture of two bodies, one body which is said to act on another, and the other receives the trace of the first. Every mixture of bodies will be termed an affection.[4]

As previously discussed, Deleuze subsumes all philosophers, including Spinoza, within Nietzsche's global concept of a 'will-to-power', which Deleuze defines as 'the element from which derive both the quantitative difference of related forces and the quality that devolves into each force in this relation'.[5] In other words, the will to power concerns 'the principle of the synthesis of forces' (NP 46). Bodily forces are either active or reactive, 'dominant or dominated depending on their difference in quantity' (NP 53). Nietzsche's theory of active and reactive forces provided Deleuze with a general framework his appropriation of Spinoza's concept of affection. The result is, according to Paolo Vignola, a philosophy that merges with that of Nietzsche to the point of synthesis, such that we can even speak of 'Nietzsche-Deleuze' (2019: 554). When two bodies, as modes of power, enter a zone of proximity (*voisinage*) with each other, their bodily forces 'differentiate' themselves immanently, at a molecular level, without reference to molar bodies or transcendentals, resulting in limitless becoming.[6] By virtue of being situated at the intersection of the relations of force, all bodies lack a defined essence (TP 262).

In the case of the interaction of an orchid and wasp, the bodies of the orchid and wasp, prior to their interaction, each constitute a 'mode of power', which is to say, two discrete networks of forces (§§ 5.2, 6.1.1): the orchid embodies an *active* network of forces, while the wasp embodies *reactive* network of force. When these two bodies entered a zone of proximity, these two networks of force form a single 'diagram' of (virtual) force that is differenciated as (actual) power, through the transfer of asignifying 'particles-signs' or singularities (in the form of pollen) from one body to the other. This differenciation of forces as power occurs at a molecular, pre-individual level, without reference to the molar bodies (*molaires organisées*) of the orchid and wasp. Hence, the resulting reterritorialization of the orchid and the deterritorialization of the wasp are not predicates of molar bodies, a point to which I shall return when we consider Christ's 'becomings' (§§ 15–17). Through this transfer of singularities, the bodies of the orchid and wasp are temporarily interlinked in two asymmetrical becomings. Likewise, when the networks of forces of human and heavenly bodies listed in 1 Thess. 4.16-17 were differenciated as power, the bodies are 'suddenly seized and caught up in the clouds, … in the air'. Thus, through a temporary suspension of our attention on molar bodies, we can grasp the two attributes of a body as a mode of power: first, its capacity for motion and, second, its capacity to affect, and be affected by, other bodies.

If we wish to understand what a body can do, whether it be the body of an orchid, a wasp, a human being or Christ – we must understand *what diagrams of force a body enters into*, and how these networks of forces are differenciated as power. According to Spinoza the capacity of a body to affect, and be affected, is not a constant property of a body but is a property that fluctuates according to 'the nature of the body affected and at the same time from the nature of the affecting body, so that one and the same body may be moved differently according to the differences in the nature of the body moving it' (1985: I, 460). As Deleuze explains, each body can only be 'defined by the ensemble of relations which compose it, or, what amounts to exactly the same thing, by its power of being affected'.[7]

1.1. Rhythms of intensity: Joy and sadness

Since the differenciation of forces as power occurs at a molecular, pre-individual level, without reference to molar human beings, molecular events are *imperceptible*. We cannot experience the flows of 'particles-signs' directly; we cannot experience the circulation of molecules and atoms, of energy, much less, the alteration of time, all of which connect the body to the plane of immanence (Guattari 1996: 160). What is more, owing to the irreducibly *synthetic* character of affect, we cannot trace affects back to the material, libidinal or discursive events that caused them.

However, while a body cannot experience molecular events directly, it *does*, nonetheless, experience the *aggregate value* of such molecular events as a *rhythm* of bodily intensity. Rhythm discloses the 'logic of the senses' in relation to these events (FB 31–8). In other words, the *rhythm* of bodily intensity is a 'sign' of the intensities that caused them.[8] Spinoza associates the rhythm of a *rising* bodily intensity with the sensation of joy (and such related affects as love and hope). When a body, as an active mode of power, 'enters into composition with' another body, the 'affect' of joy may result. Similarly, he associates the corresponding rhythm of *declining* bodily intensity with the sensation of sadness (and such related affects as hate, fear, depression, paranoia and envy) (1985: I, 499–500, 524–6). Thus, when a human body, as a reactive mode of power, enters into composition with another body that threatens its coherence, it may experience the sensation of sadness (SPP 19). Thus, the fluctuating relations between active and reactive variously increase and decrease, aid and restrain, 'our body's power of acting ... and thinking' (Spinoza 1985: I, 500).

In *Nietzsche and Philosophy*, Deleuze states that while active forces affirm the virtual possibilities of life, reactive forces impede such active forces: 'Reactive force ... limits active force, imposes limitations and partial restrictions on it and is already controlled by the spirit of the negative' (NP 56). Joy is the power of action. When Jesus sent seventy men ahead of him into the towns, they 'returned with (the sensation of) joy' over their power of action: they rejoiced, exclaiming, 'Lord, even the demons are subject to us in your name!' (Lk. 10.17). And when the man, having lost a sheep, goes into the wilderness and finds it, he too is filled *with joy*, owing to his power of action; he then invited his friends and his neighbours to rejoice with him (Lk. 15.6-7). But those who lose a family member through death experience sadness owing to the loss of their power of action, which is to say, their powerlessness to overcome the power of death (Mt. 5.4). The painter France Bacon was particularly drawn to the human body in its falling rhythm because, according to Deleuze, it is the outer threshold of the falling rhythm – with all its immobile waiting, spasms and screams – that manifests the body's 'convulsive pain and vulnerability' (FB 21).

Based on this analytic of active and reactive forces, a great many affects can be arranged along a spectrum that runs from a high-intensity joyful body to a low-intensity sad body. These rising and falling rhythms, and the corresponding sensations of joy and sadness, are 'signs' of the molecular events that caused them.[9] Deleuze, drawing inspiration from Spinoza, de-psychologizes not only the affects of joy and sadness *but also thinking, perceiving and remembering* (Braidotti 2019: 473). Thinking, perceiving and remembering are not the volitional acts of an ontological subject, as Descartes maintained, but inhuman affects arising from the differentiation of forces. Hence, Deleuze argues that there is an exteriority and contingency to thought in the sense that it is beyond our control (Vignola 2019: 552–66).[10] By introducing affect as the *inhuman* factor, Deleuze displaces the primacy of Cartesian subject, as an ontological 'I', that is in control of its own thoughts (WP 169).

2. The two planes of literature

Having established the spatiotemporal dimensions of the human body as a 'mode of power', and the related concepts of affect and rhythms of intensity, we can now ask, how this theorization of the body advances us towards a new interpretive space from which to ask, what *Christ's* body can do in the canonical Gospels? But prior to answering this question, we must take care to distinguish between *two distinct planes* in literature, a molar and molecular plane respectively. Of course, the most familiar plane in literature is the molar plane. This plane consists of literary forms – genres, themes, motifs – and subjectified literary characters. But through a temporary suspension of our attention to this molar plane, it is also possible to discern, at a deeper level, a *molecular plane*, which is composed of non-subjectified bodies, as modes of power, in spatiotemporal relations of force to other bodies. Through the disruption of the narrative of molar characters, the molecular plane is liberated. This plane reveals, what Deleuze terms, 'matters of fact', which is to say, the forces that act upon bodies and bring about the rising and falling rhythms of bodily intensity (FB 7, 13, 151, 154).

This molecular plane is asignifying. Being free of linguistic categories of thought, literary forms and subjectified characters it contains *has no meanings to decipher* and no story to tell. But something is happening all the same. *For the forces operating in this plane are productive, not representational*. They produce pure difference and unheard of 'becomings' that cannot be reduced to linguistic categories of sameness.

When we read the canonical Gospels, we are faced with the molar and molecular planes simultaneously. The task of analysing the molecular plane can be likened to being a bird in flight, looking down on the world below. From this bird's-eye perspective, we observe 'broad, motionless lines' that the movements of bodies compose, 'the points at which the lines join, cross or separate' (Sarraute 1963: 108).[11] When we view the canonical Gospels from the bird's-eye perspective, the narrative is likewise disrupted.[12] Literary characters appear to us only as 'subjectless individuations' or, what Nathalie Sarraute terms, 'envelops' of semiotic particles in motion. Characters, including Christ, the disciples, the Pharisees, the sick and demon-possessed, are all 'envelops' of semiotic particles, modes of power in relations of force with other bodies, which collectively compose a multiplicity or 'bloc of becoming' (§ 3).[13] As D&G explain, they are all subjectless individuations, figure of desire, in 'relations of movement and rest, speed and slowness between unformed elements, or at least between elements that are relatively unformed, molecules and particles of all kinds' (TP 266). The interpretation of these 'subjectless individuations' entails a machinic theorization of characters. For example, in *Kafka: Toward a Minor Literature*, D&G observe how all of Franz Kafka's literary characters are 'figures of desire' (K 28). By metamorphosing into a 'monstrous bug', Gregor Samsa became a figure of intense liberated desire *in motion*, seeking a way of escape (K 12–13). In *The Trial*, the main character (known simply as 'K') is a figure of desire *in motion*, moving from room to room, office to office, seeking justice (K 49). Likewise, the main character in *The Castle* is also a figure of desire in motion, trying to establish a liaison with the castle machine.

Likewise, the canonical Gospels present Christ as a figure of desire *in motion*, a desiring machine that travels from village to village, and place to place, establishing intense connections with other desiring machines, such as the bodies of the sick, women, demoniacs and tax collectors. Though we, as interpreters, continue to employ the term 'Christ' as a matter of convenience to designate this saintly 'figure of desire', as a kind of pointer, this 'Christ' is not a molar subject: he is a desiring machine in motion, which machinically connected with other desiring machines to precipitate events: the 'proper name does not indicate a subject. … The proper name fundamentally designates something that is of the order of the event' (TP 264). By virtue of his machinic relations to other bodies within blocs of becoming, Christ's body was in a constant state of transformation (§§ 15–17).

3. A symptomology of the Gospels

Even though the molecular plane of literature is asignifying, it is not closed off to analysis. Through a temporary suppression of our focus on the familiar molar plane, we can observe not only bodies entering into machinic relations with other bodies, but we can also detect the 'symptoms' arising from such interactions. For every 'symptom' is a sign of a molecular event (LS 170).[14] The affects of joy and sadness constitute two obvious examples of Deleuze's so-called 'symptomatological' approach to literature: joy and sadness are 'symptoms' of molecular events. They are signs of the eruption of pure difference, which cannot be reduced to linguistic categories of sameness. Through the detection of such symptoms, we can analyse how the bodies of the literary characters are formed as modes of power. To analyse such symptoms, we must first become sensitive to how bodies enter into composition and exchange intensities with other bodies; we must become *sensitive to the signs* they emit.[15] In *Proust and Signs*, Deleuze likens the vocation of the interpreter of symptoms to becoming an 'apprentice', or an 'Egyptologist':

> There is no apprentice who is not 'the Egyptologist' of something. One becomes a carpenter only by becoming sensitive to the signs of wood, a physician by becoming sensitive to the signs of disease. Vocation is always predestination with regard to signs. Everything that teaches us something emits signs. (PS 5)

How does one become sensitive to the 'signs' emitted by bodies in the Gospel narratives? This is clearly not an exegetical task, for these signs are not linguistic signifiers (§ 8.3.1). They are not even of the order of referentiality. Signs destabilize, rather than facilitate, direct reference to information or linguistic concepts. What then do signs in literature do, if not communicate linguistic concepts? Signs are symptoms of the differentiation of active and reactive forces between non-subjectified bodies (LS 170). They are asignifying in the sense that they transmit *intensities*, not concepts, to the body of the reader, without detouring through linguistic codification of signifiers and signifieds. In other words, signs provide ways of entering into relation with truth, which is a truth that *has been liberated from language and linguistic concepts*.

3.1. Deleuze's *Proust and Signs*

Let us delve deeper into the world of literary signs, with a turn to Deleuze's analysis of Proust's *Recherche*. In part 1 of the first edition of *Marcel Proust et les signes* (1964), Deleuze developed a fourfold typology of signs, consisting of worldly signs, signs of love, sensuous signs and signs of art. Deleuze defines 'worldly signs' (*signes mondains*) as stereotypical signs of social convention; these signs are discernible in culturally appropriate conversation, and in the observance of the social forms and customs (PS 7). So-called 'sensuous signs' (*signes sensibles*) are signs that help us grasp the past in terms of its inseparability from the present moment through the intervention of involuntary memory. Sensuous signs may occasion joy and sadness and, at other times, force us to reinterpret the past. Part 2 of *Proust and Signs* (added to the second French edition in 1970) is significantly titled 'The Literary Machine'. Here, Deleuze recasts his study of Proust's *Recherche* in terms of the *machinic production* of signs. Deleuze develops a tripartite system of signs consisting of, first, a composite of natural and artistic signs; second, a composite of worldly signs and signs of love; and third, signs of 'universal alteration' (e.g. aging, illness and death), which are reminiscent of lines of rigid segmentarity (Pombo Nabais 2013: 133–55, cf. § 6.1). Finally, in the conclusion to part 2 (added to the third French edition in 1973, which served as the basis for the English translation), Deleuze recasts his typology of signs into a binary model. Deleuze groups sign together on the basis of whether they are discursive or nondiscursive (PS^f 205–19, PS 110–18). Thus, in these three successive editions, one also finds different approaches to the concept of a sign, as well as different explanations of the process of fiction. What is more, Deleuze's typology of signs becomes increasingly simplified, changing from a fourfold typology of signs, to a tripartite model, and lastly to a twofold typology. We should not be disappointed by Deleuze's apparent unwillingness to formulate one, totalizing typology of signs because the signs in literature are by nature ambiguous and elusive, and the mapping of signs is always an experimental process. Arnaud Bouaniche observes how signs operate according to a process of mere 'signalling' to the reader (2007: 73). Thus, the importance of signs in literature lies not in the preciseness by which they can be classified into a universal typology, but in the changes they trigger *in the body of symptomatologists*, and especially in their thoughts, perceptions and unconscious. As previously discussed, Deleuze argues that thinking and perceiving are not the volitional acts of an ontological subject but inhuman affects arising from the differentiation of forces (§ 14.1.1). Hence, there is an exteriority and contingency to thought in the sense that it is beyond our control. For the body is machinic. Deleuze posits a kind of intelligence that is arrived at through our encounters with signs in literature and art. Contrary to the Cartesian model, the body of the reader, so conceived, is not distinct from literature (much less from the world at large) but, as mode of power, the body of the reader is more like an 'envelop' – to borrow Nathalie Sarraute's term – a kind membrane that captures signs, and such signs alter our body's dynamics of power. The shock of these signs can even induce different affects. Hence, *the question of the efficacy of literature must, in the first instance, be considered at the level of aesthetic experience*. From this vantage point, the 'sense' of a sign in literature is inextricably tied to the affects it induces in the body of the reader. But this is not the whole story, for *aesthetic experience is also the entryway to the faculties* (Pombo Nabais 2013: 93–4). Affects, in turn, trigger thoughts and perceptions in the reader.[16] It follows that reading the Gospels entails becoming sensitive to how the signs in these narratives become expressed in their own bodies, and sensitive to the types of thinking and perceiving they induce.

Intensities in literature also induce changes in the unconscious of the reader. For the unconscious, like the human body, is machinic: it too is produced through the *intersection* of the external world, literature and art (as expression), on the one hand, and the internal forces of the human body (as content). Literature, as a machine of *pure expression*, acts directly on the unconscious, injecting it with fresh intensities which may trigger fresh becomings. The unconscious is positioned at the intersection of territorialized existence and abstract machines, at the intersection of the 'organism' and the 'body without organs' (Guattari 1995: 58–9). In other words, the unconscious is a *machinic* unconscious (*inconscient machinic*). Hence, Guattari maintains that the unconscious is not a 'theatre', as Freud supposed, wherein the tragedy of Oedipus is interminably rehearsed through the triangulation of the father, mother and son. The unconscious is a *factory* that incessantly *produces new connections* with the external world. What is more, the unconscious is not a closed, linguistically structured system, which operates according to the laws of signifiers, as Lacan supposed: it is a *rhizome* – an open system of asignifying forces – that *improvises coordinates* of self-reference with the world. Thus, the unconscious truly is an open system. Within the neurotic, stratified and territorialized body of the interpreter truly resides a machinic unconscious of pure difference. Engagement with the signs of literature can increase our body's power of acting and thinking, and even function as a catalyst for new forms of desiring-production.

Conclusion

What can a body do? What difference does 'in-betweenness' make to individual bodies? Drawing inspiration from Spinoza's question, Deleuze de-psychologizes the molar subject, turning the human body into a mode of power. Every human body constitutes a network of forces that interacts with other bodies. Every network of forces is a quantity, which is either active or reactive in relation to the network of forces of other bodies. These active and reactive networks of forces differentiate themselves immanently at a *molecular* level, without reference to molar bodies. The body of Christ can be analysed as a mode of power, a figure of desire, that entered into machinic relations to other bodies within blocs of becoming (multiplicities). This Christ journeyed from place to place, forming multiplicities with other bodies through acts of teaching, healing, feeding and ultimately through the manner of his dying (§§ 15–17). Hence, Christ's body was always passional: it was always a production of productions. While these molecular events are imperceptible, the *aggregate value* of such events is manifested by the fluctuating rhythms of bodily intensity. Spinoza associates the rising rhythm of bodily intensity with the affect of joy, and the corresponding declining rhythm of intensity with the affect of sadness. These affects are not feelings or emotions of molar persons but 'symptoms' or 'signs' of prior molecular events within non-subjectified bodies.

A schizoanalysis of what Christ's body can do entails that an important distinction be made between the familiar plane of *molar* plane of literature, which consists of literary forms and subjectified literary characters, on the one hand, and the *molecular* plane, composed of non-subjectified bodies, as modes of power, in spatiotemporal machinic relations to other bodies. The interpretation of these non-subjectified bodies entails a machinic theorization of character. Literary characters, such as Christ, the disciples and the Pharisees, are all figures of desire, modes of power in relations of force with other bodies, which collectively compose a multiplicity or 'bloc of becoming'. The body of Christ is machinic: it is a desiring machine *in motion*, travelling from village to village, and place to place, establishing intense connections with other desiring machines, including the bodies of the sick, women, demoniacs and tax collectors. By virtue of these machinic relations, Christ's body was in a constant state of transformation, in relation to other bodies, as dimensions of a shared block of becoming.

Deleuze develops a symptomatological approach to literature which interprets bodily affects as 'signs' of the differentiation of forces that caused them. To carry out a symptomology the Gospels requires, we must become sensitive to the signs that the bodies of literary characters emit. These signs have no linguistic meanings and no story to tell. But something is happening all the same. For signs are symptoms of the production of pure difference, of unheard of 'becomings', which cannot be reduced to linguistic or theological categories of sameness. Such signs provide the reader with a way of entering into a relation with the truth of the Gospels, which is a truth liberated from linguistics signification and theological concepts.

We, as readers, cannot control our encounters with these signs because they function machinically on our bodies, changing the dynamics of its power. The shock of these signs can induce different affects such as joy and sorrow in us. Thus, the question of the efficacy of literature can be considered at the level of *aesthetic experience*. But aesthetic experience is *the entryway to the faculties*. Therefore, affects can also induce new thoughts and perceptions in the reader. It follows that reading the Gospels entails becoming sensitive to how the signs in these narratives are expressed in our own bodies, aware of what affects they produce and what thinking and perceiving they induce. These signs may also trigger changes in the unconscious of the reader. For the unconscious is also machinic. The unconscious is a *factory* that incessantly *produces new connections* with the external world; it is a *rhizome* that *improvises coordinates* of self-reference with the world. If we are fortunate, the signs in the Gospels will function as a catalyst for new forms of desiring-production.

15

Molecular becomings of Christ: Becoming-woman

Those who try to keep their (molar) life will lose it, but those who lose their (molar) life will keep it.

Lk. 17.33

In the canonical Gospels, the body of Christ, as a figure of desire, journeyed from place to place entering into multiplicities with other bodies through acts of teaching, healing, feeding and ultimately through the manner of his dying (§ 14.2). We cannot understand Christ, if we do not comprehend what his machinic body was capable of doing, and specifically how Christ gradually lost his molar body by entering into composition with other bodies, thereby incarnating pure difference. For the body of Christ was always a *production*, or rather, a production of productions. Christ explains this general principle in the plainest possible words: 'Those who try to keep their [molar] life will lose it, but those who lose their [molar] life will keep it' (Lk. 17.33, Mt. 16.25). In other words, if you try to hold onto your molar life – if you try to bring your bodily 'becoming' to a halt – you will end up losing your life, because *molar existence is a delusion* (§ 10). The attainment of *true* life – molecular life manifesting pure difference – only comes at the cost of losing one's territorialized, stratified life as an 'organism', and embarking upon a series of 'becomings'.

While there is no proper ordinal advancement through a series of becomings, D&G arrange three 'becomings' in particular on a spectrum ranging from the somewhat molecular 'becoming-woman' (*devenir-femme*) to the fully molecular 'becoming-imperceptible' (*devenir-imperceptible*) (§ 17), with 'becoming-animal' (*devenir-animal*) occupying 'a median region' between two points (§ 16). This spectrum of increasing molecularity ranges from becoming-intense with respect to binary gender (male/female), to becoming more intense in terms of the human/nature (or human/animal) binary, to becoming extremely intense with respect to existence in general (sentient existence/imperceptible). Since women and animals inhabit non-majoritarian modes of existence, on the periphery of apparatuses of power, their bodies are already more intense than the bodies of men (TP 116–17). All three becomings are 'molecular' in the sense that they occur without reference to molar subjectivity. Taken together, these 'becomings' amount to a break-up gesture with one's socially constructed molar subjectivity, which is to say, the amount to 'losing' of one's molar life to save one's molecular life. The life of Christ entailed a progressive loss of his molar identity, a process that ranged from 'becoming-woman' through 'becoming-animal' to 'becoming-imperceptible'.

1. Becoming and multiplicities

All 'becomings' entail the formation of multiplicities (§ 3). Indeed, D&G state that 'becoming and multiplicity are the same thing' (TP 249). All machines are passional! For what would a lone wolf-machine be without a multiplicity (pack) of wolves? Owing to their combinatory power, machines couple with other machines to form multiplicities and thereby give rise to countless 'becomings'. Hence, in the Gospel narratives, there are no autonomous machines, not even a lone Christ machine. Christ, as a figure of desire, was always coupling with other machines and forming alliances, even illicit unions, and forbidden loves.

Deleuzo-Guattarian philosophy is sensitive to countless types of becomings in literature such as Captain Ahab's 'becoming-whale', D. H. Lawrence's 'becoming-tortoise', Gregor Samsa's 'becoming-bug' in Kafka's 'The Metamorphosis', and Christ's 'becoming-demon' (§ 16.3). Such becomings do not entail imitation or mimesis. Captain Ahab did not become a whale, nor did D. H. Lawrence become a tortoise.[1] Likewise, Christ's 'becoming-woman' and 'becoming-animal' did not entail Christ imitating a woman or becoming like a demon. For 'becoming' is never about conforming to a linguistic category. Becoming is always an incarnation of pure difference. The unheard of 'becomings' of Christ, which I shall discuss in Chapters 15–17, do not correspond to linguistic concepts or theological meanings. But they are real nonetheless, for through such becomings Christ incarnated pure difference in his own body.

2. Christ becoming-woman: The entryway to other becomings

D&G maintain that becoming-woman 'possesses a special introductory power' (TP 248). For 'all becomings begin with, and pass through, becoming woman (*devenir-femme*)'. Becoming-woman is 'the key to all other becomings' (TP 277): 'because it is not too from removed from the binarism of phallic power' it can serve as the entryway to other 'sexed becomings' (Guattari 2009: 229; cf. Semetsky 2010: 87–102). Just as the male/female gender binarism delivers human bodies over to the phallic power at work in society, so also does the 'becoming-woman' deliver human bodies from the same phallic power.[2]

'Becoming-woman' does *not* entail transforming into a molar woman, identifying as a woman or presenting oneself *as* a woman; indeed, 'becoming-woman' does not even function at the level of molar subjects.[3] It lacks linguistic coordinates altogether. For 'becoming-woman' is connected to diverse minoritarian forms of sexual existence, what D&G term 'real transsexualities, continuums of intensity' (TP 147), that have been historically oppressed and prohibited. Hence, *there is an entire micropolitics of 'becoming-woman'* that is connected to becoming-queer, becoming-lesbian, becoming-gay, becoming-gender fluid and becoming-trans (Nigianni 2009: 157). Indeed 'Whatever shatters norms, whatever breaks from the established order' is related to becoming-woman (Guattari 2009: 230). Hence, D&G even speak of 'homosexual Christs' (AO 369). But that which all expressions of 'becomings-woman' share in common is that they are all *molecular* processes of singularization, without reference to the male/female binarism (D 119, TP 275–6).

2.1. Why is theology opposed to becoming-woman?

'Becoming-woman' attracts the opprobrium of systematic theologians because they can only conceive of essentialized identities and lawful unions. Theology considers molar male and female genders to be *essential forms*, which are locked in an asymmetrical linguistic binarism: for 'God created humankind in his image, ... male and female he created them' (Gen. 1.27). Hence, systematic theologians can only think in terms of essentialized identities and lawful unions.

In linguistic terms, the signifier 'woman' is 'non-man'. The term 'woman' is subordinated to, and defined in terms of, the primary term, 'man'. Implicit within this man/woman linguistic binarism is the contrast between 'same' versus 'different', with 'different' (woman) being subordinated to, and defined in terms of, the 'same' (man). Therefore, systematic theology must oppose *all* forms of 'becoming-woman', everything that escape this binarism, as a matter of principle. However, in real life, no individual fully coincides with either pole of this man/woman binarism. As Brian Massumi has observed, individuals do not *possess* gender: an individual *is gendered* by language to one degree or another (1992: 87–8). Thus, gender cannot be destratified without dismantling the linguistic strata which overcode it (§§ 7.3.2, 10.2). In 'becoming-woman' the body is destratified from the three 'great' strata (§ 7.1), the strata of the organism, signification and subjectification, and especially from the strata of the Phallus as a despotic signifier.

Of course, the category of 'man', as defined by traditional theology, is the quintessential *molar* subject. Hence, there can be no 'becoming-man' that corresponds to 'becoming-woman' because 'man' is majoritarian *par excellence.* Man, being the majoritarian standard, cannot be saved because all becoming is 'becoming-minoritarian' (TP 291). Simply existing as a molar 'man' comes at the cost of self-alienation and self-repression. 'Man' can be saved only by entering into minoritarian processes, the gateway to which is 'becoming-woman'. As Guattari explains, in the process of 'becoming-woman', man 'detaches himself from the phallic types inherent in all power formations' to enter into the diverse modalities of becoming-woman (2009: 229–30).

This same requirement applies to women. There is no salvation for molar 'woman' because the female body is also produced through the stratification on the basis of the male/female binarism. In short, the bodies of (real) women, like the bodies of men, are an *effect of phallic power*. Mary, the mother of Jesus, is the paradigmatic molar woman (§ 10.1.3). Mary sexually submitted to the Father God, as a symbolic representative of the Phallus: she acquiesced to this power with the words, 'Let it happen to me as you have said' (Lk. 1.38). And with these words of consent, her body was overcoded by phallic power. Hence, the story of the annunciation of Mary is a tale of the subjection of woman to the same despotic signifier, upon which all male authority and subjectivity depend: the Phallus.

3. Christ becoming-woman

Christ entered into (*entre dans*) 'becoming-woman' when he healed the woman who had suffered from a chronic haemorrhage of blood (Mk 5.24-34, Lk. 8.42b-48). Prior to their encounter, Christ and this woman comprised two discrete bodies. Their bodies were *in a non-relation*. Each body, as a mode of power, possessed the virtual capacity to affect, and be affected by, other bodies (§ 14.1.1). In the case of this healing story, Christ's body comprised an *active* network of forces, with the capacity 'to heal', whereas the woman's body comprised a *reactive* network of forces, with the corresponding capacity 'to be healed'.

The story of the healing of the haemorrhagic woman can be analysed in terms of the formation of a multiplicity. Like a wasp alighting on an orchid (§ 5.3), the body of this woman coupled with the body of Christ and formed a multiplicity. At the precise moment when she touched Christ's cloak, these two bodies entered into a zone of proximity. Mark's text is remarkably precise in its narration of this molecular event: at the very moment when the woman 'touched his cloak' (Mk 5.27), Christ experienced a flow of power (δύναμις), which is to say, a flow of *asignifying* intensities, pass *out of his body*: being 'immediately aware that power had passed out of him' (τὴν ἐξ αὐτοῦ δύναμιν ἐξελθοῦσαν), Jesus turned about in the crowd and asked, 'Who touched my clothes?' (Mk 5.30). While Christ's molar could not experience this molecular event directly, Christ, as a molar subjectivity, did experience the *aggregate value* of this event as a loss of bodily intensity. This affect of a loss of bodily intensity was a 'sign' of the intensities that caused them (§ 14.1.1).

When these semiotic singularities flowed from Jesus' body to the body of the woman, the boundaries of their bodies became indistinct. Through a flow of power, both bodies entered into asymmetrical 'becomings' *with reference to one another*. Through intra-action, the woman became *deterritorialized*, while the body of Christ became simultaneously *reterritorialized*. The body of the woman was *deterritorialized* by the flow of power from Christ's body; this transfer of power enacted a kind of recording of the powers of Christ's body onto her own. For his part, Christ entered into a 'becoming-woman' when his body was *reterritorialized* through the same transfer of power. Through this reterritorialization, Christ did not become a molar woman. But his identity was hybridized through this transfer of power. As a result, Christ's identity becomes blurred, for the body of the woman is now capable of transporting Christ's powers to other bodies. Likewise, following Christ's reterritorialization onto the woman's body, the woman did not become like Christ: that which was transferred was *asignifying* power, not a linguistic meaning. Like Christ's body, her body became hybridized.

This transfer of power was a *non-reversible* event – indeed two asymmetrical events, reterritorialization and deterritorialization – in which the identities of both Christ and the woman were permanently changed. The 'sign' or 'symptom' of this differenciation of power was the physical healing of the woman (§ 14.3): 'Immediately her hemorrhage stopped; and she felt in her body that she was healed of her disease' (Mk 5.29). Having experienced this healing, she disappeared into the crowd, like a wasp in flight, reterritorializing Christ's power wherever she goes. Through her 'line of flight', her body *functions as an extension of Christ's power*, which she transports to countless other bodies. We, as reader of this healing story, are left to wonder what happened next. We have so many unanswered questions. Does this story even have an ending? For in her 'becoming-Christ' she was transformed into a figure of intense, liberated desire. Hence, this is a story of the production of productions. What new multiplicities did *her* body form? What flows of power did it initiate? And what use did these other bodies make of Christ's bodily power?

Conclusion

Within the body of a molar subject abides a *molecular* 'body without organs' that is bestowed with the virtual capacity for novel 'becomings'. This is 'good news' for us because there is no salvation for the molar subject – the stratified 'organism' – except by way of molecular 'becomings'. In answer to the question, 'what must I do to be saved?', Christ does not equivocate: 'Those who try to keep their [molar] life will lose it, but those who lose their [molar] life will keep it' (Lk. 17.33). In short, saving your molecular life requires losing your molar life. Salvation always entails processes of 'becoming'.

Deleuzo-Guattarian philosophy is sensitive to countless types of 'becomings' in literature. The canonical Gospels are storehouses of Christ's 'becomings' and all such 'becomings' begin with the *formation of a multiplicity* through aleatory alliances between machines. In the Gospel narratives, as in life, there are no autonomous machines. For what would a lone Christ be? In the Gospels, whenever two machines couple and exchange semiotic flows, 'becomings' are sure to follow, and Christ, as a figure who was always animated by desire, had a particular affinity for aleatory couplings.

D&G arrange three specific 'becomings' on an increasing scale of intensiveness running from 'becoming-woman' through 'becoming-animal' to 'becoming-imperceptible'. Viewed from the perspective of the molecular plane, the life of Christ entailed a gradual loss of his molar subjecthood by 'becoming-woman', 'becoming-animal' (§ 16) and, finally, 'becoming-imperceptible' (§ 17). Of course, between these three 'becomings' there were countless other intermediate becomings, which are far too numerous to chronicle in this chapter.

D&G maintain that 'becoming-woman' serves as the entryway to all 'becomings' because woman is not too far removed from phallic power. For this reason, they argue that 'becoming-woman', more than any other becoming, 'possesses a special introductory power'. In 'becoming-woman' the overcoded human body becomes destratified with respect to the three 'great strata' – the strata of the organism, signification and subjectification – and especially from the Phallic despotic signifier. Needless to say, becoming-woman lacks molar coordinates: this becoming does not entail becoming *like* a molar woman. *For 'becoming' is never about conforming to a linguistic category.* Becoming is always an incarnation of pure difference. Thus, 'becoming-woman' is also the entryway to becoming-queer, becoming-lesbian, becoming-gay, becoming-trans, becoming-gender and becoming-gender fluid.

There is no salvation for molar man, for he is the quintessential molar subject. Simply existing as a molar man comes at the cost of profound self-alienation. This same logic applies to women, for the female body is also stratified by phallic power in terms of the male/female binarism. Hence, there is no salvation for molar woman either. In the Christian tradition, Mary, the mother of Jesus, is the paradigmatic molar woman: she sexually submitted in an act of obedience to the Father God, as a symbolic agent of the Phallus. Hence, even the body of Mary was overcoded by the Phallus. Even *she* had to enter into 'becoming-woman' to be saved.

Christ entered into 'becoming-woman' by forming a multiplicity with the body of a haemorrhagic woman (Mk 5:24-34). Like all becomings, this is a story of the formation of a multiplicity through the coupling of machines. The text of the Gospel of Mark is remarkably precise in its narration of this coupling of machines: at the precise moment when the woman touched his cloak, Christ experienced a flow of power passing out of his body (Mk 5.30). Through this flow, both bodies participated in an asymmetrical becoming with reference to one another: Christ entered into a 'becoming-woman' through the *reterritorialization* of his body's power into the body of the woman; this same transfer of power enacted a *deterritorialization* in the body of the woman. Thereafter, her deterritorialized body functioned as an extension of the Christ's power following her 'line of flight' into the crowd. We, as readers, are left to wonder what happened next. What new multiplicities did *her* body form? What use did those whom she later encountered make of Christ's bodily power? In asking such questions, we have clearly abandoned the traditional quest for the theological meaning of this healing miracle and embarked upon a schizoanalysis of the body of Christ, as a figure animated by desire, that continuously formed multiplicities with other bodies. Hence, this healing narrative illustrates a general principle concerning the entirety of Christ's life: it was always a *production of productions*. For what is the purpose of desire, if it is not producing life-changing connections?

16

Christ becoming-animal: An affair of sorcery

When Jesus got out of the boat, a man with an unclean spirit came from the tombs to meet him. … Then Jesus asked him, 'What is your name?' He replied, 'My name is Legion, for we are many.'

Mk 5.2, 9-10

Innumerable 'becomings-animal' (*devenir-animal*) are possible, some of which are quite famous, such as the 'becoming-wolf' of the Wolf-Man, the 'becoming-horse' of Little Hans, the irresistible 'becoming-whale' of captain Ahab, the 'becoming-ox' of King Nebuchadnezzar (Dan. 4.29-30) and the 'becoming-demon' of Christ (Mk 5.1-20, Lk 8.26-33).[1] For Christ's encounter with an entire legion of demons in the country of the Gerasenes was also an affair of 'becoming-animal'.[2]

Regardless of the form it may take, becoming-animal always entails participations with the power of a pack, with a multiplicity, that deterritorialize one's body from its human territory. Becoming-animal is possible because the human body is positioned at the shifting boundary that separates humans from their own inherent animality. For there is truly 'no separation between [human] bodies and nature' (Cimatti 2019: 504). In their working, and in their playing, human beings are never very far removed from their own animality, from their inner wolves and demons (TP 28, 208). Becoming-animal provides a way of *escape* from one's tidy territorialized humanity: For 'to become animal is to participate in movement, to stake out the path of escape in all its positivity' (K 12–13). It is an *immanent* process that entails a line of flight from the human/nature binarism.

Of course, 'becoming-animal' is highly problematic for systematic theologians, for the same reason that 'becoming-woman' is problematic: theology considers the molar human to be an *essential form*, which is locked in an asymmetrical linguistic binarism with animal, as well as with woman. Theology is rigid on this point. For it can only conceive of essentialized identities and lawful unions. Therefore, it must oppose all forms of 'becoming-animal', just as it opposes all forms of 'becoming-woman', as a matter of principle. In a section of *A Thousand Plateaus* entitled 'Memories of a Theologian', D&G make this same point: 'Theology is very strict on the following point … human beings cannot become animal. That is because there is no transformation of essential forms; they are inalienable and only entertain relations of analogy' (TP 252). In contrast to theology, D&G do not attribute any distinct ontological status to human beings against animals, or nature in general: 'becoming-animal' is always about *human* animality.

If we deterritorialize the linguistic categories of theologians, their objections lose their force. Indeed, there is a strong connection between deterritorializing language and 'becoming-animal'. For in becoming-animal the body crosses a threshold 'where all forms come undone, as do all the significations, signifiers and signifieds, to the benefit of … nonsignifying signs' (K 13). As Felica Cimatti observes, 'when language is no longer a territorializing device, the possibility of becoming-animal finally shows itself' (Cimatti 2019: 500–1). The logic that the 'subject' does not exist, in the absence of the linguistic subject versus object binarism, can also be applied to becoming-animal. For becoming-animal also moves in the direction of relinquishing the 'subject' through a life characterized by 'absolute immanence' (ES 27). Cimatti goes so far as to suggest that 'animality is the horizon of the philosophy of the future' (2019: 506).[3] In their book *Kafka: Toward a Minor Literature*, D&G develop their theory of becoming-animal that aims at destratifying the unified ontological subject altogether; they observe how Franz Kafka, in depiction of Gregor Samsa becoming a 'monstrous bug' (*ungeheuren Ungeziefer*), in his short story 'The Metamorphosis', performs a *dispersion* of his own self by decoding his individual perspective as a totalizing matrix (K 58). In becoming an insect, Gregor Samsa is transformed into a figure of intense, liberated desire, seeking a way of escape:

> To the inhumanness of the 'diabolical powers' there is the answer of becoming-animal: to become a beetle, to become a dog, to become an ape … rather than lowering one's head and remaining a bureaucrat, inspector, judge, or judged. … To become animal is to participate in movement, to stake out the path of escape in all its positivity. (K 12–13)

1. Two principles of becoming-animal

According to D&G there are two principles of becoming-animal: contagion through a pack and alliance with an anomalous individual. The first principle entails modes of propagation. In becoming-animal, 'it is never filiations which are important, but alliances, alloys; these are not successions, lines of descent, but contagions, epidemics, the wind' (D 69). 'Becoming-animal' always involves *contagions* cross-fertilizations and aleatory alliances with a pack or multiplicity as a mode of propagation (TP 239): for 'animals are packs, and ... packs form, develop, and are transformed by contagion' (TP 242). Wolves travel in a pack, and a wolf pack is a wolf-multiplicity, a 'wolfing', a 'wolf-machine', formed through contagion (TP 2, 32, § 3.1). Likewise, a legion of demons is demon-multiplicity. Of course, even Christ travelled in a pack, in a pack of disciples. Regardless of what form it takes, whether a pack of wolves or a pack of disciples, a swarm of rats or cloud of bats, 'becoming-animal' always entails *forming a multiplicity through contagion*: 'We do not become animal without a fascination for the pack, for multiplicity within us, human and nonhuman' (TP 239–40). As the case of the Gerasene demoniac demonstrates, contagion through a pack may even take the form of hostile occupations and monstrous unions. Indeed, 1 Pet. 5.8 warns of the danger of demons that prowl 'around like a roaring lion, seeking someone to devour' which serves as a reminder of the possible dangers inherent in becoming-animal.

Most theologians have a horror of propagation by contagion. For they deal in patrilineal kinships, lawful unions, genealogies and especially *filial relations*, both human and divine. Indeed, many theologians assert that Christ advocated for filial relations, and that his mission defended 'familialism' as a central value of the kingdom of God. How easily we forget that, in the Gospel of Mark, Christ disowns his relatives: he asked the crowd gathered around him, 'Who are my mother and brothers?', and then answered his own question, 'Whoever does the will of God is my brother, sister, and mother' (Mk 3.31-35) (§ 6.3.2). He even announces his intention to *disrupt* family relations in general (Lk. 12.51-53): 'If anyone comes to me and does not hate his father and mother, wife and children, brothers and sisters, yes, and his own life also, he cannot be my disciple' (Lk. 14.26, cf. Mt. 10.37). Follow me, he says, and 'let the dead bury the dead' (Mt. 8.22, Lk. 9.60). John the Baptist, who announced the advent of Christ's mission, even attacks the foundational doctrine of Judaism, namely that 'the alliance with God through a filiation that goes back to Abraham' (AO 133). According to John, a patrilineal kinship going back to Abraham means nothing, 'for God can raise up out of these stones children for Abraham' (Mt. 3.9). Thus, familialism was not a core value for all Christ groups. The Christ of the Gospels often decontextualizes the family as the primary locus of societal relations and resituates family members within an expanded series of networks within an expanded social field of marginalized people – fishermen, tax collectors, lepers, sex workers and sinners of all kinds – which was exterior to patrilineal kinships and genealogies. Christ invites such would-be followers to embrace that way of life that exceeds the family through the creation of the energetic connections with others. On the basis of these observations, it can be argued that Christ's mission was based on the first principle of 'becoming-animal': contagion through a pack.

Indeed, did Christ himself not teach that the kingdom of God spreads by contagion? Did he not teach that the kingdom of God spreads like a culture of yeast that *infects* a lump of dough, when yeast, wheat and water are mixed (Lk. 13.20-21, § 3). Jesus' teachings were like a contagion of yeast that *infected* those who listened to them. And he considered those who were so infected to be his true 'brother, sister and mother' (Mk 3.31-35, § 5.3.2).[4] The kingdom of God seems to be more like a revolutionary contagion, like an epidemic, than a set of theological propositions: it is like seeds that are scattered here and there, some falling 'on good soil, where it produces a crop – a hundred, sixty or thirty times what was sown' (Mt. 13.8). Christ taught that love is a *holy epidemic* that spreads by contagion.

This holy epidemic is the opposite of the first error of desiring, in which desire becomes overcoded as lack and insufficiency (§ 10). True love does not arise out of a lack or privation of an object of desire. There is a micropolitics of love. For love always produces connections, solidarity, with others. True love is a production of productions. Thus, in the canonical Gospels, there is also an entire micropolitics of becoming that is associated with those who are infected by this holy epidemic. All this is to say that the life of Christ incarnated the first principle of becoming-animal: propagation through contagion with a pack.

D&G's second principle of becoming-animal is the corollary of the first principle: namely, wherever there is pack, *there will always be an anomalous individual*. What exactly is this 'anomalous' individual? The 'anomalous' is the border- or liminal-point of a pack: the anomalous is the one with which an alliance must be made in order to connect with the power of the pack (TP 243): 'every animal swept up in its pack or multiplicity has its anomalous (*anomal*)' (MP 298, TP 243).[5] In the case of the Gerasene demoniac, the anomalous was the spokesperson of the pack of demons, the one who explained to Christ, 'My name is Legion, for we are many' (Mk 5.9-10, Lk. 8.30-31). And, as I shall explain below, sorcerers are experts in connecting with an anomalous individual.

2. Becoming-animal as an affair of sorcery

Taken together, the first principle of contagion through a pack, and the second principle of alliance with an anomalous individual, make becoming-animal *an affair of sorcery*, at least at the level of pragmatics (TP 506). A sorcerer (μάγος), not a 'priest', is required for all 'becomings-animal' because, while sorcerers know little about patrilineal kinships, genealogies and filial relations, they are *experts* in propagation by contagion by connecting with the anomalous.

A sorcerer forms a multiplicity with the pack by receiving an intensity from the outside, from a multiplicity. The reception of an intensity shakes up his own bodily molecularity, allowing his body to function in a new way. At the level of pragmatics, forming such a multiplicity with a pack often entailed the use of special materials such as faeces, eggs, herbs, gold and myrrh. Through the manipulation of special materials, the sorcerer connects with the anomalous point of the pack, and thereby enters into heterogeneous participations with the power of the pack, even entering into 'becoming-god', such as 'becoming-Helios' and 'becoming-Myrrh'.[6] In his 'becoming-god' he undergoes a disjunctive synthesis that ranges from 'I am molar man who is connected to the power of god' to 'I am molecular man with the powers of god' (§§ 3, 4.2.2). To reorganize his bodily molecularity in this way – to enter into such a 'becoming-god' – the sorcerer must form an alliance with the anomalous point of a pack that deterritorializes his body.

This special vocation of the sorcerer brings us back to the life of Christ. We must not forget that three sorcerers (μάγοι), following a deterritorialized star, brought the infant Christ such special materials as gifts (Mt. 2.1, 11): they presented him with gold, frankincense and myrrh, a veritable sorcerer's toolkit. Imagine Mary's surprise! The value of gold, frankincense and myrrh lay not in their symbolic value, as theologians suppose, but in their usefulness in forming an alliance with the pack.[7] The infant Christ, who was worshipped by sorcerers, spent the remainder of his life performing feats of sorcery. According to the Infancy Gospel of Thomas, Jesus, at the age of five, played at being a sorcerer. He 'made soft clay and fashioned from it twelve sparrows … and clapped his hands and cried to the sparrows, "Off with you!", and the sparrows took flight and went away chirping'.[8] On another occasion he later caused a boy who had angered him to be 'withered up completely' (*Inf. Gos. Thom.* 3), and he restored to life another boy who had died (*Inf. Gos. Thom.* 10). As an adult, Jesus continued to perform acts of sorcery (Horsley 2014): he turned a few loaves and fishes into enough food for five thousand people (Mk 6.33-44), he walked on the turbulent sea of Galilee (Mk 6.45-52), stilled a violent storm (Mk 4.37-41), healed a deaf man with spittle and a magic word, '*Ephphatha*' (Mk 7.31-37, cf. 8.22-26) and, on another occasion, turned one hundred and fifty gallons of water into wine (Jn 2.6-9). He even became invisible after blessing bread at a meal in Emmaus (Lk 24.13-35) (§ 17.2). Hence, we should not be surprised that the Gospel of Matthew portrays Jesus as the new Moses, who was the *most famous sorcerer in antiquity*.[9] After all, with the help of a miraculous rod (Exod. 7.8-13), Moses conjured the ten plagues upon Egypt (Exod. 7.14–12.42), and divided the Red Sea into two (Exod. 14.1-31). In the second and third centuries of the Common Era, Jesus' reputation as a sorcerer spread far and wide. Sorcerers invoked the name of Jesus as sorcerer in their own magic spells. To drive out demons, one such spell specifies the precise words which must be spoken: 'I conjure you by the god of the Hebrews, *Jesus*.'[10] All this is to say that the second principle of 'becoming-animal' – alliance with an anomalous individual – requires a sorcerer. For only sorcerers are experts in propagation by contagion. The infant Christ, who was worshipped by sorcerers, practised sorcery throughout his life, and was revered by sorcerers after his death.

3. Christ becoming-animal

The first principle of contagion through a pack, and the second principle of alliance with an anomalous individual, make becoming-animal an affair of sorcery. Christ's encounter with the Gerasene demoniac was likewise an affair of sorcery (Mk 5.1-20, Lk 8.26-33). At the outset of the story, the narrator explains that a legion of demons had taken over a man's body. When confronted by this monstrous pack of demons, Christ acted as a sorcerer, as one with expertise: he knew that to form an alliance with a pack of demons, a sorcerer must deal with its anomalous individual, which in this case was the demon's spokesperson. When Christ questioned the demoniac, asking 'What is your name?', it is the spokesperson of the demons who replied, 'My name is Legion, for we are many' (Mk 5.9, Lk. 8.30). This 'legion' of roughly five thousand demons was considerably larger and more powerful than the pack of seven demons that took over the body of Mary Magdalene (Lk. 8.2). The reply of this anomalous individual was infused with fear: 'What have you to do with me, Christ, Son of the Most High God? I beg you, do not torment me' (Lk. 8.28). Terrified at what might happen next, this anomalous individual begs

Christ for permission for the pack of demons to *reterritorialize* into a nearby herd of swine (Lk. 8.32).

Prior to their interaction, the body of Christ and the legion of demons constituted two separate bodies. But when Christ grants the demons permission to reterritorialize, his words of authorization were defined less by their linguistic content than by what they caused 'to move, to flow, and to explode' (AO 133). Through this transfer of semiotic power, both bodies participated in asymmetrical processes of 'becoming'. For through this exchange of semiotic power, a 'Christ-demon-man' assemblage was formed for the briefest possible moment. From the perspective of the legion of demons, this transfer of semiotic power enacted a kind of *deterritorialization* of Christ's bodily power onto it. But, from the perspective of Christ, his bodily power was *reterritorialized* through the same transfer of power: for the legion of demons had become, de facto, an extension of Christ's bodily power. Through a flow of power, the body of Christ and the body of the legion of demons entered into asymmetrical 'becomings' *with reference to one another*. Christ entered into a 'becoming-animal' when he formed a multiplicity with a legion of demons, while the legion of demons entered into a 'becoming-Christ'.

Through this reterritorialization, Christ did not become a molar woman. But his identity was hybridized through this transfer of power. As a result, Christ's identity becomes blurred, for the body of the woman is now capable of transporting Christ's powers to other bodies. Likewise, following Christ's reterritorialization onto the woman's body, the woman did not become like Christ: that which was transferred was *asignifying* power, not a linguistic meaning. Like Christ's body, her body became hybridized. Through this reterritorialization, Christ did not become a demon. But his identity was hybridized through this transfer of power. His identity became blurred, for the legion of demons was now capable of transporting Christ's powers to other bodies, such as the herd of swine.

What happens next are a complex series of deterritorializations and reterritorializations. The legion is *deterritorialized* a second time when it departs from the body of the demoniac. (The healing of the demoniac is a 'sign' of this second deterritorialization.) Next, the legion of demon undergoes a *reterritorialization*: being dispossessed of the body of the demoniac, the legion of demons is *reterritorialized* into another body, a herd of swine. The herd of swine, being violently affected by this injection of demonic intensities, and by the consequent formation of a monstrous demon-swine multiplicity, is taxed beyond its capacity for recuperation: it *deterritorializes* by stampeding over a cliff, plunging to their death in the sea below. And who knows what additional reterritorializations of the power of Christ's body occurred after that. Did the legion of demons depart on another line of light and transport Christ's power to other bodies? All that we can be sure of is that, minimally, the formation of the initial 'Christ-demon-man' assemblage gave rise to two reterritorializations and three deterritorializations, not to mention the destruction of a great many swine! Thus, from a molecular perspective, it is impossible, in practice, to separate out Christ's becoming-demon from countless other interpenetrations and productions of desire that followed. We, the readers, are always left in a constant state of wondering about what would have happened next.

We have no way of judging all these unheard-of reterritorializations and deterritorializations, for they do not correspond to the linguistic categories of language. The 'Christ-demon-man' multiplicity does not convey an essential theological truth that we must commit to memory. These becomings are neither true nor false. They do not symbolize anything. Nonetheless, in each step of this elaborate sequence, *difference, not sameness, functions as the horizon for change and transformation*: in each stage, 'different relates to different by means of difference itself' (DR 41). At each step, becoming is always a manifestation of pure difference. All that we, as readers, can do is try to keep all these manifestations of difference in sight at the same time, as machines and multiplicities waver between processes of decomposition and reorganization.

4. Conclusion

Becoming-animal occupies a medial region in D&G's spectrum of becomings between becoming-woman and becoming-imperceptible. Becoming-animal is possible because the molecular human body is positioned at the boundary between its humanness and its inherent animality. In their working and playing, human beings are never far removed from their own inherent animality, from their inner wolves and demons (TP 28, 208). Thus, in becoming-animal, human beings do not transform into something apart from what they already are. In short, becoming-animal is always about *human* animality. It always entails deterritorializing from our *human* territory to be reterritorialized in *the territory of their own animality*. Thus, what is at stake in becoming-animal is our own molecular animality, and the neutralization of the human/animal and human/nature linguistic binarisms that stratify our bodies. Becoming-animal poses a problem for systematic theologians. For theologians locate the human being at the very centre of an entire ontology of Being. Indeed, theology is rigid on this point: 'human beings cannot become animal' (TP 252). D&G reject theology's claim that human beings possess a distinct ontological status: human beings are nothing apart from nature.

D&G formulate two principles of becoming-animal: contagion through a pack, and alliance with an anomalous individual. The first principle concerns modes of propagation: becoming-animal always involves contagions, cross-fertilizations and aleatory alliances with a pack or multiplicity. Even Christ taught that the kingdom of God spreads *by means of contagion*, like a culture of yeast infecting a lump of dough (Lk. 13.20-21, § 3). His teachings were like a contagious virus that infected those who heard them. He even declared that only those who were so infected were his true 'brother, sister and mother' (Mk 3.31-35). Thus, there is an entire uncomfortable micropolitics of becoming-animal, outside the comfortable, familialism of theology. This micropolitics is connected to the lives of those who were infected by this holy contagion, termed the 'kingdom of God'; it is connected to a miscellany of marginalized people of all kinds, who are exterior to the world of patrilineal kinships and reassuring family genealogies. The second principle of becoming-animal is the corollary of the first: wherever there is pack or multiplicity, there will always be an anomalous individual. In the case of the Gerasene demoniac, the anomalous point was the spokesperson of the pack of demons.

Taken together, the principle of contagion through a pack and the principle of alliance with an anomalous individual make 'becoming-animal' an *affair of sorcery*. Christ was well practised in the ways of sorcery: worshipped by three sorcerers in his infancy, he practised sorcery as a young boy, and indeed throughout his life, and following his death, he was revered by sorcerers for centuries. Hence, Christ's 'becoming-animal' is to be expected. He entered into his 'becoming-animal' when he formed a multiplicity with a legion of demons (Mk 5.1-14). His body was *reterritorialized* into the legion of demons, while the legion of demons was simultaneously *deterritorialized* as a 'becoming-Christ'. Next, the legion of demon undergoes a *reterritorialization*: being dispossessed of the body of the demoniac, the legion of demons is *reterritorialized* into another body, a herd of swine, transporting Christ's power in the process. And who knows what additional reterritorializations of the power of Christ's body occurred after the herd of swine stampeded over the cliff? Can a legion of demons be drowned?

As the story of the Gerasene demoniac demonstrates, there are no autonomous machines (bodies) in the Gospels but only machines coupling with other machines, that couple with other machines. In the Gospels, whenever two machines couple and exchange semiotic flows, 'becomings' are sure to follow, and Christ, as a figure who was always animated by desire, had a particular affinity for aleatory couplings. Multiplicities are formed through temporary aleatory couplings between machines, through flows of power from body to body. Becoming-animal is always a production of productions.

17

Christ's becomings-imperceptible: Martyrological, magical and cosmic

When Jesus was at table with them, he took bread, blessed and broke it, and gave it to them. Then their eyes were opened, and they recognized him. And he vanished from their sight.

Lk 24.30-31

If becoming-woman entails an entry point to 'becoming-molecular' (*devenir-moléculaire*), and becoming-animal moves in the direction of increasingly molecularity, where do these becomings lead? D&G's unequivocal answer is, 'Without a doubt, toward becoming-imperceptible', for 'the imperceptible is the immanent end of becoming, its cosmic formula' (TP 279). In Deleuzo-Guattarian theory, the human body dissolves at both the micro and macro levels, respectively, into a cloud of particles-signs with no boundaries whatsoever, on the one hand, and into the vastness of the cosmos, where space contracts and time dilates, and joins in the cosmic process of all becoming: for 'everything becomes imperceptible, everything is becoming-imperceptible on the plane of consistency, which is nevertheless precisely where the imperceptible is seen and heard' (TP 252). In becoming-imperceptible, 'there is no longer a Self that feels, acts, and recalls' but only 'a glowing fog, a dark yellow mist' that has affects and movements, and speeds.[1] Christ's many incarnations of pure difference culminated in diverse becomings-imperceptible as his body formed rhizomes with almost anything whatsoever. Logion 77 of the Gospel of Thomas describes Christ as an all-pervading light that forms a rhizome with such mundane objects as stones and pieces of wood:

> I am the light that is over all things. I am all: from me all things came forth, and to me all attained. Split a piece of wood; I am there. Lift up the stone, and you will find me there. (*Gos. Thom.* 77, Miroshnikov 2018: 269–73)

Philip Sellew observes how logion 77 describes Christ's presence, after it escaped from the form of a physical body, as continuing only in ambiguous forms by conjugating with things, even in the darkest of places, such as in pieces of wood and under stones (2006: 51). While this resurrected Christ-stone-machine and Christ-wood-machine continued to emit Christ's illuminating presence, this presence was imperceptible to most onlookers. Thus, logion 77 reminds us how easy it is to overlook Christ's diverse becomings! Do we really know what Christ 'becomings' were possible?

The canonical Gospels narrate numerous instances of Christ becoming-imperceptible including: (1) a martyrological 'becoming-imperceptible' at his crucifixion, when he experienced the loss of his molar subjecthood (Mk 14.53-65); (2) a magical 'becoming-imperceptible', when he became invisible during a meal in the village of Emmaus (Lk. 24.13-35); and finally (3) a cosmic 'becoming-imperceptible, 'when his body was dispersed in the bodies of an oppressed humanity (Mt. 25.31-46). What all three of these Christ's 'becomings' share in common is that, in each case, Christ's body forms a multiplicity with other machines by which he enacted his own teaching: 'Those who try to keep their [molar] life will lose it, but those who lose their [molar] life will keep it' (Lk 17.33). Salvation always entails processes of 'becoming'.

1. Christ's martyrological becoming-imperceptible

The first of Christ's 'becomings-imperceptible' may have occurred at his crucifixion, at a time when his molar existence was being deterritorialized. For to 'lose one's life' is an extreme form of deterritorialization (Lk. 17.3). Through the spectacle of his betrayal, public humiliation and torture Christ experienced a *loss of face*, a deterritorialization of his faciality. As D&G observe, human subjecthood dissolves 'when the face is effaced, when the faciality traits disappear' (TP 128). Through a *loss of faciality*, a human being becomes imperceptible: the 'one who is tortured is fundamentally one who loses his or her face, ... a becoming-molecular the ashes of which are thrown to the wind' (TP 116).

The same loss of faciality is evident in the fourth Suffering Servant Song (Isa. 52.13–53.12), a text which functions in the background of all the canonical passion narratives. For the Septuagintal version of this Servant Song describes the servant of the Lord as one 'whose face (πρόσωπον αὐτοῦ) is turned away', one who was 'dishonoured and not esteemed' (Isa. 53.3b). When Jesus stood before the Sanhedrin, he too was dishonoured, and his face was the focus of abuse: the chief priests 'spat on his face and struck and slapped him' (Mt. 26.67). Through the conventional form of his execution, death by crucifixion, his molar selfhood was dismantled. He became merely one of many criminals. He became nobody. He became *imperceptible*.

2. Christ becoming-imperceptible as an affair of sorcery

Other 'becomings-imperceptible' are attested *after* Christ's resurrection. During a meal in the village of Emmaus, the resurrected Christ 'vanished (ἄφαντος ἐγένετο) from sight' (Lk. 24.31). *This* 'becoming-imperceptible' was an affair of sorcery, at least at the level of pragmatics (TP 506, § 16.2). In the Hellenistic world, magic was practised widely, and was closely integrated with Jewish, gnostic and pagan religious practices (Horsley 2014). Invisibility spells were widely practised in the Hellenistic world. For example, one invisibility spell directs the sorcerer to 'Say to the god Helios, "I abjure (ὁρκίζω) you by your great name, … Make me invisible, Lord Helios … in the presence of any man until sunset"' (Preisendanz 1928: I, 222–31). At the level of pragmatics, becoming invisible typically involves the use of special materials, and following precise steps, in accordance with local practices (LiDonnici 1999: 227–44).

As previously discussed, Christ was well practised in the ways of sorcery (§ 16.2). Therefore, it is not surprising that it is possible to establish points of symmetry between the narrative account of Christ becoming invisible at a meal in the village of Emmaus and the invisibility spells in the Greek magical papyri. Invisibility spells generally entailed the three steps: first, take hold of a special object; second, invoke the name of a deity;[2] and finally, perform an action with the object, whereby the sorcerer becomes imperceptible.[3] We find the same sequence of events at the meal in Emmaus. At the meal in Emmaus, first, Christ 'took hold of bread'; second, he invoked the name of God (εὐλόγησεν) and 'gave thanks' (Lk. 24.30) and finally, he performed an action with the bread, he 'broke it and began to give it to them', at which point, Christ 'vanished from their sight' (Lk. 24.30-31). He became 'invisible' (ἄφαντος), or at least almost so, if one considers the bread as a visible sign of his continued presence. The crucifixion brought an end to Christ's molar subjecthood. At this moment, the body of the resurrected Christ, having already dispensed with the limitations of bodily existence, was *deterritorialized* absolutely: he entered into a becoming-imperceptible.

3. Christ becoming-imperceptible as a cosmic event

My third example of Christ 'becoming-imperceptible' is drawn from Matthew's parable of the last judgment (Mt. 25.31-40). In this parable the spirit of Christ forms a rhizome with the oppressed of the world. At the outset of this parable, the Son of Man sits on a throne like a king and praises the righteous for having provided him with food, drink, clothing and care when he lay sick and in prison. The righteous, confused by this unmerited praise, ask, 'Lord, when was it that we saw you hungry and gave you food, or thirsty and gave you something to drink?' (Mt. 25.37). In reply, the Son of Man explains how he had *been present* in the bodies of the hungry and thirsty, stranger, naked, sick and prisoner to whom they had showed acts of compassion (Mt. 25.40).

This parable teaches that when the physical existence of Christ had ceased, all that remained of him was the endless proliferation of his spirit in the lives of the oppressed. Like a contagion of yeast spreading through a lump of dough, his spirit spread throughout the bodies of oppressed humanity. The crucifixion, which brought an end to Christ's molar subjecthood simultaneously liberated his *molecular* life (Lk. 17.33). Henceforth, his spirit was no longer localized presence. Through the annihilation of his molar subjecthood, and freed from the constraints of material existence, his spirit formed a multiplicity with the hungry and thirsty, stranger, naked, sick and prisoner. In addition to the micropolitics of becoming-woman and becoming-animal, there is also a micropolitics of becoming-imperceptible. From the marginalized and oppressed, Christ's becoming-imperceptible enacted a kind of reterritorialization of his life-force into theirs: 'I am the stranger in your midst.' Hence, those who perform acts of love on the marginalized and oppressed encounter the veritable presence of Christ in their midst. The lesson of Matthew's parable of the last judgment is clear: salvation proceeds by forming multiplicities with Christ through acts of love to strangers.

Through Christ's diverse martyrological, magical and cosmic becomings-imperceptible, he seems to declare to the world, 'My molar life is nothing,' 'I am in bread,' 'I am in the stranger in your midst.' These three becomings-imperceptible imply a single process, which is the process of gradually losing one's molar life to recover one's molecular life (Lk. 17.33). We have no way of judging these many becomings-imperceptible for they do not correspond to the linguistic categories of language, much less to a theological meaning. Each of Christ's becomings-imperceptible was a manifestation of pure difference. They are all *spiritual* in nature for the incarnation of pure difference is the very essence of the spiritual.

Conclusion

Becoming-woman and becoming-animal move in the direction of becoming-imperceptible, which is the immanent goal of all becoming. The life of Christ was traversed by strange becomings-imperceptible. This chapter has explored three such becomings: martyrological, magical and cosmic. Christ's becomings-imperceptible began with his torture and crucifixion, through which he suffered a *loss of face*, and molar subjectivity was deterritorialized (Mk 14.53-65). For what is death if not an extreme form of deterritorialization? In the village of Emmaus, Christ entered into another 'becoming-imperceptible', which was an affair of sorcery: like so many sorcerers before him, he deterritorialized *absolutely* through the act of blessing and distributing a ritual object, bread (Lk. 24.30-31). Finally, Matthew's parable of the last judgment narrates Christ's cosmic becoming-imperceptible (Mt. 25.31-40), in which his molar selfhood became absolutely dispersed through the formation of a multiplicity with all the poor, oppressed and persecuted of the world. Indeed, all of Christ's becomings-imperceptible proceeded through the formation of multiplicities. One wonders what other becomings of Christ we have missed: Christ's 'becoming-bread-and-wine' (Mk 14.12-26), 'becoming-wind' (Mk 4.35-41), 'becoming-water' (Mt. 14.22-33)?

All of Christ's 'becomings' throughout his life were incarnations of *pure difference*. Through these becomings, he seems to say, 'I am woman. I am animal. I am nobody. I am bread. I am the stranger in your midst.' No two of these becomings are alike. These events cannot be traced back to linguistic categories of sameness, much less to theological meanings. Nonetheless, through these 'becomings', Christ demonstrates that saving one's molecular life always comes as the cost of losing one's molar life: it always entails *incarnating pure difference in one's own body*. A schizoanalysis of Christ's many becomings entails discerning how Christ's molar body gradually *ceased to be*, while his molecular body was simultaneously engaged in a process of *becoming*. Mapping this double structure of Christ's ceasing and becoming takes us into the very heart of the virtual forces of Being.

18

The nomad Jesus and the Galilean war machine

Jesus said, 'Foxes have dens, and birds of the air have nests; but the Son of Man has nowhere to lay his head.'

Mt. 8.20

Not only does every animal possess its own territory, but every human being as well. Hence, we are *surprised* when Jesus declares that he has no territory: while foxes and birds have their own territories, he 'has nowhere to lay his head' (Mt. 8.20, Lk. 9.58). Perhaps Jesus' nomadic way of life was ill-suited to territoriality. The earliest sources of the synoptic Gospels present Jesus as an 'outlandish' character, an itinerate teacher and healer 'without land', who spent the last years of his life travelling from village to village, away from the familiar territory of kith and kin, with no final territory in view.[1] He even cut himself off from his family, preferring the company of those who were estranged from their territories, marginalized and low-social-status people (§ 16.1). Hence, it is not surprising that his disciples were sometimes perplexed by this *nomadic* wanderer.

1. Jesus: A Galilean Jew

Over the last forty years many scholars have rooted the historical Jesus in the context of Galilean Judaism, as an itinerate Jewish peasant who travelled from town to town.[2] This Jesus was a Jew, born into a Jewish family, who followed the Jewish law, or Torah (Mk 1.40-44, Mt. 5.17-20). His public ministry was announced by a Jewish prophet named John. His first followers were Jews, some of whom believed that key events in his life were the fulfilment of the Jewish scriptures (Mt. 1.23, 2.6, 18, 23).[3] Some even viewed him as a new Moses, who provided the definitive and final interpretation of the Torah (Mt. 22.35-50). Jesus sometimes debated with Jewish religious leaders, who challenged his interpretation of Torah (Mk 2.7). The so-called 'Jesus movement' that formed around him was a reform movement *within* Judaism. As Carl Mosser observes, this movement 'was born and nurtured in Second Temple synagogues' (2013: 523). Hence, the conclusion of Julius Wellhausen, formulated a century ago, has not lost much of its force:

> Jesus was not a Christian but a Jew. He did not proclaim a new faith, but he taught to do the will of God. For him as well as for the Jews the will of God was contained in the law and in the other holy scriptures counted as part of them. Yet, he showed another way to fulfill it [sc. the will of God] than the one the pious Jews followed.[4]

Many contemporary scholars likewise argue that there is no compelling evidence to suggest that this historical Jesus directly established a religious movement that was separate from Judaism.[5] But this is not the whole story. For the Jesus movement was not a sui generis religious movement. There is a connecting pathway, albeit in dotted lines, between the Jesus movement and other messianic movements that emerged in Galilee and Judaea in response to intense political–economic pressures. For life for the peasant class in the villages was harsh under Roman rule: factors such as double taxation by the state and priestly aristocracy, concentration of landownership in the hands of city elites, poor harvests and drought, followed by debts and land confiscations, were felt most acutely by the rural population (Horsley 2010: 1008). In response to Roman rule, various Jewish messianic movements arose and some successfully resisted Roman rulers for periods of time (Horsley 2003: 13–45). Zealot groups such as the Sicarii, representing the political and revolutionary side of messianism, attacked the Romans and anyone who cooperated with them; they attempted to install John of Gishala as messiah (65–66 CE). On the quietistic end of the messianic spectrum, the Qumran community seems to have expected three messiahs: a sacerdotal messiah of Aaron, who would preside over a battle against the Romans, a royal Davidic messiah who would defeat the Gentiles and usher in God's kingdom and a messianic prophet, who would teach about the coming of the kingdom of God. The phenomenon of social banditry represents yet another type of resistance movement to Roman rule: bands of bandits, formed around various charismatic messiahs, targeted Roman garrisons, military supply lines, local elites and large country estate holders. We should not forget that Jesus himself was crucified between two bandits (Mk 15.27-28, Mt. 27.38). It is plausible that Jesus was crucified on the charge of being a popular political agitator (Lk. 22.36). All this is to say that the years during which Jesus was alive were marked by the emergence of diverse Jewish messianic movements, which engaged in various forms of resistance against Roman rule. It seems probable that the Jesus movement was itself porously related to a rhizomatic network of messianic movements that included zealots, bandits and apocalyptic groups. Based on this historical probability, Richard Horsley has developed a contextual approach to Jesus, which he terms the 'Jesus-in-movement', paying special attention to the historical realities of Jesus' time, including the social forms of peasant life in the Galilean villages, and the political–economic pressures on them (Horsley 2003: 55–6, 2010: 99–145).

Do these Jewish messianic movements, and the general phenomenon of Jewish resistance to Roman rule, provide an alternative way of *mapping* Jesus? In posing the question in this way, you may accuse me of straying off course and into the direction of what Foucault terms 'a history of the referent' (1972: 47). You may ask, have we come all this way through Deleuzo-Guattarian theory to end in an unvarnished quest for the historical Jesus?

Without calling into question the legitimacy of writing a history of the Jesus movement against the background of Jewish resistance to Roman rule, Deleuzo-Guattarian concepts do not require a verisimilitude between the Gospel narratives and the historical Jesus movement. Two such Deleuzo-Guattarian concepts are the 'nomad' and the 'war machine'. These concepts are in no way dependent on recovering a historical Jesus. Thus, my question, 'does Jewish resistance to Roman rule in Galilee provide an alternative way of *mapping* Jesus?', is not essentially *a historical question*. As previously discussed, D&G are pioneers in philosophical 'mapping'. A 'map' is a diagram of the virtual (§ 11.1). Mapping is an experimental way of engendering new ways of perceiving and thinking. The process of 'mapping' Jesus in terms of Jewish messianic movements represents one way of enacting a new way of perceiving and thinking about Jesus. Bearing in the purposes of mapping in mind allows me to rephrase my question: 'Does Jewish resistance to Roman rule in Galilee provide an alternative way of *mapping* the "Jesus-in-movement"?' While this is not a historical question, it is a question that is inspired by our contemporary historical awareness of Jesus, as a Jew, who lived in Galilee, within the historical context of social struggle against Roman rule. Answering this question entails a *machinic* theorization of Jesus as the 'anomalous point' of a 'pack' of followers (§ 16.1), as a Jesus-in-movement within a multiplicity. It would be a bizarre situation, indeed, if the historical plausibility of this historical Jesus constituted grounds for disqualifying it as part of a mapping experiment. What then are the implications of mapping the life of Jesus in terms of a multiplicity? Was the historical emergence of the Jesus movement part of a '*productions of productions*', 'of actions and of passions' (AO 4), in first-century Galilee?

2. Nomadism and the war machine

In philosophical terms 'nomadism' is a way of life that exists on the exteriority of all totalizing systems of thought, all territories, strata, points of subjectification and, especially, exterior to the life of an 'organism' (§ 7).[6] Nomadism requires no king, priest or divine law, and all illusory transcendentals. Nomad thought does not operate in the categorically 'gridded' space created by linguistic binary opposites (Kaf. 7, 48). It dismantles all linguistic binarisms. In fact, it considers the 'same' versus 'different' binary opposition to be empty because actual human existence is naturally hyper-differentiated. In part, nomadism is a mode of imaginative, creative and experimental thought that creates 'smooth' space out of 'striated' space. In political terms, nomadism moves in the direction of more intense and more adequate investments of the social field (Villani 2019). It is a *minoritarian* movement that facilitates acts of resistance against despotic biosocial–political–technical assemblages. Nomadism's minoritarian status in no way implies that it is small in size. As Deleuze explains, a 'minority may be bigger than a majority'; the defining feature of a minority is that it 'has no model, it's a becoming, a process' (Neg. 173).

D&G define 'nomadism' in reference to two other closely related concepts, namely, the 'war machine' and 'smooth space': indeed, with uncharacteristic simplicity, Deleuze explains, 'nomadism is *precisely* this combination, the "war machine-smooth space"' (D 33). If one were to ask Deleuze, what do the nomads do?, he would answer, without equivocation, nomads *effectuate the conditions for a war machine in space*. Indeed, nomads *become* a war machine through their resistance to the State apparatus. Moses is the paradigmatic nomad. When Moses resisted the Egyptian State apparatus, he launched

> into the desert, *he began by forming a war machine,* on the inspiration of the old past of the nomadic Hebrews and on the advice of his father-in-law, who came from the nomads. This is the machine of the Just, already a war machine, but one that does not yet have war as its object. Moses realizes, little by little, in stages, that war is the necessary supplement of that machine, because it encounters or must

cross cities and States, because it must send ahead spies (armed observation), then perhaps take things to extremes (war of annihilation). (TP 417)

2.1. The war machine

The war machine (*machine de guerre*) is perhaps the greatest of all Deleuzo-Guattarian machines. What is a war machine? The war machine is *always defined in relation to the State apparatus*: it deterritorializes and destratifies the 'territorialized' and 'striated' space of the State apparatus, converting it into the 'smooth' space. Hence, contrary to what its name implies, the primary function of the war machine is not the waging of war but the conversion of 'striated' space into 'smooth' space.

But while destruction is not the primary purpose of the war machine, D&G also acknowledge that destruction often accompanies the war machine. Let the reader be warned that the war machine may entail the desecration of old beliefs and pervert familiar representations. To all who will listen, D&G call out war cry of the molecular revolution: destroy, desecrate, pervert! The war machine deterritorializes all striated space, knocking down walls, erasing borders, destroying apparatuses of capture and domination that repress individuals and communities, including the illusion of *signifiance*, the autonomous subject, universal thinking, fascisms, patriarchy and heterosexism as eternal values. But it always does so on the condition that *something new is created*. For the expression of the war machine is always tied to *ethics*: the war machine is primarily directed towards fostering new ways of thinking, acting, living in solidarity and generally towards fostering a 'people yet to come to life'. To this end, it sets out to destroy – to wage war against – all that is harmful to life.

The war machine has no stable historical characteristics or actualizations because it is an 'abstract machine'. Like all abstract machines, it possesses only virtual dimensions, functions, intensities and relations which are expressed differently in different historical contexts (§ 8.4). It exists only through its own transformations. It continuously enters into new 'revolutionary connections' in opposition to molar organizations (AO 522). A war machine 'scatters into thinking, loving, dying, or *creating* machines' (TP 356, emphasis added). Indeed, the very persistence of the war machine throughout time actually *depends upon* its capacity to adapt to different historical contexts, to be able to 'scatter' itself 'into thinking, loving, dying, or creating machines' (TP 356).

Whatever form it may take, the war machine is always a *minority* warfare. Minority people, itinerate people, the oppressed and persecuted, the migrant and exile, and religious movements can all function as a war machine. Even love can become a war machine: 'love itself is a war machine endowed with strange and somewhat terrifying powers' (TP 278–9). For abstract machines have no way of making a clear distinction between love and war, literature and life, peace and revolution. It always scatters into other machines such as the war machine. It forms a rhizome with the structure of 'and … and … and'. D&G insist that even *religion* possesses the capacity to set 'itself up as a war machine'. When religion functions as a war machine

> it mobilizes and liberates a formidable charge of nomadism or absolute deterritorialization; it doubles the migrant with an accompanying nomad, or with the potential nomad the migrant is in the process of becoming; and finally, it turns its dream of an absolute State back against the State-form. And this turning-against is no less a part of the 'essence' of religion than that dream. (TP 384)

2.2. The striated space and smooth space

As noted above, the primary function of the war machine is not war but the deterritorialization and destratification of the State's striated space (*espace strié*) and converting it into 'smooth' – deterritorialized, destratified – space. There could be no better historical exemplar of striated space than the Roman Empire. In *A Thousand Plateaus*, D&G quote Paul Virilio, who observes how

> the Roman Empire imposes a geometric or *linear reason of the State* including a general outline of camps and fortifications, a universal art of 'marking boundaries by lines', a laying out of territories, … in short, an increasingly rigid segmentarity. (1975: 120, TP 212, n. 8)

The state depends on the fixed paths of striated space in well-defined directions to restrict speed, regulate flows of all kinds – troops, decrees, commodities and money – and to measure in detail the relative movements of subjects and objects (TP 385). The striated space of the Roman Empire consisted of fixed pathways for the regulation of flows of commodities, troops, envoys, taxes, traders and slaves. It also depended on striated space for the aggregation of bodies based on heredity and filial relations, property and wealth, citizenship, gender and legal freedom. Its civic cults functioned as extensions of the social production of the city-state, by reinforcing striated space of king, priest, law and the despotic signifier (§ 7.1).

'Smooth space' (*espace lisse*) is the opposite of striated space. Smooth space is rhizomatic, non-territorialized space, lacking fixed coordinates and pathways: like a 'horizonless milieu, steppe, desert or sea', smooth space is characterized by 'variability, the polyvocality of directions' (TP 379, 382). For example, in his assertion that, for those 'in Christ Jesus', there is no longer Jewish or Greek, freeman or slave, and male or female (Gal. 3.28), Paul was attempting to create smooth space in the Galatian churches. Owing to its polyvocality, smooth space is capable of cultivating minoritarian becomings, non-filial relations and lines of escape from striated space.

The nomad is not without the land: indeed, the nomad is tied to the land, but such land is not striated space, but 'simply ground (*sol*) or support' for the nomad's customary pathways (TP 381). This land may even contain points of reference such as wells, oases, altars and meeting places in the desert. But such points of reference are of secondary importance compared to the pathways of the nomads. For a reference point is nothing more than a *relay* point: nomads arrive at a well or oasis only *to leave it behind* and move on to the next relay point; they travel 'from point to point only as a consequence and as a factual necessity', but their *life* 'is in-between' these points: 'A path is always between two points, but the in-between has taken on all the consistency and enjoys both an autonomy and a direction of its own. The life of the nomad is the intermezzo' (TP 380). Where does a nomad go? Nowhere. The nomad does not really move at all: he remains stationary, seated on his camel. Bedouin people gallop, *while seated*. Their camels move, but they do not. According to Deleuze, this feature makes nomad travel a 'stationary process'; it is a 'feat of balance', not of speed (TP 381). Whereas movement has a direction and a goal, which is attained by moving from point to point, movement in it is confined to preset paths between fixed and identifiable points. In contrast, nomad space is 'smooth', or open-ended. The nomad's journey has speed, without movement. Speed is intensive: it has *intensity* but no direction or goal.

But we must not become unduly distracted with the task of contrasting the Roman Empire and Jewish messianic groups in terms of striated and smooth space respectively. For like many Deleuzo-Guattarian concepts, *striated space and smooth space imply one another* (§ 0.1.2). These concepts provide a pair of abstract polarized coordinates that can be mapped onto various historical formations. But in historical formations, they are always actualized in *mixed forms*. There can be no doubt that Christ groups sometimes functioned in tandem with the State apparatus, reinforcing its striated space. The Didache's dualistic 'two ways' doctrine reinforces striated space in life and thought with its opposition of a way of life to a way of death (*Did.* 1-6). Hence, the primary issue for my purposes is not contrasting the Roman Empire and messianic groups in terms of striated and smooth space respectively, but simply employing these concepts to theorize nomadism and the war machine. As noted above, nomadism is a mode of imaginative, creative, and experimental thought that actually *creates* smooth space out of striated space. Nomad war is first and foremost a process of *creation*. To all who would listen, D&G call out the war cry of the war machine: *imagine, create, experiment!* The war machine is a productive force that escapes such repressive 'thinking-as-representation', which argues 'this is that', and engages instead in 'thinking-as-experimentation', which disrupts stratified and territorialized formations that repress both individuals and faith communities. How can we put the war machine into practice? Michel Foucault sets out some possible strategies:

> Withdraw allegiance from the old categories of the Negative (law, limit, castration, lack, lacuna), which Western thought has so long held sacred as a form of power and an access to reality. Prefer what is positive and multiple, difference over uniformity, flows over unities, mobile arrangements over systems. Believe that what is productive is not sedentary but nomad. (AO, preface, xiii)

At its best, early Christianity had the capacity to move beyond the borders of the State apparatus and enter 'a more indistinct zone, … where it has the possibility of undergoing a singular mutation or adaptation' (TP 383). Hence, we are faced with the question, does the concept of the 'war machine' help scholars engender new ways of theorizing early Christianities? Can we re-imagine the 'Jesus-in-movement' as a Galilean version of a 'war machine'?

2.3. The analogy of chess and go

As a starting point for trying to answer these unfamiliar questions, let us consider an analogy that D&G construct between the war machine and State apparatus, on the one hand, and the games of go and chess respectively (TP 352–3).[7] This analogy can be summarized in the following three points. First, D&G note that chess pieces are structurally *coded* to perform predetermined functions. They perform these functions by moving along fixed pathways on the 'striated' space of the chess board. The game pieces of chess, consisting of pawns, knights, bishops and rooks (comparable to the infantry, cavalry, elephants and chariotry of the Roman army), are coded in terms of a *fixed set of structural relations* in relation to the opponent's coded pieces. Indeed, even the function and movements of the most valuable pieces, the king and queen, are structurally pre-determined. Thus, within the striated space of the chess board, not only the pawns but also the king and queen are *captives* to their structural roles, as predetermined by the rules of chess. In contrast, the coded pieces of chess, the game pieces of go (called 'stones'), are *uncoded*. They lack structural relations to other pieces. All game pieces have the *same* function. What is more, they do not move along fixed pathway; pieces are simply placed on the board, rather than moved from space to space.

Second, D&G observe that the relations between chess pieces are unilateral: pieces function individually, by challenging and capturing the individual game pieces of the opponent. In contrast, go pieces do not form unilateral relations: every stone has the same anonymous, collective function. Rather than being semiologically coded, every stone has the *same* identical function. Stones act *in solidarity* with other stones in the performance of strategic functions such as bordering, encircling and shattering, making it a game of *collective* strategy.

Third, D&G observe that chess is a game of *exteriority* in the sense that chess pieces invade the (exterior) territory of an opponent. Indeed, the strategic objective of chess is to conquer the opponent's territory. In comparison, the game of go has no exteriority: it is a game without battlelines, without an opponent's territory, and indeed, even without direct confrontations: pieces are moved 'without aim or destination, without departure or arrival' (TP 353). Hence, go can be said to be a game of *interiority* in the sense that it proceeds by coding space and consolidating territories through the construction of adjacent territories.

On this basis of this analogy with the games of chess and go, D&G argue that the nomad war machine (like the game of go) has a strategic advantage over the State apparatus: the war machine employs *uncoded* bodies, each with the same *collective* function, which wage a war of *interiority*. Based on D&G's analogy with the game of go, we can ask new questions. Can the Jesus movement be theorized in terms of uncoded nomads? Did such nomads have the same collective function? Can their collective mission be theorized as part of a war of resistance waged from within the Roman Empire?

3. The nomad Jesus and the Galilean war machine

The analogy between the State apparatus and the war machine with the games of chess and go breaks down at one key point: the game of chess and the game of go are *unrelated* in terms of their rules. What is more, they are obviously played independently of each other. In contrast, the operations of the State apparatus and the war machine are *interrelated* and indeed *reciprocal* functions. There is no simple opposition between them, just as there is no simple opposition between striated space and smooth space (TP 474). In the case of the Roman Empire, Jewish messianism and the Jesus movement striated and smooth space existed only in mixtures. The dividing line between striated and smooth space was continuously being contested. Hence, when studying the Jesus movement, *it is as if one is observing the games of go and chess being played simultaneously.*

The fact that smooth and striated space existed historically only in mixtures is to be expected because they *belong to the same multiplicity*. Therefore, the schizoanalysis of the Jesus movement (and Christ groups) must be carried out at the level of multiplicities, not on the basis of individuated groups, such as the Jesus movement, much less on the level of the supposed leaders of such groups. Hence, rather than theorizing Jesus as a lone, heroic figure, who set out to organize a movement, he can be mapped as a 'nomad Jesus', as the *anomalous individual* of a pack. As previously discussed, D&G's second principle of 'becoming-animal' is that wherever there is pack, there will always be an anomalous individual, a border-point, through which one can make contact with a multiplicity (§ 16.1). The pack of disciples, which we term the 'Jesus movement', had its own anomalous individual, Jesus of Nazareth. Through this anomalous individual, the Jesus movement may have combined with other multiplicities and formed a Galilean war machine, which scattered into 'thinking, loving, dying, or creating machines' (TP 356). This Galilean war machine had only functions, arrangements, relations and dimensions.

Have I gone too far in mapping Jesus as a 'nomad' who helped effectuate the conditions of a 'war machine'? Possibly. But in philosophical terms, nomadism is a mode of experimental thought. In political terms, nomadism facilitates acts of resistance against despotic biosocial–political–technical assemblages. Therefore, the concept of nomadism raises philosophical and political questions about the strategies of the Jesus movement in relation to space. One can ask, what types of striated space did the Jesus movement attempt to reorganize and destroy? What types of smooth space did it attempt to construct? What lines of escape from striated space (if any) did it make possible, and at what price, and for whom?

Conclusion

If we temporarily bracket out the familiar Johannine 'despotic Christ' and Lukan 'passional Christ', other Christs come into focus, not the least of which is the 'nomad Jesus', who was the 'anomalous individual' of a pack of disciples, which we now term the 'Jesus movement'. Like other Jewish messianic movements, this Jesus movement seems to have emerged in response to Roman rule. But we need not become diverted by this historical hypothesis since it is sufficient that the phenomena of Jewish messianic movements in first-century Galilee provoke a new way of thinking about Jesus in relation to nomadism and the war machine.

The war machine is perhaps the greatest of all Deleuzian machines, but it is also arguably the most abstruse. Being an abstract machine, it possesses only virtual dimensions, functions, intensities and relations which are expressed differently in different historical contexts. Contrary to what its name implies, the primary function of the war machine is not to wage war but to convert striated space into smooth space. There could be no better historical exemplar of striated space than the Roman Empire. But in the case of the historical Roman Empire and Jewish messianism, striated and smooth space *existed only in mixtures*. The dividing line between them was continuously being contested. Thus, when studying the Graeco-Roman world, it is as if one is observing a game of chess and the game of go being *played simultaneously*.

D&G's primary interest lies not in questions of the precise definition of striated and smooth space but in the exploration strategies by which 'nomads' *effectuate the conditions of a war machine*, and thereby transform striated space into smooth space. The very existence of the war machine depends on the collective efforts of such nomads. For a war machine is not an organic whole, comparable to the Roman army, but is an abstract machine effectuated by nomads who wage a war against the State apparatus from *within*.

This observation brings us back to the question about whether the Jesus movement, as a type of religious movement, can be mapped as a war machine. The task of mapping the movements of a war machine, religious or otherwise, must be carried out at the level of multiplicities, not on the level of individual groups, much less on the basis of the leaders or 'messiahs' of such groups. Therefore, rather than conceiving Jesus as the heroic founder of the 'Jesus movement', it is more constructive to map him as the anomalous individual of a pack of followers, the border-point, through which outsiders made contact with a multiplicity.

While this mapping of Jesus as a nomad, and the Jesus movement in terms of a war machine, leaves some historical questions unanswered, and arguably may even ignore important historical facts, we must bear in mind that the purpose of Deleuzo-Guattarian mapping extends beyond the task of trying to make sense of the available historical evidence. After all, the battle cry of the war machine is 'imagine, create, experiment!' Schizoanalytic biblical interpretation abandons the quest to capture interior, linguistic meanings, in the sense of an objective referent, and instead directs its efforts towards forms of interpretation that find their practical coherence in destratifying and deterritorializing processes. In the final analysis, Deleuzo-Guattarian philosophy is not 'defined by what it says, even less by what makes it a signifying thing, but by what causes it to move, to flow, and to explode' (AO 133). The essence of war machine is creative line of flight, the construction of smooth space and new non-organic, non-filiative social relations: the invention of 'a people to come' (TP 377). The war machine always scatters into other machines. Therefore, the primary question *for us*, today, is not, 'Was the Jesus movement really a war machine?', but 'What can this Galilean war machine be plugged into, and what is it capable of producing?' And if someone should then ask us, 'Yes, that's fine, but what would Jesus, the nomad, do?', the answer is obvious: Jesus would strive to effectuate the conditions of a war machine.

Conclusion

The impact of the philosophy of Deleuze on the humanities and social sciences notably includes the study of theology. Kristien Justaert goes so far as to argue that the discipline of theology actually *needs* Deleuze, for only through such an encounter can theology recover from its current problems. In contrast to theology, the discipline of Christian origins has not yet encountered Deleuzian philosophy in a serious way. This prompts the question, if the discipline of theology actually *needs* Deleuzian philosophy, as Justaert maintains, then why does the discipline of Christian origins not have a similar need? Perhaps this lack of engagement can be traced back to the underlying tendencies of the discipline, which are based on a genealogical model. This model orients the discipline towards the task of recovering early Christianity's *lost origins*, with a focus on the historical Jesus of Galilee, or his lost original teachings, the earliest Jesus movement, Pauline Christianity and so forth. The discipline of Christian origins is certainly not unique with respect to its obsession with the silent beginnings of Christianity. Systematic theology also represents Christianity on a genealogical model but within a *transcendental*, rather than historical, framework: it traces 'the Church' backwards to a single point of transcendental origin, a supreme signifier, Jesus Christ, Son of God, as one might trace a mighty oak tree back to the acorn from which it grew. It is easy to interpret Christianity this way. It's comforting and one can do so almost without thinking. But is identifying the origin of Christianity as simple as this?

D&G would say that systematic theology has employed 'tree logic' to represent the past: 'All tree logic is a logic of tracing and reproduction. ... It consists of tracing something that comes ready-made' (TP 12). René Descartes famously compared the structure of Western knowledge to that of a tree. D&G argue that all Western humanist thought is modelled on what they term 'tree-logic' or 'arborescence'. A survey of the systematic theology's accounts of the origin of Christianity would demonstrate that this 'tree-logic', which traces back historical Christianity to a sui generis transcendental origin, has often served as the accomplice of domination. For it has been employed as a universalist and colonizing discourse to argue that Christianity is superior to all other religions. D&G would say that systematic theology has employed 'tree logic' to represent the past: 'All tree logic is a logic of tracing and reproduction. ... It consists of tracing something that comes ready-made' (TP 12). What benefits would come from abandoning this 'tree-logic' and instead thinking *rhizomatically*? What benefits would result if theologians theorized in terms of rhizomes instead of trees? This book entails a sustained exploration of this simple question.

Deleuzo-Guattarian 'rhizomatic' philosophy destabilizes all forms of 'tree-logic' and indeed all universalist discourses, not to mention the sui generis origins they give rise to. If the greatest impediment to interreligious dialogue is Christian theology's exclusivist claim to a sui generis transcendental origin, then D&G's philosophical concept of a 'rhizome' provides a means to facilitate new forms of dialogue and cooperation between Christians and other co-religionists including not only adherents of the five 'world' religions but also queer spirituality (§§ 3, 15.2.1), followers of the sacred spiritualities of aboriginal peoples. For 'rhizomatics' finds its theoretical and practical coherence by means of an exploration of *our relations* to Jews and Moslems, Buddhists and Hindus, to differently gendered people, to migrants and the economically exploited. In other words, *there is an entire micropolitics of rhizomatics*. The Deleuzo-Guattarian concept of a rhizome provides a new space for fostering non-universalist, non-colonizing discourses, as well as for explorations of the *interrelatedness* of these systems of thought. In short, the substitution of D&G's 'rhizomatic' model in place of the genealogical model of theology could facilitate new forms of interreligious understanding and cooperation.

Through the construction of new concepts, such as the 'rhizome', D&G invent new ways of perceiving and thinking. For Deleuzo-Guattarian philosophy privileges the virtual over the actual, 'becoming' over 'being', structural transformations over static structures and semiotics over linguistics. This philosophy views existence – including existence in the *historical past* – as an interrelation of actual and virtual, of states of affairs and forces, that are manifested as change and discontinuity, ruptures, breaks, mutations and transformations.

Through the invention of new concepts such as the machine, multiplicity, body without organs, plane of immanence, assemblage, abstract machine and war machine D&G create new ways of perceiving and thinking. The only precondition for the creation of such concepts is that they have a 'strangeness', and that they have to respond to real problems. For only through the creation of such 'strange' terms can one become 'a foreigner in one's own language' and ask new questions. Such concepts, lacking established disciplinary usages, create new ways of thinking about early Christianity.

Through the invention of new concepts, D&G turn 'thinking-as-representation' (which argues that 'this is that') into thinking-as-experimentation. What difference does the philosophical revolution of D&G make to our understanding of the early Christianity? In this book I have demonstrated that the use of Deleuzo-Guattarian concepts enables the disciplines of both theology and Christian origins to accomplish new tasks that are presently beyond their reach. For the discipline of Christian origins is presently fragmented by a wide range of methods, a restricted focus on individual texts and bifurcated disciplinary approaches that can be traced back to the theoretical division between the humanities and the social sciences. This fragmentation defines the fate of historical reasoning in our own time. The overall effect of this disciplinary fragmentation is that it is nearly impossible to think about early Christianity in its entirety. Deleuzo-Guattarian philosophy, in contrast, is a *theory of everything*: the historically actual and spiritually virtual, the discursive and nondiscursive, the body of the individual and the supra-individual bodies of groups and institutions. Hence, the reach of Deleuzo-Guattarian philosophy far exceeds the reach of any of these fragmented parts. All this is to say that D&G have provided us with a toolbox of nonrepresentational concepts and a new modality of thought, which can give rise to new insights.

One such 'strange' new concept is the 'machine'. What difference does the concept of the machine make to our understanding of the structurality of life? As I argued in Chapter 1, the Deleuzo-Guattarian 'machine' provides a powerful tool for exploring the rhizomatic relations between Christ groups and other groups and institutions in the Graeco-Roman world. Christ groups can be theorized as machines coupled with countless other machines of widely ranging types and magnitudes. This machinic dimension of Christ groups could be highly problematic, as evidenced in the notorious case of the Christ-follower machine who coupled with a sex-worker machine (1 Cor. 6.15-20): for in the moment that these two machines were connected by a flow, Paul declares that they were temporarily organized as 'one body' and 'one flesh'. In other words, the man and sex worker temporarily became *one machine*.

Early Christian texts were also machines: a Gospel or Pauline letter is a *literary* machine that coupled with other literary machines and social machines and exchanged semiotic flows (§ 8.3). However, every Christian text possessed a *semiotic* dimension in addition to its linguistic content and, through this semiotic dimension, it accomplished *strategic effects* such as the discipline and normalization of human bodies (2 Tim. 3.16-17, Heb. 4.12, § 8). D&G argue that this strategic effect of discourse is coextensive with language itself. Through early Christian literary machines (discourse), semiotic forces were injected into the bodies of Christ followers. All this is to say that discursive utterances entailed more than information: all early Christian writings *functioned as literary machines* in relation to a tangled mass of other machines (bodies) of Christ followers.

The theorization of Christ groups as machines highlights the primary role of asignifying (semiotic) flows in the genesis, change and transformation of Christ groups. Chapter 1 argued that machines – not structures – provide a starting point for mapping the historical emergence and diversification of the first Christ groups. By drawing attention to the central role of these *exterior* machinic processes, this chapter challenges some of the general tendencies of the disciplines of Christian origins and theology, at least to the extent that they prioritize the *interior* beliefs of such groups.

All machines are interconnected by flows of desire, for desire is always *desiring production*. As Chapter 2 explained, Deleuzo-Guattarian desire is a cosmic force that produces connections between machines. Everything in the Graeco-Roman world was interconnected by flows of desiring production, and Christ machines emerged at the intersection of these flows. Hence, *the history of early Christianity can be mapped as a history of desiring production*. The totality of all desiring production constitutes the plane of immanence, a one-storey universe that does not distinguish between immanence and transcendence. Whereas traditional theology presupposes that God and human beings inhabit different planes, D&G adhere to Duns Scotus's doctrine of the univocity of Being, which denies any distinction between existence and essence. Owing to the hyperfusional character of the plane of immanence, so-called 'early Christianity' cannot be condensed into a unified narrative. Hence, we must always speak of multiple early 'Christianities'. The concepts of desiring production and the plane of immanence provide new tools for the analysis of the historical emergence and diversification of Christ groups.

All machines are composed within multiplicities. A multiplicity is a complex structure that does not reference a prior unity: it is simultaneously one and the multiple. Christ compares the spread of the kingdom of God to a multiplicity of yeast that takes over a lump of dough (Lk. 13.20-21). He declared that the kingdom of God spreads like a culture of yeast that *infects* a lump of dough (Lk. 13.20-21, § 3). Similarly, Jesus' teachings were like a contagion of yeast that *infected* those who listened to them (§ 16.1). Indeed, the kingdom of God was a revolutionary contagion, like seeds that are scattered here and there, some falling 'on good soil, where it produces a crop – a hundred, sixty or thirty times what was sown' (Mt. 13.8).

The Graeco-Roman world abounded in multiplicities. Chapter 3 explained how Christ groups, as machines, were composed within diverse multiplicities, by virtue of which such groups were perpetually in flux. Hence, Christ groups possessed no essence but only dimensions and lines of intensity within multiplicities, as blocs of becoming. The intrinsic variability of Christ groups poses a problem for traditional theology because theology is based on a belief in stable essences. But the truth of early Christianity is the truth of disjunctive synthesis, which is the truth of the one *and* the multiple. The disjunctive synthesis of a multiplicity is irreducible. Therefore, the task of the theologian and scholar of early Christianity alike is not to attempt to recover early Christianity's prior unity but rather to explore the rhizomatic relations that connected Christ machines to other machines within multiplicities.

In his theoretical elaboration of multiplicities, Deleuze brings into play another distinction, and in a rather surprising way: the distinction between the virtual and the actual. Deleuze declares not only that his philosophy is nothing but 'the theory of multiplicities' but also that every multiplicity is 'composed of actual and *virtual* elements' (D 148, emphasis added). D&G theorize *the virtual as fully real*. Indeed, theirs is a philosophy that privileges the virtual over the actual, just as it privileges machinic processes over static structures (§ 1), and 'becoming' over 'being' (§ 15). The historically actual, including historically actual Christ groups, emerged from a restructuring of *virtual* relations. He argues that what Proust specifically says about the virtual in relation to memory is uniformly true of the virtual in general: that 'the virtual is opposed not to the real (*réel*), but to the actual (*actuel*). The virtual is fully real (*pleine réalité*) in so far as it is virtual', despite not necessarily being actualized. What kind of metaphysics does this non-virtual 'real' imply? By extension, in the case of the Graeco-Roman world, *purely actual Christ groups did not exist*. Scholars of Christian origins are unaccustomed to theorizing the virtual (non-actualized) dimension of Christ groups in the Graeco-Roman world, for they deal only in historically actual entities. Surely, such an investigation is compromised from the outset. What is gained by overlooking the most fundamental aspect of early Christianity?

Chapter 4 turns to the question of the historical emergence of Christ groups. It begins with the question, which came first, Christ or Christ groups? Theologians give primacy to a transcendental Christ. But D&G cannot accept a solution based on the ontological dualism of Plato. We can theorize the historical emergence of Christ groups *immanently* in terms of a 'body (of Christ) without organs', which is formed through autoproduction, without reference to a transcendental plane. Through disjunctive synthesis, each 'body of Christ without organs' formed a surplus-value 'Christ'. The resulting 'body of Christ without organs' oscillated between its paranoiac and attractive poles. At its paranoiac pole, it seemed to be truly *without organs* (members), or at least exist a body *without need* of organs (1 Cor. 11.3). But at its attractive pole, it functioned as a *unified* body of Christ '*without* (discrete) organs' (1 Cor. 12.27). Thus, the Corinthian 'body of Christ without organs' existed in a state of constant contradiction.

The Graeco-Roman world was heavily territorialized, and every 'body of Christ without organs' *was territorialized by it*. Chapter 5 discussed how the interpretation of the Christ groups requires an understanding of the principles by which Christ groups were territorialized. The possession of a territory constitutes a primary condition for every animal: 'Foxes have dens and birds of the air have nests' (Mt. 8.20, Lk. 9.58). Not only foxes and birds but every animal – including *human* animals – possess their own territories. The territory of a Christ group entailed more than a physical space. First and foremost, a territory is a set of *structural relations* that control, regulate and repress flows of desiring production.

But the primary focus of Deleuzo-Guattarian philosophy is not territorialization but processes of deterritorialization. To be deterritorialized is to become abstracted from a set of structural relations and the flows they regulate. Every aspect of territorialized Christianity was subject to deterritorialization and reterritorialization. Consequently, Christ groups were not static, deterministic structures but were changeable formations continuously vulnerable to being destabilized and transformation. Indeed, the primary focus of Deleuzo-Guattarian philosophy is not processes of territorialization but how territories are destabilized, and how territories participate in event-oriented processes of transformation. In short, D&G are primarily interested in machinic processes of *deterritorialization* by machines. To be 'deterritorialized' is to become abstracted from a set of structural relations and the flows they regulate.

In simple terms, deterritorialization entails becoming 'outlandish'. The paradigmatic example of deterritorialization is the story of the Exodus of the Hebrew people, who were deterritorialized from the territory of Egypt and adopted an 'outlandish' life of nomadic wandering for forty years (Exod. 13.17-21). The Gospel of Matthew narrates how three sorcerers left their territory in the East and became 'outlandish' in pursuit of a deterritorialized star (Mt. 2.1,

11). Of course, Jesus was also an outlandish character: an itinerate preacher, who wandered from village to village, connecting with people on the margins of society, men with leprosy, a woman with chronic bleeding, not to mention gluttons, drunkards and tax collectors (Mt. 11.19). He journeyed from place to place, establishing connections with others, by debating, teaching and healing.

Chapter 6 explored the territorialization and deterritorialization of the canonical Gospels considered as literature. Deleuzo-Guattarian philosophy is premised on an intrinsic connection between literature, life and philosophy: literature is an expression of life, and writing literature can be a means of thinking through the philosophical questions which life poses. D&G theorize the functions of territorialization, deterritorialization and reterritorialization in literature based on a threefold typology of lines: lines of rigid segmentarity, lines of supple segmentarity and lines of flight. These lines can be arranged on a spectrum ranging from *molar* lines of rigid segmentarity to *molecular* lines of flight, with lines of supple segmentarity occupying a medial position between these two poles. All literary characters in the Christian Gospels are positioned at the point of *convergence* of these three types of lines. These lines in the Gospels do not pose a problem of theological meaning because they are *asignifying* in character: they have functions, not meanings, and these functions produce *affects*. When viewed from the vantage point of lines, the Gospels are defined less by their theological meanings than they are by the types of lines that traverse them.

Christ groups were not only territorialized but were also 'stratified'. Stratification is a process that overcodes human bodies on the basis of idealized transcendentals. Three strata in particular lie before us, whose specificities and interrelations must be examined. Chapter 7 discussed how D&G single out 'three great strata' owing to their harmful effects on the human body: the strata of the organism, signification and subjectification. Stratification is characteristic of the 'despotic socius', which overcoded human bodies on the basis of the vertical alliance of a despot-god (as surplus value) to despotic signifier (chief god as idealized transcendental). Through the process of stratification, human bodies become indistinguishable from the system of social production that formed them. D&G marvel at how, through the external overcoding of desire in terms of law, an ideal signifier, and lack, human 'desire can be made to desire its own repression' (AO 115).

In the Roman Empire, as a notable manifestation of the despotic socius, citizens were stratified through the vertical filiation of the Roman emperor (as a despot-god) to the god Jupiter (as a despotic signifier). In Rom. 13.1-4, Paul assimilates Christianity's Father God to the stratified structure of the Roman Empire, asserting that the authority of Roman governors was guaranteed by this Father God. However shocking Paul's terrifying logic may be from a contemporary theological perspective, when considered in *structural* terms, nothing about Paul's assertion is surprising: for this 'Father God' fulfils the *same* structural function in Paul's imaginary Roman Empire as did the pagan god Jupiter in *actual* Roman Empire. The logic of stratification is *always the same*: obedience to a despotic signifier takes the form of obedience to an earthly despot as 'despot-god'.

When human desire is stratified, an 'organism' is formed that experiences lack in relation to Law, that is, as a Subject that is denied by Law what it desires. Hence, the starting point of the 'organism' is prohibition. In the specific case of the Roman Empire, law (or the gods) collectively supplied a set of despotic signifiers for the construction of a sociopolitical hierarchy. But idealized law is essentially unknowable because it is without content. Idealized law is a pure form that produces forms of empty repetition: connections, repetitions and repressions. But this idealized Law, despite being an empty form, nonetheless had the power to set in motion the pervasive judgment of all aspects of life and to induce guilt and punishments with respect to human bodies. Hence, the purpose of such law is not to prevent transgression but the opposite: to make transgression, judgment and the accumulation of guilt possible. Through the accumulation of debt, the 'body without organs' of individual Christ followers was imprisoned as an 'organism' and put under the control of the Roman Empire as a despotic socius. However, by following their own cartographies of productive desire, every such Christ 'organism' retained the virtual capacity to disrupt the stratification of its desire by entering into new experimental assemblages: for a virtual 'body without organs' is always present within an actual 'organism'. Hence, stratification and destratification are concurrent processes. Indeed, D&G remind us that, while 'stratification in general is the entire system of the judgment of God', it is equally true that 'the body without organs, constantly eludes that judgment, flees and becomes destratified, decoded, deterritorialized' (TP 40). Indeed, the primary theme of D&G's *Anti-Oedipus* is a call for subjectivity – whether the subjectivity of individuals or groups – to destratify, and to cease functioning as an organism by constructing new cartographies of self-reference.

Christ groups can also be mapped as biform social assemblages. As discussed in Chapter 8, one of the most striking features of such biform assemblages is that there was *no direct causality* between the discursive and nondiscursive iterative practices. But D&G theorize an immanent non-unifying cause that connects them indirectly, which they term an 'abstract machine' or power/knowledge 'diagram'. This diagram can be imagined as a kind of 'electric circuit' that provided a network of pathways for the flow of intensities. Every Christ assemblage presupposed an historically specific abstract machine that linked Christian discourse to the systems of power. Thus, all early Christian discourse was social in both its origin and destination. As 2 Tim. 3.16-17 and Heb. 4.12 illustrate, Christian discourse did not function independently of the world, representing theological 'truths' from the outside, but was always coordinated with networks of power and the social practices. This chapter concluded that every Christ social assemblage effectuated its own, historically specific abstract machine, which coordinated its discourses with its iterative practices.

Chapter 9 discussed how Christ assemblages were also located at the intersection of two mega-abstract machines, the molar Roman 'ecumenon' and molecular 'planomenon'. The ecumenon diagrammatically coordinates the entire field of social assemblages, as an architectonic unity of systems, within the State apparatus. The ecumenon of the Roman Empire operated in the background of Christ social assemblages, attracting them towards their territorialized and stratified poles. Through the ecumenon, Christ groups functioned as extensions of the social production of the Roman Empire. But the planomenon also operated in the background of Christ assemblages, attracting them towards their deterritorialized and destratified poles, triggering processes of deterritorialization and destratification.

On the basis of these opposing mega-abstract machines, D&G distinguish between two types of God, a 'God of religion', which operated in the ecumenon, and a 'schizo God', which functioned in the planomenon of the plane of immanence, while the abstract machine of the Roman Empire, the 'ecumenon', was constantly stratifying the bodies of its citizens. Hence, all small groups, such as Christ groups, were characterized by repressive determinism. But owing to the functioning of the 'planomenon', such groups also preserved virtual degrees of freedom. Owing to the functioning of these competing abstract machines, this chapter argued that a schizoanalysis of Christ groups must be two pronged, with due attention directed towards both the role of the Roman ecumenon and its God of religion, *and* the planomenon and its schizo God, in theorizing the proliferation of early Christianities.

The three 'great strata' (discussed in Chapter 7) are closely related to three errors of desiring production. Chapter 10 explored how the primeval myth of the 'fall' of Eve bears a striking similarity to D&G's 'three errors of desire', namely, the errors of lack, law and the signifier. While theological anthropology traces humanity's insufficiency before God and guilt back to the 'fall' of Eve, this chapter argues that Eve's 'fall' was not a primordial 'fall' into sin, as Augustine supposed, but a 'fall' into a *delusion* founded on the idealization of lack, law and language.

Lacan argues that there is no escape from the ontological and ahistorical delusions generated by the symbolic order: 'desire-as-lack', and the errors connected with lack, law and language are an inescapable human condition. At the point when a child enters the symbolic register of lack, law and language, it becomes an 'oedipal' subject for whom the 'real' becomes the 'impossible real' (*réel impossible*). With the disappearance of the 'real', there is no way to escape from the illusion of 'reality'. However, D&G are not so pessimistic: they argue that the stratification of human desire *can be reversed* by disrupting the processes of social production that overcoded desire in the first place (§§ 7, 10). Hence, this chapter argued that Eve's 'fall' was a *felix culpa*, a 'happy fall' – at least for us – inasmuch as it serves as the starting point for ways of desiring that are *disengaged from lack*. The discursive lives of Thecla and Maximilla in the Apostolic Acts may have had a role in helping Christ followers 'fall out' of this delusional system of thought and awaken to the possibilities of life disengaged from desire-as-lack.

Chapter 11 turned to the topic of discursive constructions of Christ in the canonical Gospels. Every discursive construction of Christ entailed a regime of signs, which is a 'specific formalization of *expression*' in relation to nondiscursive 'content'. By virtue of such regimes of signs, every Christian discourse functioned *as expression* within a biform social assemblage in relation to 'content' (nondiscursive formations), through the coordination of a power/knowledge 'diagram' or 'abstract machine' (§ 8.4). Just as structures in general are subordinate to machinic processes (§ 1.1), so also are *linguistic* structures subordinate to regimes of signs (§ 1.3). Just as structures in general are subordinate to machinic processes (§ 1.1), so also are *linguistic* structures subordinate to regimes of signs (§ 1.3). Language – including the Hellenistic Greek of the New Testament – operates primarily as a *linguistic codification of a power/knowledge diagram*. Only secondarily is language a vehicle for the storage and retrieval of ideas and information: *language is a semiotic flow before it is a linguistic code*. Different regimes of signs produced different constructions of Christ, and every linguistic signification of Christ was part of the *regime of truth*. In sum, all early Christian texts were formed by regimes of signs, and all regimes of signs functioned within power/knowledge diagrams. To explicate these regimes of signs, D&G employ 'mapping' as an analytical tool (§ 0.4). A map is not a representation. Maps are rhizomatic in the sense that they are *open* systems with multiple entryways and exits (§ 0.3). Every map is connectable to other maps. D&G employ 'mapping' to explore the *exteriority* of systems in relation to other systems. In the case of their fourfold typology of regimes of signs we must bear in mind that these four regimes *imply one another*.

D&G's typology of regimes of signs does not signal a turn towards structuralism: D&G are more interested in the deterritorialization of regimes of signs than they are in the structure of the regimes in their separateness. For theirs is a philosophy that privileges the virtual over the actual, and machinic transformations over static structures. Like all structures, regimes of signs are *open* systems that retain the capacity for transformation. While it is true that regimes of signs manifest predictable, stable behaviours over short periods of time, it is equally true that over extended periods of time they possess the virtual capacity to self-organization on a molecular level. Indeed, every regime of signs involves four virtual deterritorializing functions: a generative, transformative, diagrammatic and machinic function, which endows it the capacity for transformation (§§ 3.2, 5.3, 11.2).

Of particular importance for all such deterritorializing functions is the 'scapegoat mechanism', which is a machinic function. In literal terms, the term 'scapegoat' designates the goat, described in the book of Leviticus, that carried away the sins of the Israelites on the Day of Atonement (Lev. 16.7-10, 20-22). Western scholarship has abstracted the scapegoat concept from its Levitical roots and employed it in diverse ways, such as in the context of the study of violence in religion. In Deleuzo-Guattarian philosophy, any human being or animal that is deterritorialized from a regime of signs or social assemblage is a 'scapegoat'. In other words, a scapegoat is a *machine* that acts on the exteriority of structures (§ 1).

The history of the multiplication of Christs in early Christianity can be written as a history of the scapegoat mechanism. Viewed from this perspective, the 'despotic Christ' of the Gospel of John (§ 12) and the 'passional Christ' of the Gospel of Luke (§ 13) represent little more than temporary monuments within a succession of deterritorialized Christs. Thanks to D&G's concept of a regime of signs, we can now, for the first time, write a history of the transformation of Christs within regimes of signs. When we recognize the interrelation between constructions of Christ and regimes of signs, new questions present themselves. Instead of asking, who was Christ?, and, what was the theological meaning of his life?, schizoanalysis asks, on the basis of which regimes of signs were different

Christs produced?, and within which Christ assemblages and power/knowledge diagrams did they function?

Chapter 12 demonstrates that the Gospel of John displays a dominance of the 'signifying despotic regime of signs', which, in turn, produced a relatively stable 'despotic Christ'. In this Gospel, the Father God, functioning as a 'despotic signifier', provides the ultimate reference point for the entire Johannine signifying system. Through the vertical filiation of Christ to this Father God, Christ becomes a son of God, and thereby acquires the *surplus value* of a 'despot-god'. Christ's status as the face, and voice of God, simultaneously displaces the face and voice of the Father God, who is thereby reduced to silence. Henceforth, Christ speaks on behalf of the Father God, and truth emanates from his face and spreads out in every widening discursive circles. The interpreters of Johannine discourse consigned all that exceeded this signifying structure to the category of 'sin'. To stabilize itself against the incursions of pure difference, the Gospel of John required a scapegoat to *take away* all that it consigned to the category of 'sin' (Jn 1.29, 36): it required a scapegoat to take away 'everything that resisted signifying signs, ... everything that was unable to recharge the signifier' (TP 116). The scapegoat mechanism is a *machinic function*, one which is not tied to molar subjects (§ 6.1.1, 14). As D&G observe, *even a despot or king can function as a scapegoat*. Like King Oedipus, the Johannine Christ functioned structurally as both a king and a scapegoat. This Christ could function structurally as both king and scapegoat because *structural functions are not tied to molar subjectivities.*

Through his torture of the Cross, Christ lost his despotic *faciality* and was transformed into a *faceless* scapegoat. He thereby became the 'inverted figure of a king' (TP 116). For 'the one who is tortured is fundamentally one who loses his or her face' (TP 116). But even in the moment of his extreme torture, Christ is hailed the '*king* of the Jews' (Jn 19.19). Somehow those who witnessed his crucifixion recognized the 'inverted figure' of a *king* (TP 116). Christ, the very *face* of God, became a *faceless* scapegoat to take away this 'sin of the world'. By taking away all that escaped the Johannine circularity of signs, Christ as scapegoat stabilized the signifying despotic regime, allowing it to perpetuate itself thereafter.

The Gospel of Luke displays a dominance of the 'passional subjective regime of signs', which produces a 'passional' prophetic Christ. Chapter 13 explains how this 'passional Christ' is the inverse figure of the Johannine 'despotic Christ'. This prophetic Christ, having entered into a lonely and passional relation with his point of subjectification – the Hebrew God – cut himself off from the religious officials aligned with the Jerusalem Temple. In point of fact, this is the story of a *double betrayal*: for having betrayed the Jewish signifying despotic regime, Christ, in turn, was betrayed by it. Through betrayal Christ was transformed into the perfect scapegoat. In his cry of dereliction on the Cross, Christ accuses the despotic signifier of *betrayal*, crying out, 'My God, my God, why have you forsaken me?' Having betrayed the signifying despotic regime, and having been betrayed by it, Christ's cry of dereliction transforms his death into a *great spectacle of betrayal*.

Chapter 14 introduces the topic of Christ's many 'becomings'. What difference does 'in-betweenness' make to individual bodies? In the Gospels, Christ's body can be analysed as a 'mode of power', a figure of desire, that entered into composition with countless other bodies. Christ travelled from place to place, forming multiplicities with other bodies through acts of teaching, healing, feeding and ultimately through the manner of his dying. Christ's life was always a production of productions. While these molecular events are imperceptible, their aggregate value is manifested as 'symptoms' or 'signs'. On the basis of this insight, Deleuze develops a 'symptomatological' approach to literature that interprets such 'signs' in relation to the molecular events that caused them. A symptomology of the Gospels requires sensitivity to the signs that are emitted by their literary characters. Viewed from this molecular perspective, these 'signs' provide a way of entering into a relation with the truth of the Gospels, which is a truth liberated from linguistics, exegesis and theology.

Christ teaches that there is no salvation for the molar subject, except by means of molecular 'becomings': saving one's molecular life requires losing one's molar life. In other words, salvation always entails 'becoming'. Chapter 15 discussed how the Gospels are a storehouse of Christ's 'becomings'. The entire life of Christ entailed a progressive loss of his molar subjecthood by becoming-woman, becoming-animal and finally by becoming-imperceptible.

Becoming-woman serves as the entryway to all 'becomings' because woman is not too far removed from the Phallus. There is an entire micropolitics of 'becoming-woman' that is connected with becoming-queer, becoming-lesbian, becoming-gay, becoming-gender fluid and becoming-trans. For 'whatever shatters norms, whatever breaks from the established order' is related to becoming-woman. Hence, D&G even speak of 'homosexual Christs'. That which all expressions of 'becomings-woman' share in common is that they are all *molecular* processes of singularization, without reference to male/female binarism. 'Becoming-woman' attracts the opprobrium of systematic theologians because they can only conceive of essentialized identities and lawful unions. Indeed, such theology opposes all forms of becoming-woman because it considers male and female gender to be essential forms: 'woman' is 'non-man'. But no person possesses an essential gender: a person is only gendered by language to one degree or another. Christ entered into his 'becoming-woman' when he formed a multiplicity with a haemorrhagic woman; and in her 'becoming-Christ' she was transformed into a figure of intense, liberated desire. We ask, what new multiplicities did *her* body form? What flows of power did it initiate? And what use did these other bodies make of Christ's bodily power? Hence, like all of Christ's becomings, this is really a story of the production of productions.

Becoming-animal is possible because the human body is positioned at the boundary between the human being and its own inherent animality. Chapter 16 explains why becoming-animal also poses a problem for systematic theologians: for theologians locate the human being at the centre of an entire ontology of Being. But D&G reject this human-centred ontology. They formulate two principles of becoming-animal: contagion through a pack, and alliance with an anomalous individual. The first principle concerns modes of propagation: becoming-animal always involves contagions, cross-fertilizations and aleatory alliances with a pack or multiplicity. Christ taught that the kingdom of God spreads *by means of contagion*, like a culture of yeast infecting a lump of dough (Lk. 13.20-21, § 3). His teachings were like a contagious virus that infected those who heard them. He even declared that only those who were so infected were his true 'brother, sister and mother' (Mk 3.31-35). Thus, there is an entire uncomfortable micropolitics of becoming-animal that is outside the comfortable familialism of theology. Taken together, the principles of contagion through a pack and alliance with an anomalous individual make 'becoming-animal' an *affair of sorcery*. We must not forget that three sorcerers (μάγοι), following a deterritorialized star, brought the infant Christ gold, frankincense and myrrh, a veritable sorcerer's toolkit of special materials as gifts (Mt. 2.1, 11). Their value lay not in their symbolic value but in their capacity to *connect* the sorcerer to the anomalous individual of a pack.

Christ was well practised in the ways of sorcery: worshipped by sorcerers in his infancy, Christ practised sorcery as a young boy and throughout his life, and following his death he was revered by sorcerers. Christ entered into his 'becoming-animal' when he formed a multiplicity with a legion of demons. Through a flow of power, the body of Christ and the body of the legion of demons momentarily entered into asymmetrical 'becomings' *with reference to one another*: Christ entered into a 'becoming-animal' when he formed a multiplicity with a legion of demons, while the legion of demons entered into a 'becoming-Christ'. In each step of the sequence of becomings that followed, difference, not sameness, functioned as the horizon for change and transformation.

Becoming-imperceptible is the immanent end of all becomings. Chapter 17 explores three of Christ's 'becomings-imperceptible', beginning with martyrological becoming-imperceptible: during his crucifixion, Christ suffered a loss of face, and his body ceased to be bound by molar subjectivity. Christ's second 'becoming-imperceptible' was an affair of sorcery: he was deterritorialized absolutely through an act of blessing, breaking and distributing bread: he thereby became invisible. Matthew's parable of the last judgment narrates Christ's cosmic becoming-imperceptible, in which his molar selfhood was dispersed through the formation of a multiplicity with the poor, oppressed and persecuted. Like a contagion of yeast spreading through a lump of dough, his spirit spread throughout an oppressed humanity (Mt. 25.31-40). Thus, all of Christ's becomings-imperceptible entailed the formation of multiplicities. A schizoanalysis of these becomings entails discerning how Christ's molar body gradually *ceased to be*, while his molecular body was engaged in a process of *becoming*. The crucifixion, which brought an end to Christ's *molar* subjecthood, simultaneously liberated his molecular life. He had truly kept his life by losing it (Lk. 17.33). His spirit was no longer localized presence. Through the annihilation of his molar subjecthood, and by being freed from the constraints of material existence, his spirit *formed a multiplicity with the oppressed*. Hence, not only is there a micropolitics of becoming-woman and becoming-animal, but there is also a micropolitics of becoming-imperceptible. Mapping the double structure of Christ's *ceasing and becoming* takes us into the very heart of the virtual forces of the plane of immanence.

Finally, Chapter 18 takes up an exploration of Christ 'becoming-nomad' and the 'war machine', which is perhaps the greatest of all Deleuzian machines. Not only does every animal possess its own territory, but every human being as well. Hence, we are *surprised* when Jesus declares that he has no territory: in contrast to foxes and birds, which have their own territories, he 'has nowhere to lay his head' (Mt. 8.20; Lk. 9.58). Perhaps Jesus' nomadic way of life was ill-suited to territoriality. It is not surprising that his disciples were sometimes perplexed by this nomadic wanderer.

In philosophical terms, 'nomadism' is a way of life that exists on the exteriority of all totalizing systems of thought, all territories, strata, points of subjectification and, especially, exterior to the life of an 'organism' (§ 7). Nomadism requires no king, priest or divine law. Nomad thought does not operate in the striated space of linguistic binary opposites. In fact, it considers the 'same' versus 'different' binary opposition to be empty because all human being are naturally hyper-differentiated.

What do the nomads do? The *effectuate the conditions for a war machine in space*. Indeed, nomads *become* a war machine through their resistance to the State apparatus. The war machine, being an abstract machine, possesses only virtual dimensions, functions, intensities and relations which are expressed differently in different historical contexts. Contrary to what its name implies, the primary function of the war machine is not war but converting striated space into smooth space. To the extent that the nomad war machine does engage in destruction, such destruction is supplemental: the war machine destroys in order to create. Destruction is not the purpose of the war machine but may accompany it (TP 416). This is not to imply that there is a simple opposition between religion and nomadism. Deleuze argues that even religion has the capacity to function as a war machine, an observation that allows us to map the 'Jesus movement' as a type of Galilean 'war machine'.

The purpose of such mapping the 'Jesus movement' as a 'war machine' extends beyond the task of making sense of the available historical evidence. For nomad war is first and foremost a process of *creation*. The battle cry of the war machine is 'imagine, create, experiment!' It creates, affirms and populates smooth space with 'strange new becomings, new polyvocalities' (AO 211). The war machine engages in the invention of 'a people to come' (TP 377).

Therefore, the primary question for us is not, 'was the Jesus movement really a war machine?', but 'what can this Galilean war machine be plugged into, and what is it capable of producing?' Effectuating the conditions of a war machine entails learning how to engage in conflict in ways that maximize our connections to others and our collective capacities. For the true measure of value of a war machine is its ability to facilitate the emergence of ethical forms of life, thought and action. Hence, in reply to the question 'What would Jesus, the nomad, do?', the answer is obvious: Jesus would strive to effectuate the conditions of a war machine.

Notes

Introduction

1 *L'Anti-Oedipe* (1972) was translated into English and published in 1983 as *Anti-Oedipus: Capitalism and Schizophrenia* (notably with the addition of a new preface by Michel Foucault). Four years later Brian Massumi translated *Capitalisme et Schizophrénie, tome 2: Mille plateau* (1980) as *A Thousand Plateaus: Capitalism and Schizophrenia*, published in 1987. The close connection between these two volumes is indicated by their shared title in the French editions, and by their shared subtitle in the English translations: *Capitalism and Schizophrenia*.

2 Guattari's first clinical development of schizoanalysis, entitled *Cartographies Schizoanalytiques*, was published in 1989 (Genosko 2002; Guattari 2012). Its translator, Andrew Goffey, describes this book as 'one of the last big books of French theory' ('Introduction', in Guattari 2012: xv). Guattari also published on the subject of 'schizoanalysis' in *Psychanalyse et transversalité*, published the same year as *L'Anti-Oedipe*, and in *L'inconscient machinique*, published in 1979, a year before *Mille plateau*. In many ways, *L'inconscient machinique* functions as the companion volume to *Mille plateau*, even though it was largely ignored at the time by English-speaking scholarship until 2011, when it was available in English translation.

3 For examples of the application of Deleuzian philosophy to theology, see: Bryden (2001); Crockett (2002, 2010, 2011); Goodchild (1996a, 1996b); Higgins (2010); Justaert (2010); Kaufman (2007); Keller (2003); Ramey (2012); See and Bradley (2016); Shults (2014a, 2014b); Simpson (2012); Watson (2005).

4 Descartes, as quoted by Martin Heidegger in his essay 'What Is Metaphysics?' (1998: 277).

5 Deleuze does not dispense with transcendence altogether but instead accords it a derivative status by defining the concept of transcendence in terms of immanence (§ 2.2). In the opinion of Philip Goodchild, Deleuze's philosophy of immanent transcendence provides 'an alternative "topos" to think the divine and salvation' (2001: 157). Ronald Faber goes so far as to describe Deleuze's philosophy of pure difference as 'the infinite, univocal, affirmative, and self-differentiating essence of God' (2002: 216).

6 I employ the term 'Christ group' throughout this book, instead of 'church', on the grounds that no Christian 'church', with a canon of scripture, bishops, doctrines and creeds, existed prior to the fourth century of the Common Era. In prior centuries

Christ groups did not agree on such basic issues as table fellowship, circumcision, the authority of the Jewish scriptures, the role of women or the nature of Christ's body. For example, that which some scholars habitually term 'early Christianity' was not a unified movement of near identical groups but a *diverse* set of historical phenomena, which proliferated in the centuries prior to the Constantinian revolution of Nicene Christianity in the fourth century (Boyarin 2004).

7 The expression 'caught in the true' (*dans le vrai*) was coined by Georges Canguilhem (Foucault 1972: 223–4). These 'rules' of discourse are *not* ahistorical, transcendental laws that 'hovered' over actual Christian texts in an ethereal Platonic realm. The distinction between 'texts' and 'rules' is merely a *modal* distinction. Just as one can conceptually distinguish between the colour and shape of an object, even though they are two properties of the same object, similarly a text and its rules of formation can likewise be distinguished but never separated in practice because they operate in a mutually generative manner. The rules of discourse are always immanent within the discursive process of the accumulation of texts in an associative series over time. When viewed from the perspective of the plane of immanence, within which all texts emerge, these rules are more like specific kinds of *changing relations* between textual bodies that collectively permitted the emergence of some texts, while simultaneously prohibiting the emergence of other kinds of (possible) texts, within the same associative discursive series.

8 This notion of 'meaning as use' can be traced back to Ludwig Wittgenstein (LS 146). Paolo Vignola argues that we must treat Deleuze's concepts as 'meta-stable entities, capable and transforming and being transformed' by those who experiment with them (2019: 558). Indeed, this is precisely the same advice that D&G provide us in *What Is Philosophy?* (WP 28).

9 Other concepts can be arranged as three-point spectrum, such as milieux > territory > strata (§§ 5, 7); rigid lines of segmentarity > subtle molecular lines > lines of flight (§ 6); becoming-woman > becoming-animal > becoming-imperceptible (§§ 15–17).

10 See § 11.2 for my discussion of 'mapping'.

1 The rise of the Christ machines

1 My reference to 'flows' of money alludes to the collection of money that 'flowed' from various Christ groups to the 'poor' in Jerusalem. Paul agreed to take up this collection at the Jerusalem conference (Gal. 2.10) and subsequently gave directions during its organizing phase (1 Cor. 16.1-4, 2 Cor. 8-9), and completion (Rom. 15.25-28).

2 Deleuzo-Guattarian philosophy also has roots in the failure of French structuralism in the 1960s, which was idealist in terms of its subordination of historical

expressions of symbolization, culture and identity to deep ahistorical, autonomous structures. Structuralism was unable to account for the historical transformation of structures over time and the 'event' quality of history.

3 Deleuze's first condition states that a structure must include 'at least two heterogeneous series, one of which shall be determined as "signifying" and the other as "signified"' (LS 50). In other words, one series is active ('expression'), while the other is reactive ('content') (§ 8). The second general condition states that 'each of these series is constituted by terms which exist only through the relations they maintain with each other' (LS 50). For within any structure there are no absolute terms but only differential relations of interdependence, a phenomenon termed negative value. According to the principle of negative value, the value of any single term in a series is determined *negatively* by its place within the series, as a whole, as a *system of differences*.

4 On the priority of the virtual dimension of the 'real' see § 3.2.

5 In his article entitled 'Machine and Structure' (1969), Guattari critically reviewed Deleuze's *Différence et répétition* (1968) and *Logique de sens* (1969). This review was subsequently reprinted in Guattari's *Psychanalyse et transversalité*, published in 1972 (Guattari 2015: 318–29, 1984: 111–19). This essay precipitated Guattari's first face-to-face meeting with Deleuze, which led to their collaboration (Thornton 2017: 454–5, n. 1).

6 'Singularities' or 'particles-signs', being both matter and energy, particle and wave, virtual and real, are in a non-relation to the distinction between signifiers and signifieds, expression and content (§§ 8.4, 12, n. 1). Singularities perform non-linguistic, asignifying transfers of force (Genosko 2008).

7 All applications of French structuralism were based on the premise that structures (comparable to the signifying structures of language) shape many dimensions of human society. Structuralism, as a movement, began with Claude Lévi-Strauss, who argued that the symbolic structures within human societies, such as kinship systems, can be analysed in the same way that Saussure analysed language. In the wake of Lévi-Strauss' discovery of the structurality of human social practices and myths, others recognized the applicability of Saussurian theory to literary criticism (Roland Barthes), mythology (A. J. Greimas), psychotherapy (Jacques Lacan), developmental psychology (Jean Piaget), neo-Marxism (Louis Althusser) and biblical studies (Leach and Aycock 1983; Patte and Patte 1978).

8 On the basis of the base–superstructure schema, Marx famously argued that 'the mode of production in material life determines the general character of the social, political and spiritual processes of life, … their social being that determines their consciousness' (Marx 1978: 4). As Marx observed, 'What else does the history of ideas prove than that intellectual production changes its character in proportion as material production is changed? The ruling ideas of each age have ever been the ideas of its ruling class' (1959: 26; cf. Calhoun 2002: 22).

9 Louis Althusser, publishing about the same time as Guattari, also elaborated his own structuralist version of Marxist theory, which he termed 'aleatory materialism' (Althusser 2006).
10 Scholars who employ social scientific approaches, such as John Kloppenborg, also recognize that Christ groups 'can be thought of as social networks – arrays of people related to one another by multiple connects' (2019: 56).
11 Owing to their inherent power, curses accompanied the declaration of punishments (Gen. 3.14, 16, 4.11), the utterance of threats (Jer. 11.3, 17.5; Mal. 1.4) and they were even employed as weapons (e.g. Judg. 9.57; Prov. 11.26, 30.10).
12 According to the speech act theory of J. L. Austin, when one performs such a locutionary speech act, one usually performs an illocutionary and perlocutionary speech act at the same time (Austin 1975).

2 Desiring production and early Christianities

1 This myth of angels in heaven, preserved in Gen. 6.1-4, was later expanded, first in *1 En.* 1, 6.1–8.2, and later in *T. Reub.* 5.1–7.
2 Here I follow Lacan's direction that the neologism '*objet a*' be left untranslated, whereby it acquires 'the status of an algebraic sign' that carries multiple meanings (see 'Translator's note', in Lacan 2002: xi). According to Lacan, desire is neither an appetite for satisfaction, nor a demand for love, but the difference that results from the subtraction of the first from the second. According to Lacan, the residual status of desire constitutes its very essence (1977: 286–7).
3 The term 'Watchers' designates the two hundred angels who rebelled against God after the flood of Noah; cf. *1 En.* 1.5-7, 9, 15, 16.2, cf. Jude 1.6 (Milik 1976: 7–21; Nichelsburg 2012: 165–73).
4 Lacan's algebraic formula for the structure of fantasy is $\$ \lozenge a$. In this formula, the *poinçon* symbol ($\lozenge$) represents a relation of conjunction–disjunction, that is, a contradictory relation between a divided subject ($\$$) and *objet a*.
5 As I argue in Chapter 10, when Eve gazed upon the fruit in the garden, she also constructed a fantasy, *objet a*, namely, a fruit that would make her 'like divine beings knowing good and evil' (Gen. 3.4).
6 On D&G's dependence of Lacan see §§ 5.2, 7.1, 9. Deleuze admits, perhaps begrudgingly, his indebtedness to Lacan, saying, 'There's no question that we're all the more indebted to Lacan, once we've dropped notions like structure, the symbolic, or the signifier, which are thoroughly misguided, and which Lacan himself has always managed to turn on their head to bring out their limitations' (Neg. 14).

7 There can be no 'subject' of desire because the subject is a 'molar' formation produced through the capture and organization of desiring production (Masumi 1992: 47–8, 52–7, 61–4).
8 Heraclitus, as quoted by Plato, *Cratylus*, 402a.
9 Other notable influences on Deleuze include Henri Bergson's concept of 'vital impetus' (*élan vital*) (Marks 1998) and Spinoza's concepts of movement and affect (§ 14.1).
10 In the following year Paul Ricoeur took up the same 'NFM construct' in his book, *Freud and Philosophy* (1965). Ricoeur grouped together Nietzsche, Freud and Marx as 'three masters of suspicion', each of whom looked upon the contents of consciousness as, in some sense, *false* with respect to conscious alienated from itself through class interest and ideology, in the case of Marx, repressed libidinal desire, in the case of Freud, and reactive ressentiment, in the case of Nietzsche (1970: 32–3).
11 Freud tied the libido to the pleasure principle, which is manifested positively as a quest for pleasure, and negatively as the avoidance of displeasure. Freud famously argued that all forms of personality development are expressions of repressed libido.
12 On Marx's base–superstructure schema see §§ 1, § 7.1.1. Guattari argues that group subjectivity, like individual subjectivity, possesses its own laws, forms of transference, fantasy and resistance (2015: 93–4, 130). See my discussion of how a 'subjected group' (*groupe assujetti*), characterized by societal repression, can deterritorialize and become a 'subject group' (*groupe-sujet*), capable of constructing its own cartographies of self-reference (§ 10.2).
13 As Philippe Mengue explains, Deleuze developed an original interpretation of Nietzsche, beginning with *Nietzsche and Philosophy* and *Difference and Repetition*, in which he reorients the Nietzschean system of active and reactive forces. Through the combination of his own interpretation of Nietzsche with his interpretation of other philosophers, Deleuze creates in his own thought a 'Nietzsche mutation'. As Mengue observes, 'Deleuze does not become Nietzschean without Nietzsche becoming Deleuze' (2000: 177). The result is, according to Paolo Vignola, a philosophy that merges with that of Nietzsche to the point of synthesis, and indeed indistinction, such that we can even speak of 'Nietzsche-Deleuze' (2019: 554).
14 On Guattari's 'machinic unconscious', see § 14.3.1.
15 *Anti-Oedipus* never employs the term 'plane of immanence'. However, D&G employ this term frequently in *A Thousand Plateaus*, where it is comparable to Lacan's register of the 'real' (*réel*). Lacan argued that the 'real' cannot be expressed in language, for entry into language entails an irrevocable alienation from the real. In contrast to the 'real', Lacan employs the term 'reality' (*réalité*) that signals the *disappearance of the real*. The term 'reality' designates that which human beings take to be the external world, which is an illusion generated of the symbolic register.

16 In the history of philosophy there have been two formulations of the univocity of being, those of Duns Scotus and Spinoza (Redell 2014: 46). Deleuze adopted, through Heidegger, Duns Scotus's doctrine of the univocity of Being expounded in his *Opus Oxoniense*. This doctrine denies any distinction between existence and essence. In *Difference and Repetition* Deleuze remarks that Duns Scotus understands univocal being as being 'indifferent to the distinction between the finite and the infinite, the singular and the universal, the created and the uncreated' (DR 39).

17 Felice Cimatti argues the dualism of transcendence versus immanence is an effect of the framework of language, which can be traced back to language's splitting of the living human being into two parts, a mind which thinks, and a body which is the slave of the mind. This mind–body dualism is the origin of countless other dualisms including the dualism of transcendence and immanence (2019: 497).

18 Platonic philosophy assigns to the things of the material world the status of imperfect copies of perfect transcendental 'forms' or 'ideas' (ἰδέαι) on a transcendental plane. Thus, Platonism and Neoplatonism subordinate the differences between human beings to their essential sameness based on their shared transcendental form.

19 See my discussion of God as a 'disjunctive synthesis' in § 4.2.2. Deleuze cannot be understood apart from the post-war French reception of Heidegger, and especially Heidegger's rejection of so-called 'ontotheology', and his reawakening of the question of Being (Justaert 2007). Clayton Crockett suggests that a renewal of theology may be possible by 'explicating and implicating the unconditional power of immanence' (Crockett 2010: 6).

20 Deleuze, Guattari and Stivale (1984: 15). Philip Goodchild has argued that Deleuze's philosophy of immanent transcendence provides 'an alternative "topos" to think the divine and salvation' (2001: 157). Likewise, Kristien Justaert observes how Deleuze's conceptualization of 'immanent transcendence opens up a new way to understand an incarnational God of the cosmos, who is 'non-hierarchical, non-representable … and at the same time, as immanent' (2012: 36). In *What Is Philosophy?*, D&G state that 'Christ was incarnated once, in order to show, that one time, the possibility of the impossible', which is to say that immanent transcendence is real (WP 59).

3 The rhizome: Multiplicities and the virtual dimension of Christ groups

1 The term 'Oedipus' in the subtitle of the original French edition of *Capitalisme et Schizophrénie, tome 1: L'Anti-Oedipe* (and in the main title of the English translation) functions as a shorthand for the ontological assumptions of Freudian and Lacanian psychoanalysis. At a basic level, 'Oedipus' refers to the Oedipus complex of

classical psychoanalysis, and to related Oedipal processes that root psychosexual development in the inner dynamics of Lacan's 'daddy–mommy–me' triangle (Flieger 1999: 219–40). 'Oedipus' is also D&G's code word for the modern subject within the capitalist socius, which reduces every aspect of life to the nuclear family, as the starting point for social exploitation within the capitalist field (§ 10.1.3). In capitalism, the function of father can be transferred to almost anyone: a 'boss, the foreman, the priest, the tax collector, the cop, the soldier, the worker' (AO 265).

2 DR 208, DR^f 269, cf. B 42–3, 96–8, DI 44.
3 Deleuze's concept of the 'essence of pure things' does not imply a pre-existing Platonic order but 'an ongoing power of creation ... an originary difference and an individualizing force' (PS 48). Signs express an essence, but they do not reveal an essence. An essence is the relation between a physical sign and its sense. It possesses an autonomous reality that is independent of objects, truths and subjects, and is irreducible to the subject apprehending it (PS 37–8). Such Deleuzian 'essences' can be said to be 'Platonic' with respect to their nonmaterial, nonactual ideality, but they are Leibnizian in their individuality.
4 Differen*t*ial ('t') relations are *virtual* points of resonance between two pre-signifying series (DI 179; Thornton 2017: 462). Through resonance 'two heterogeneous series converge toward a paradoxical element, which is their "differentiator"' (LS 50–1). Differen*t*ial ('t') relations are *actualized* as 'differen*c*ial' ('c') relations between singularities. Hence, all differencial relations depend on prior differential relations. 'Repetition' entails the never-ending resonance of differen*t*ial relations between *virtual* points of interaction, which may be actualized as differencial relations.

4 The autoproduction of a body of Christ without organs

1 For the term μέλος can be translated as both 'part' and 'organ' (Bauer and Danker 2000: 628, § 1).
2 This chapter does not distinguish between virtual 'differentiation' and 'differenciation' as a process of actualization (§ 3.2). For *Anti-Oedipus* does not employ the term 'differenciation', and hence does not distinguish between these two processes, at least at the level of terminology.
3 Through repression, some flows are downgraded, while others are upgraded. While the resulting categorical grids are context dependent, all categorical grids impose on the 'body without organs' the 'forms, functions, bonds, dominant and hierarchized organizations, organized tendencies' (TP 159).
4 Deleuze's concept of disjunctive synthesis can be traced back to Emmanuel Kant, who employed it to present the idea of God. In Deleuze's view, Kant presents God

'as the principle or master of the disjunctive synthesis', as the sum of all possibilities, insofar as this sum constitutes an 'originary material' (LS 294-5).

5 See my discussion of surplus value in §§ 1, 7.1.1. All three of D&G's 'social machines' (socii) depend on the creation of surplus value (specifically, a chief, king and capital), and in each case is linked to social control.

6 The verb 'to miraculate' is derived from the memoire of Daniel Paul Schreber (1842-1911), who suffered from paranoid schizophrenia. In his memoire entitled *Memoirs of My Nervous Illness*, Schreber chronicled the progress of his disease. One morning, he woke up with the thought that it would be pleasant to 'succumb' to intercourse 'as a woman' (i.e. a reference to anal intercourse). As his psychosis progressed, he believed that God had *miraculously* turned his body into a woman's body by sending sunrays directly into his anus. In other words, Schreber's 'organ' (anus) was 'miraculated' by God so that his body seemed to emanate from God as a quasi-cause. Schreber figures prominently in the opening pages of *Anti-Oedipus*, as D&G's primary example of an empty BwO (AO 2, 16, 18); see Nigianni (2009: 157).

7 Lane (1971-8: I, 9-10, no. 13); Kloppenborg and Ascough (2011: no. 53).

8 See my discussion of the religious association in Philadelphia (Asia Minor) dedicated to Zeus Saviour as a surplus value in § 7.1.2.

9 D&G's theorization of the third passive synthesis received fresh stimulus when Ilya Prigogine and Isabelle Stengers published *Order Out of Chaos* in 1979, which argued that the classical version of thermodynamics applied only to closed systems, which is to say, to predictable, deterministic systems, whose range of behaviour can be accurately predicted by standard methods of calculation. While dynamical systems behave like closed systems over brief periods of time, they manifest long-term unpredictability and display forms of self-organization or 'autoproduction'. When an intense flow of energy is injected into dynamical systems, they are pushed beyond their virtual attractors (thresholds) into a zone of sensitivity in which minor increases in energy are amplified and force the system to change beyond its powers of recuperation. When a bifurcation point, or 'schiz', is reached, dynamical systems spontaneously self-organize and achieve a new phase space (1984: 177). Guattari's first application of phase space theory was published in 1989 under the title *Schizoanalytic Cartographies*.

5 Territorializations and deterritorializations: On becoming outlandish

1 The French term *milieu* has a variety of meanings including 'surroundings', 'medium' (as in chemistry) and 'middle'. All these meanings are all relevant to understanding D&G's concept of a *milieu*.

2 D&G borrowed the term 'territorialization' from Lacan's theory of the psychosexual development of children, where it is closely tied to the imaginary register, which revolves around the relation of the 'self' to the 'other'. Prior to 'territorialization' the infant experiences its world without any separation or demarcation of boundaries. But over time, the infant's body becomes 'territorialized' into specific erogenous zones (mouth, anus, penis, vagina). When a mother pays special attention to such zones, the process of territorialization accelerates, as does the territorialization of the mother's body (breast, lips, voice and look). When the child enters the imaginary order it 'logicizes' its mother as 'other', as 'not-me'. When a child perceives itself as being in a dyadic relation to its mother, it forms an 'ideal-ego' (§§ 3.1, 5, n. 5). Lacan argues that entry into the imaginary register entails a fundamental *misrecognition* owing to the fact that a child's body is always less separate, more closely related to his mother's body, and generally less bounded and more chaotic, than it perceives (Lacan 2002: 2; Sloterdijk and Heinrichs 2011: 147).

3 Gospel of Thomas, logion 65, Mk 12.1-9, expanded in Lk. 20.9-12 and Mt. 21.28-46.

4 As Kloppenborg observes, the Gospel of Mark has omitted some steps: it was also necessary to construct a wine press, water wheels, a room for laborers to sleep and other rooms for the amphorae of wine (2006: 279–96).

5 1 Cor. 11.18-23, Acts 2.42, 46, 20.7, *Did.* 7.1-4, 14.1, Jude 12.

6 Origen quotes the pagan writer Celsus, who criticized Christianity for attracting 'the foolish, dishonorable and stupid, and only slaves, women and little children' (*contra Celsus* 3.44). In his reply Origen points out that Paul's words are not '*none* of you were wise by human standards' but '*not many* were wise according to human standards, *not many* of you were powerful, *not many* were of noble birth' (1 Cor. 1.26).

7 D&G also borrowed the term 'reterritorialization' from Lacan, who employed it psychoanalytically to designate the reverse process of 'territorialization', that is, a process of freeing desire from the imaginary and symbolic registers, from the Oedipal (nuclear) family and Oedipal representations of desire.

8 Deleuze connects Lacan's term 'deterritorialization' with Herman Melville's use of the adjective 'outlandish' in his novel Moby Dick: 'That mortal man should feed upon the creature [Whale] that feeds his [oil] lamp, and … eat him by his own light, as you may say; this seems so outlandish a thing'; Melville also refers to Queequeg, the son of a South Sea chieftain, as an 'outlandish individual' (Melville 1961: 291, cf. 49).

6 Deterritorialization in the Gospels: A typology of lines

1 Fitzgerald (1945: 69–84); cf. MP 242–3, TP 198–200. In Plateau 8 of *A Thousand Plateaus*, entitled '1874 – Three Novella', or 'What Happened?' D&G carry out an

analysis of the literary genre of the novella on the basis of three types of lines (TP 192–207).

2 D&G translate Fitzgerald's term 'break' as '*coupures*', which is closely related to the term '*coupes*' (sections), a term which appears frequently (*coupes immobiles*) in *Cinéma 1* (IM 9–11, 17–18).

7 The stratification of Christ groups in the Roman despotic socius

1 This structural argument has no bearing on the question of the existence or non-existence of God but only concerns the structural function of the idealization of the concept of God as a 'despotic signifier' in the sociopolitical organization of the Roman Empire as a 'despotic socius' (§ 12.2.1).
2 See my discussion of the concept of 'surplus value' (§ 4.2.2), and the terms 'despot-god' and 'despotic signifier' (§§ 12.2.1-2, 12.3.1).
3 In this chapter I have translated the term *signifiance* as 'signification', instead of employing the French term 'without modification' (see § 11.1.1), as Brian Massumi recommends in his English translation (TP ix).
4 According to Lacan, there is no pre-given desire which is subsequently regulated by law. Human desire is born out of the process of legal regulation: 'desire is essentially the desire to transgress, and for there to be transgression it is first necessary for there to be prohibition' (1992: 83–4).
5 Paul's concepts of law, sin and debt are all components of his 'judicial' model of salvation, according to which, sin is a transgression of God's laws, and everyone who transgresses God's laws has incurred a debt to God, which cannot be paid (Rom. 3.23, 6.23). But through his death and resurrection, Christ, who was innocent, paid off this debt. Christ followers appropriate this benefit through faith. In contrast, according to Paul's 'participationist' model of salvation, *sin is not transgression* against God's laws but rather is a cosmic power that enslaves people (Rom. 5.13, 21, 6.12, 17). Through his death, Christ defeated the cosmic power of sin, and through their baptism, Christ followers participate in Christ's cosmic victory, and are thereby freed from the power of sin (Rom. 6.18). Paul does not differentiate clearly between the judicial and participationist models.
6 A common analogy for the structuralist perspective is the game of chess (§ 18.2.2). By analogy, the despotic socius, considered as a structure, can be said to have functioned like a chess game. Chess pieces are *structurally coded* to perform predetermined functions. Likewise, in the despotic socius, acts of obedience and acts of transgression were both 'moves' that were *permitted* by the 'rules' of this structure.

7 Frederick Engels divided the history of civilization into three stages of economic production on the basis of the social relations between the control over material resources and modes of production: namely, first, the stage of so-called 'savagery' (*Wildheit*), centred around a tribal chief, as the period in which human beings appropriated products in their natural state; second, a stage of 'barbarism', centred around a despot, when human beings learned to breed domestic animals and practise agriculture; and third, the stage of 'civilization', centred around capital, when humans began to develop industry. What these three historical stages of economic production share in common is that *the structure of social production changed whenever the nature of the surplus value changed* (from a chief, to a despot, to capital, as surplus value) (Engels 1972).
8 D&G's 'despotic socius' was developed based on Marx's so-called 'Asiatic' mode of production, which reflects Marx's attempt to account for the stagnation of economic development in countries such as China, resulting from the superimposition of an impersonal bureaucracy on a primitive agrarian economy. While this mode of production was relatively unimportant in Marx's argument, it was reprised by Karl Wittfogel in his *Oriental Despotism* (1957).
9 The surplus value of the modern capitalist socius is capital. Capitalism decodes the former territorial and despotic socii to recode them for the production of capital as surplus value (AO 364).
10 Deleuze's theory of 'surplus value' is rooted in Karl Marx's base–superstructure schema (§ 1). Through the expenditure of labour power, capitalism *adds value* to the commodity value of goods, resulting in the production of capital as a *surplus value*. Despite the fact that the production of surplus value *depends on the proletariat*, the continuous accumulation of capital gives rise to the delusion that capital possesses an autonomous existence *apart of* the workers that create it (Marx 1976: 169; Neocleous 2003: 683).
11 The Seleucid, Ptolemaic and Hasmonean dynasties can each be analysed as a paranoiac body without organs. In these dynasties, all flows of obeisance, obedience, tribute and taxation converged upon a king (§ 7.1). At its paranoiac pole, the citizens ('organs') do not belong to the king as *surplus value* but are merely related to his body as points of disjunction. The king, as surplus value, seems to have an autonomous existence apart from these flows emanating from these organs. But at its attractive point, the same king, as surplus value, *attracts* the citizens to himself, creating the illusion that the citizenry emanates from him as its quasi-cause and unifying power.
12 In terms of linguistic structures, such hierarchical relations are termed 'sequencing' relations. Such relations create a structure that maintains the possibility for graduated dependencies (McLean 2015: 52–3).
13 Similarly, in 1 Cor. 11.7-9, Paul arranges men/husbands in a hierarchical position, which is subordinate to God, but superior to women/wives, based on Gen. 1.27,

reasoning that man is the glory of God but woman is 'the glory of man'. While women seem to be granted power and 'authority' (ἐξουσία) over their own heads in 1 Cor. 11.4-16, Paul's closing arguments remain focused on the subordination of women to men.

14 For the Greek term *kyrios* (κύριος) can be translated as both 'master' or 'Lord'.

8 Christ groups as social assemblages and abstract machines: Discourse and power

1 D&G's distinctive term for concrete machines (*machines concrètes*) is *agencement*, a term which is very close in meaning to Foucault's *dispositif* ('mechanism'). Their first systematic attempt to develop a theory of assemblages is found in chapter 9 of *Kafka: Toward a Minor Literature,* entitled 'What Is an Assemblage?' (K^f 145–57, K 81–8). Since D&G never present their theory of assemblages in toto, nor systematize their assemblage theory, this chapter represents my own synthesis of their concept of an assemblage in relation to the Christ groups as biform social assemblages.

2 Acts 18.3, 20.34; cf. 1 Thess. 2.9; 2 Thess. 3.8, 1 Cor. 4.12 (Kloppenborg 1996: 24).

3 In his essay, entitled 'A New Cartographer (*Discipline and Punish*)', Deleuze takes up Foucault's distinction between the 'visible' and 'articulable' (*énonçable*), found in Foucault's study of Bentham's panopticon. Deleuze employs these terms to designate the nondiscursive and discursive components of social assembles respectively (F^f 31–51, F 23–44).

4 Cf. 1 Cor. 11.18-23, Acts 2.42, 46, 20.7, *Did.* 7.1-4, 14.1, Jude 12.

5 In *A Thousand Plateaus* D&G curiously introduce the Danish linguist Louis Hjelmslev as a 'geologist' who analysed the stratification of language (TP 43). Hjelmslev can be said to be a 'geologist' only in the sense that his planes of expression and content provided D&G with a model for their analysis of geological 'strata' (nondiscursive and discursive planes) in biform social assemblages (§ 8). In this sense, one might term the analysis underway in *A Thousand Plateaus* is a *geological* affair. This 'geophilosophy' aims at *releasing* the 'asignifying' potentials of material systems that lie latent within them.

6 Ferdinand de Saussure subordinated actual acts of communication (*parole*) to the ideal structure of language (*langue*). Like an iceberg, the great majority of which remains submerged beneath the surface of the water, Saussure's theory privileged the hidden structural dimension of language over acts of actual instances of human communication.

7 Louis Hjelmslev theorized linguistic formations in terms of 'planes', rather than individual linguistic signs (as Saussure did) because linguistic signs are not compartmentalized units of meaning. Isolated signs do not have meanings but

'values', which are determined *negatively* based on their positions within a system of signs, as a system of differential differences. This phenomenon is termed 'syntagmatic' value (*signifiance*). As Hjelmslev observes, 'In absolute isolation no sign has any meaning; any sign-meaning arises in a context, but which we mean a situational context or explicit context' (1969: 45).

8 Hjelmslev likened 'content-form' to a fishing net: 'Just as an open net casts its shadow down on an undivided surface', so also does content-form cast a 'net' over amorphous thought, gathering it in and organizing it as a content-substance (1969: 57).

9 Hjelmslev developed a new linguistic model based on the 'expression plane' and 'content plane', allowing him to distinguish between the 'form' of content and the 'substance' of content, and the 'form' of expression and the 'substance' of expression (§ 8.3.1).

10 According to Foucault, the human body is the essential component for the operation of power relations in society. The body is a place where the minute and local institutional practices (such as in factories, schools, universities, state administrative offices) are linked with the large-scale organization of power and body-moulding techniques to render the body useful and productive. This so-called 'bio-power' remains relatively hidden through its expression in different institutional settings.

11 See Beate Bollmann's discussion of the buildings used by professional associations (1998), David Balch's study, and Balch and Weissenrieder study, of houses (2012), and Pierre Gros's analysis of the floor plans of purpose-built *scholae* used by associations (1997). All such structures functioned as the 'form of content'.

12 A 'paradigmatic' domain is an associative field of interrelated words that belong to a single conceptual category, such as words having to do with attitudes and emotions, with psychological faculties, learning, knowing, thinking, power and force, time, agriculture and building. Collectively, paradigmatic domains establish the cultural assumptions that lay behind human cognition. For example, in Judaism and Pauline Christianity, the terms περιτομή (circumcision) and ἀκροβυστία (uncircumcision) were in a complementary relation, which established a normative dualism for Jewish self-definition.

13 As Ronald Bogue observes, in the case of Jeremy Bentham's Panopticon, 'prison and delinquency are reciprocally determined, but their relationship is not one of structural homology, nor is it one of infrastructure to superstructure, signified to signifier, or thing to word' (1989: 131).

14 In the centuries following the translation of the Septuagint, this text came to be read as 'scripture' by Jews, without reference to the Hebrew parent text. According to Marguerite Harl, the Septuagint had relative autonomy from the Hebrew text, and was considered comprehensible on its own terms (2001: 184).

15 D&G presuppose a distinction between the term 'force' (*puissance*), which entails *virtual* potential, in contrast to the term 'power' (*pouvoir*), which designates the *actualization* of force. Through the differenciation of networks of force, power is organized/actualized in a 'diagram' (§ 14.1.1).

9 The God of religion and the schizo God

1 So-called 'normative Judaism' of the Hellenistic world can be said to be 'covenantal' in the sense that it presupposed that Israel's place in God's overall plan was determined by God's prevenient grace in choosing Israel as a separate people and establishing the mosaic covenant with them (Deut. 4.31, 2 Macc. 8.15, *Pss. Sol.* 9.10, CD 6.2, 8.18).
2 According to Paul, God never intended that the Jewish law should serve as a path to salvation (Gal. 2.21, 3.21). He argued that no one can keep *all* the laws, and the transgression of a single law brings about a curse (Gal. 3.13). He goes so far as to contend that the was intrinsically unfulfillable (Gal. 3.10, Rom. 3.23). In Romans, he argues that the law served to 'multiply sin' in order that grace may abound (Rom. 5.20, cf. 4.15). Hence, living under the law (Gal. 4.5a) was also a form of slavery (Gal. 4.3, cf. 4.7-9, 24-25, 5.1, 2.4-5).
3 For example, 'panopticism' can be said to be an ecumenon, that is, an abstract machine of the socius that was independent of any specific instantiation of it, such as the form of Bentham's Panopticon. For 'panopticism' was also operative in 'systems of centralized observation' such as the insane asylum, the factory, the military schools and the modern penitentiary, as well as in 'devices' (*dispositifs*) such as standardized test, modes of physical exercise, and techniques of family counselling. In short, 'panopticism' was a *generalized function*, an 'abstract machine', that created an environment in which one constantly feels that one is under constant surveillance.
4 A Deleuzian 'Idea', as one type of multiplicity, is a set of differential relations. To philosophize using Ideas entails conceiving 'the multiple in the pure state', which is to say, to conceive of this heterogeneous arrangement of oppositional concepts as 'a substantive' (TP 32). For 'difference is internal to the Idea; it unfolds as pure movement, creative of a dynamic space and time which correspond to the Idea' (DR 24). Thus, in *Difference and Repetition* Deleuze explains that the 'Idea' of God requires oppositional concepts such as a 'God of love' and a 'God of anger' (DR 191). On this point, Deleuze also cites Nietzsche who 'never stops saying that there are active and affirmative Gods, active and affirmative religions' (NP 143).

10 The myth of Eve: Falling into, and out of, delusion

1 LeRon Shults has observed how the three errors of desire are evocative of concepts found in the story of the 'fall' in Genesis 3, namely, the concepts of the privative (lack of the fruit in the middle of the garden), the punitive (the three curses of God) and the palliative (the expulsion of Adam and Eve from the garden) (2014a: 171).
2 Augustine, *De Nuptiis et Concupiscentia*, II, xxvi, 43. Similarly, in Sir. 25.24-26, Eve is blamed for all the sin in the world: 'Sin began with a woman, and because of her we all die.' The Life of Adam and Eve, which is a Christianized work, also narrates the details of Eve's transgression, with special emphasis on Eve's culpability (Anderson and Stone 1999; Anderson 2000; Arbel 2012: 5–6; Tromp 2005: 158–9).
3 The phrase 'grammar of God' alludes to a comment made by Nietzsche in *Twilight of the Idols* (1888), in which he observes that even if God is dead, 'we are not getting rid of God because we still believe in Grammar' (Nietzsche 1954: 483). Nietzsche's notion of the 'grammar of God' supplied a basis for Deleuze's non-representational theology: 'Theology is now the science of non-existing entities, the manner in which these entities – divine or anti-divine – Christ or Antichrist – animate language and make for it this glorious body which is divided into disjunctions' (LS 322).
4 Pierre Klossowski has called for a revival of theology, arguing that theology has necessary function as the overarching 'grammar' within which Western thinking moves. Michel Foucault observes how Klossowski, inspired by Nietzsche's comment, employed this 'grammar of God' as an *empty structure* for his own philosophy. By so doing, Klossowski reduced theological concepts to the status of simulacra (Foucault 1998: 123–35; Kaufmann 2007; Smith 2009: 8–21).
5 Jacques Derrida argued that all structures have a centre, which is an element that functions as the ultimate reference point for everything else in the structure. This centre functions can be said to function as a 'transcendental signifier' in the sense that it is the one element that stabilizes every other element in the structure (1978: 278–80).
6 §§ 7, 7.2, 10.1, 10.1.2. In Lacanian theory, *l'Autre* (Other) designates the overarching linguistic structure of language (*langage*) (§ 2). For language is a system without positive terms but only relative differences.
7 With the advent of law begins the creation of spiritualized debt (guilt). The imposition of an idealized law gives rise to the 'organism', who desires to transgress the law, and then feels guilty when s/he does. D&G argue that the creation of spiritualized debt is more important than law itself (AO 194–5).
8 The divided subject ($) is constituted by lack (§ 13.1.2). It is divided by modelling itself as an ideal-ego (§§ 3.1, 5, n. 2) in relation to how it would like to be seen by the 'big Other' (*l'Autre*), and in relation to language (*l'Autre*).

9 The actual/virtual relation is about individuation (§ 3.2). A human being is not free to choose a particular outcome but only has the capacity to affirm what is virtual in that moment. Deleuze hails Kierkegaard's Abraham as a 'hero' of repetition on the grounds that, through his leap of faith, he authenticated the 'imperatives of Being' in his own life.
10 The term 'Apocryphal Acts' designates a group of five texts, written by different authors at different times. The Acts of Paul and Thekla, dated c.170–180, was widely disseminated in the early Christian antiquity. The Acts of Andrew can be dated c.200–210 (Klauck 2008).
11 Ehrman (1998: 177–82); Lypsius and M. Bonnet (1972: I, 235–72); Schneemelcher (1963: II, 361–4).
12 Jean-Daniel Kaestli observes that in the Apostolic Acts, chastity 'is not an exclusively feminine concern' (1986: 129). In the case of the story of Agrippa's concubines, the preaching on sexual continence is also directed towards men: 'men too ceased to sleep with their wives, since they wished to worship God in sobriety and purity' (Acts Th. 34). Elsewhere, men are also exhorted to chastity, such as in the story of the bridegroom (Acts Th. 6), the young man, Siphor, and Iuzanes (Acts Th. 6, 33, 42, 100–5, 139–58). Andronikos, the husband of Drusiana, also agrees to live with his wife like a 'brother' (Acts John 83) (McLean 2017).
13 Lanzillotta (2007); Lypsius and Bonnet (1972: II^1, 39–42); Schneemelcher (1963: II, 410–12).

11 On several regimes of signs and several Christs

1 The author of the Gospel of Matthew, recognizing this is a 'hard' saying in Mark, softened it to read, 'Why do you ask me about what is good? There is only one who is good' (Mt. 19.17).
2 The 'presignifying' regime exhibits a horizontal plane of organization: a tribal chief is installed at the center of a horizontally organized 'territory' of clans, from which position he receives tribute and offers benefaction (§ 7.2).
3 D&G's delineation of these two Christs is based on Jean Paris's analysis of how the poles of the 'despotic Christ' and 'passional Christ' operate in Western art (1965).
4 The term 'scapegoat', literally 'escapegoat', was coined by William Tyndale for his 1530 translation of the Bible. The Revised Version (1884) translated the Hebrew term more literally as 'the goat designated for Azazel', but retained Tyndale's term, 'scapegoat', in the margin.
5 The scapegoat ritual began by the casting of lots to determine which goat would be set apart for the purification of the Temple, and which would be employed for the ridding of the transgressions of the people (Lev. 16.16, 21). The two lots were inscribed respectively '(intended) for YHWH [Yahweh]' and '[intended] for Azaz'el'. Following

the transfer of transgressions to the head of the god for Azaz'el, a messenger would lead the goat away from the Temple into the desert where it was abandoned.

6 On the expression '*sur place*', see MP 444, 473, 509, 602, 623, cf. 36, 84, 103, 198.

7 Walter Bauer (1971) advanced the thesis that so-called Christian 'heresy' *preceded* orthodoxy chronologically. More recently, Gerd Lüdemann (1996) has similarly argued that so-called 'heretical' groups represent more authentic and original forms of early Christianity (Ehrman 2003; cf. Riley 2000). Daniel Boyarin argues that so-called 'orthodox' Christianity formed in the late fourth century of the Common Era as a product of intentional practices of boundary-drawing in light of recent church councils (2004).

12 The despotic Christ and the signifying despotic regime of signs

1 As previously discussed, Louis Hjelmslev subdivided language as a signifying system into two independent planes, expression and content (roughly equivalent to Saussure's signifiers and signifieds), each operating according to a different set of rules (§ 8.3.1). The plane of expression is comprised of an associative field of signifiers, whereas the plane of content is composed of an associative field of interrelated signifieds. Hjelmslevian linguistics recognizes that the plane of expression and plane of content have different forms, and therefore do not interact directly (§ 8.3-4). It is this non-relation between the planes of expression and content that makes language as system of signs unique.

2 On despotic signifiers, see §§ 4.2.2.1, 7, 7.2, 10.1.2.3, 12.2.1.

3 Lacan represents the 'absent Other' (Autre) of signification with the grapheme S(A̶), which is to say, a signifier (S) of the 'absent Other' (Autre) (2002: 300–2).

4 The semantic value of any linguistic sign is determined *negatively* in terms of its place within a system of signifiers, which is a system of differences. Signification entails the syntagmatic process (*signifiance*) of signifiers pointing to other signifiers, and the parallel paradigmatic process of signifieds pointing to other signifieds (which have a conceptual, non-linguistic form).

5 This structural argument has no bearing on the question of the existence or non-existence of God but only on the structural function of the idealization of the concept of God as a 'despotic signifier'.

6 See my detailed comments on the concept of 'surplus value' in §§ 2.2, 4.1.1.1, 7.2.1.

7 In general terms, Christ's status as despot-god is probably polemically modelled after the deification of Julius Caesar and Octavius. Adolf Deissmann's pioneering work on the polemic parallelism between the cult of Christ and the cult of the Caesars is still of great value. He concludes, 'Thus arises the polemic parallelism

between the cult of the emperor and the cult of Christ, which makes itself felt where ancient words derived by Christianity from the treasury of the Septuagint and the gospels happened to coincide with the solemn concepts of the despotic cult which sounded the same or similar' (1995: 342). Indeed, many of the terms that were most closely associated with the cult of the emperor, terms such as the terms 'saviour', 'salvation' and 'gospel', were adopted by Gentile Christology. An inscription from Priene (Ionia), dated 9 CE, records a letter from the Proconsul of Asia, Paulus Fabius Maximus to the Asian provincial assembly in which he declares the birthday of Caesar Augustus (23 September, 63 BCE) to be a new beginning for all of humanity (Hiller von Gaertringen 1968: no. 105; Sherk 1969: no. 65). He then proceeds to commemorate the many benefactions realized through the reign of Augustus, whom he declares to be a 'saviour' (σωτήρ) sent by divine providence, who has brought peace to the world. In this letter, the proclamation of the life and benefactions of Augustus is termed the 'gospel' (εὐαγγέλια, *ll*. 37, 40). In response to this letter, the provincial assembly passes a decree of fulsome praise to Augustus as their 'god' and 'saviour', for his many benefactions ('salvation').

8 Jn 2.1-11, 4.46-54, 5.2-9, 6.1-14, 6.16-21, 9.1-12, 11.1-44.
9 Jn 6.35, 51, 8.12, 58, 10.7-11, 14, 11.25, 14.6, 15.1.
10 John the Baptist declares Christ to be the 'Lamb of God' that 'takes away the sins of the world' (Jn 1.29, 1.36). In the Gospel of John, Christ is crucified on the fourteenth day of the month of Nisan, the day *before* Passover (not the fifteenth day of Nisan, as in the Synoptics), which is the day that the Passover lambs were slaughtered.
11 Burkert (1979: 65); Girard (1986: 89–91); Vernant (1973: 114–13).
12 It is notable that Christ is portrayed as a scapegoat in the Epistle of Barnabas 7.4-7, in Justin Martyr's *Dialogue with Trypho* (40.4, 95.2), in Tertullian's *Against Marcion* (7.7-8), in Origen's *Homilies on Leviticus* (10.1-2), and in Clement of Alexandria's *Miscellanies* (7.33).

13 The passional Christ and the passional subjective regime of signs

1 Or Isa. 58.6, according to Septuagintal versification.
2 Isa. 1.1, Zech. 1.7-8, Hos. 1.1, Joel 1.1, Nah. 1.1, Hab. 1.1.
3 Hence, the series of woes pronounced by Christ against the scribes and Pharisees (Lk. 11.49-50) resemble the indictments of the Israelite prophets (Lk. 10.21-22, 11.2-4, 22.29-30, 23.34, 46, 24.49). Similarly, the parable of the tenants (Mk 12.1-12, Lk. 20.9-19, Mt. 21.28-46) focuses on a familiar prophetic image (Ps. 80.8-13, Isa. 5, Jer. 2.21, 12.10, Ezek. 15.1-6, 19.10, Hos. 10.1).
4 Mk 13.1-2, 14.58-61, 15.39, Mt. 26.57, 62-63, 65, Lk. 19.45-48, Jn 2.13-16, 19.

14 What can Christ's body do?

1. Colombat (1999: 208); Giofkou (2015: 1–10). D&G express their admiration for Kierkegaard who, like an acrobat, was able to leap back and forth between the plane of philosophy and the plane of literature (WP 67).
2. See my discussion of Christ becoming-woman, becoming-animal and becoming-imperceptible (§§ 15–17).
3. In the case of the parable of the sower, each of the seeds that the farmer scatters in the field is also a 'body' as a 'mode of power' (Mk 4.1-9). In this case, each seed has the capacity to be affected by other bodies: to sprout, to be scorched and withered by the sun, to be choked out by weeds and sometimes to grow into a mature plant that produces more seeds. In this latter case, the differential relations of force between the bodies – between seeds, soil, water droplets and the sun – are differenciated as power within a block of becoming (multiplicity), namely, the field of the farmer.
4. Gilles Deleuze's lecture, 'Spinoza's Concept of Affect', Cours Vincennes – 24 January 1978 (obtained from http://www.webdeleuze.com/php/sommaire.html).
5. See my discussion of Nietzsche's 'will to power' and Deleuze's use of Nietzsche in § 2.3.1.
6. D&G make an important distinction between 'force' (*puissance*), which is a set of 'differential' relations on the *virtual plane*, and 'power' (*pouvoir*), which is the actualization of force on the *actual plane* of organization as a set of 'differencial' relations.
7. Gilles Deleuze, *Cours Vincennes* (24 January 1978), as quoted by Hardt (2015: 215–22).
8. In his monograph, *Francis Bacon: The Logic of Sensation*, Deleuze discusses how Francis Bacon sets out to 'render visible forces that are not themselves visible', especially as manifested by the falling rhythm (FB 48). Bacon's human bodies are figures of meat and bone, upon which operate the elementary forces of life, which stress and deform it, dissipating its natural intensity. Bacon was particularly interested in the falling rhythm, and especially the breaking point at which it reaches its outer, almost unbearable limit (FB 21). In his 'Study after Velázquez's Portrait of Pope Innocent X' (1953), Bacon strips out all narrative elements by depicting the pope screaming *unseen*, hidden behind a curtain from all possible witnesses. The function of the pope's scream 'is to render visible' the forces that cause the sad passions and a hatred for life (FB 51).
9. As Rosi Braidotti observes, Deleuze is sometimes heralded as the 'philosopher of joy' because his philosophy 'cultivate(s) joy as a sort of exercise in increasing our ontological capacities' (2019: 475). Deleuze affirms the shear wonder of joy in his declaration that 'the most beautiful thing is to live on the edges, at the limit of her/his own power of being affected, on the condition that this be the joyful limit

since there is the limit of joy and the limit of sadness'; Deleuze's lecture, 'Spinoza's Concept of Affect' (www.webdeleuze.com/php/sommaire.html).

10. The human body can be theorized as a sensitive, self-organizing system, with many different dimensions: physical, biological, chemical, emotional, social, semiotic, cultural, existential, religious, ethical, economic and cognitive. On a day-to-day basis, this system passes through a predictable repertoire of behaviours (attractors) in response to various external and internal forces. Fluctuations in these forces trigger pre-patterned, qualitative changes in behaviour (bifurcation) to return the system to homeostasis.

11. Nathalie Sarraute describes how Marcel Proust is torn between these two planes, and how he extracts from his characters 'the infinitesimal particles of an impalpable matter', but then glues all of the particles back into a coherent form, the envelope of this or that character (1963: 108–11).

12. In *Francis Bacon: The Logic of Sensation*, Deleuze discusses how Francis Bacon disclosed the molecular, non-narrative plane in his paintings by employing the technique of isolation: he isolates his figures by painting them within the three disconnected panels of a triptych, or by surrounding them with backgrounds of intense colour, and by encircling them in ovals of colour. His purpose is to *disrupt any possible narrative* and to block all representation. This absence of narrative is most obvious in his triptychs, such as in the four crucifixion triptychs. In the case of his first crucifixion triptych, entitled 'Three Studies at the Base of a Crucifixion' (1944), Bacon painted an isolated body in each of the three triptych panels. By isolating these bodies, he eliminated the spectators needed to create a narrative relation between the panels. There is no narrative progression in the triptych panels from left to right, or from right to left, nor does the central panel have any kind of univocal role. Indeed, these panels are unable to tell any story because no one is present to witness what happens to Bacon's tortured figures. Only an 'attendant' – who is not a spectator – is depicted in one panel. But since this 'attendant' does not see anything, there is no witness to tell a story. By disrupting the possibility of narrative and representation, Bacon's paintings are freed to reveal the invisible forces that act upon the body, especially as manifested by the two primary 'rhythms of sensation', the rising and falling rhythms (FB 13).

13. D&G note how Proust's *Recherche* often composes blocs of becoming: 'Proust was able to make the face, landscape, painting, music, resonate together. Three moments in the story of Swann and Odette. First, a whole signifying mechanism is set up. … The other lines, of landscapity, picturality, and musicality, also rush toward this catatonic hole and coil around it, bordering it several times' (TP 185).

14. Deleuze notes that the term 'symptom' is derived from Greek *symptoma* (σύμπτωμα) which can designate a 'fortuitous event', a 'mischance' or 'accident' (LS 170).

15 Gilles Deleuze's lecture, 'Spinoza's Concept of Affect'.
16 'Perception' is a kind of selecting of what has interest for one's own needs, and corresponding discarding of what is not of interest (Bergson 1991: 37–8). Daniela Angelucci compares perception to the practice of selecting one photographic image from among many (2019: 572).

15 Molecular becomings of Christ: Becoming-woman

1 To the objection raised against D. H. Lawrence, 'Your tortoises aren't real!', he answered, 'Possibly, but my becoming is real, even and especially if you have no way of judging it' (1962: 1154).
2 The 'phallus' is the pre-eminent Lacanian symbol for all the laws, authorities, and social and linguistic structures that exercise control over life. Lacan draws an important distinction between a man 'being' the phallus within the symbolic register and merely 'having' a phallus (2002: 271–80).
3 Luce Irigaray has accused Deleuze of denying the maternal verities of sexual life (Irigaray and Howie 2008: 79). Deleuze does not deny sexual difference but only argue that sexual difference does not lie at the foundation of subjectivity (Massumi 1992: 86). The gendered subject easily becomes stratified whereby gender becomes the product of power. What is needed is to de-subjectify gender by means of multiplication and diverse combinations. The social production of gender ties all human bodies, including the bodies of woman, to systems of power. Tamsin Lorraine has recently made use of Irigaray's own theory to redress some of the apparent oversights in Deleuze's concept of becoming-woman, arguing that since women enter the symbolic order differently than men, 'the project of becoming-woman is going to be radically different for women and men' (1999: 20–3).

16 Christ becoming-animal: An affair of sorcery

1 Wolf-Man: TP 26, 28, 30–1, 34–5, 37–8, 239, 249, 250; Captain Ahab: TP 243–4, 248, 250, 304, 306; Little Hans: TP 4, 257–60, 63–4, 304.
2 Demons are classed as animals in Deleuze's bestiary: they are demonic animals. A demon is not an Oedipalized animal, a favourite family pet, a cat or dog. Every demon belongs to a pack of demons.
3 Almost fifty years have passed since Michel Foucault argued that the concept of the autonomous subject is 'an effective artifact of a very long and complicated historical process of moving through these various discursive fields', which can

be traced back to the Enlightenment (1977a: 194). Throughout the twentieth century, this autonomous subject has been challenged by social constructivist theories of knowledge, including phenomenology, existentialism, structuralism and psychoanalysis. From a post-structural perspective, the autonomous 'subject' is an effect of multiple overlapping discourses. Over the last twenty years the concept of the autonomous subject has come under repeated criticism by object-oriented approaches to knowledge (Clough and Halley 2007; Thrift 2008). Bruno Latour's actor-network theory (2005), Graham Harman's object-oriented philosophy (2002), Alan Smart and Josephine Smart's posthumanism (2017) and Quentin Meillassoux's speculative realism (2008) all reject the subject/object dualism.

4 The genealogies of Matthew and Luke (Mt. 1.1-16, Lk. 3.23-38) trace the filiation of Christ back to a hereditary point origin, Abraham (Mt. 1.1) and Adam (Lk. 3.38) respectively.

5 D&G note that the French term '*anomal*' originally had the sense of something 'outside the rules', or something that 'goes against the rules'. He traces this obsolete meaning back to the Greek term *anomalia* (ἀνωμαλία). Every animal is fundamentally a band, a pack, a multiplicity (TP 241). They argue that the whale Moby Dick was an anomalous individual. Ahab must strike at Moby Dick to get at a pack of whales.

6 For example, in a love spell for the attraction of a woman, the sorcerer conjures the power of the deity, Myrrh, by burning myrrh in a vessel (Preisendanz 1928: IV, no. 1496–1595; Betz 1992: 67).

7 On the use of these materials in magic see Preisendanz (1928: 4–5, 13, 67, 104, 160).

8 *Inf. Gos. Thom.* 2.2-5, Hennecke (1963: 392–401).

9 Moses' fame as a sorcerer attested in Pliny's Natural History (30, 11), who credits him with starting his own school of sorcery. Jews and Gentiles circulated magical texts under Moses' name (Gager 1972: 134–61). One such text was *The Eighth Book of Moses* (Betz 1992: 172, n. 2). A spell 'for those possessed by demons' requires the sorcerer to draw on the power of Moses, who brought ten plagues against Egypt: 'I conjure you by the one who appeared to Israel in a shining pillar and cloud by day, who saved his people from the Pharaoh and brought upon Pharaoh the ten plagues because of his disobedience' (Betz 1992: 96–7).

10 Another spell for exorcism directs the sorcerer to say, over the head of a demon-possessed man, the following spell: 'Hail, God of Abraham; hail God of Isaac; hail, God of Jacob; Jesus Chrestos, the Seven. Bring Iao Sabaoth; may your power issue forth from him, NN, until you drive away this unclean daemon Satan, who is in him.'

17 Christ's becomings-imperceptible: Martyrological, magical and cosmic

1 TP 163, quoting Henry Miller's *Tropic of Capricorn* (1961: 239).
2 One such invisibility spell directs the sorcerer to 'Say to Helios, "I abjure (ὀρκίζω) you by your great name, ... Make me invisible, lord Helios...in the presence of any man until sunset"' (Preisendanz 1928: I, 222–31). The Greek verb, to invoke, abjure (ὀρκίζειν), means 'to solemnly command/bind somebody by magically invoking the deity'. The same verb is used in Acts 19.13, which describes Jewish exorcists invoking the Jewish God the purpose of exorcism: 'I abjure (ὀρκίζω) you by Jesus whom Paul proclaims.'
3 One such invisibility spell directs the sorcerer to smear his whole body with an oily mixture (Preisendanz 1928: I, 222–31). Another spell directs, 'If you wish to become invisible, rub just your face with the concoction, and you will be invisible for as long as you wish' (Preisendanz 1928: I, 247–62). Another spell directs the sorcerer to take hold of an object such as 'fat or an eye of a night owl and a ball of dung rolled by a beetle and oil of an unripe olive and grind them together until smooth' (Preisendanz 1928: I, 222–31).

18 The nomad Jesus and the Galilean war machine

1 On the idiomatic use of the term 'outlandish', see § 5. The summary statements in the synoptic Gospels repeatedly portray Jesus as one who taught and healed in villages, village assemblies and private houses (e.g. Mk 1.38-39, 6.6b); see Horsley (2001: 178–83); Horsley and Draper (1999: 228–49).
2 Aviam (1995); Horsley (1995: 190–3); Sanders (1985); Vermes (1983, 1993, 2010).
3 On this point, the conclusion of Julius Wellhausen's has not lost much of its force:

> Jesus was not a Christian but a Jew. He did not proclaim a new faith, but he taught to do the will of God. For him as well as for the Jews the will of God was contained in the law and in the other holy scriptures counted as part of them. Yet, he showed another way to fulfill it [sc. the will of God] than the one the pious Jews followed. (1905: 113; translated by Betz 1998: 2)

4 Wellhausen (1905: 113); translated by Betz (1998: 2); cf. Horsely (2012); Vermès (2010); Theissen and Winter (2002); Sanders (1995); Crossan (1994); Betz (1998); Hoheisel (1978: 13–20).
5 Michael Bird has argued that Jesus was attempting to enact the restoration of Israel (Bird 2006). It matters little whether John Dominic Crossan is correct in his assertion that Jesus was a radical revolutionary, who did *not* found Christianity

(1991), or David Flusser is correct in his assertion that Jesus *accidentally* caused Christianity (2001). In neither scenario does Jesus directly establish a non-Jewish movement.

6 Despite their frequent references in *A Thousand Plateaus* to the characteristics of historical nomads, such as Attila and Genghis Khan (TP 351–423), D&G's concept of 'nomadism' is a non-representational, non-geographical descriptor of assemblages that are characteristic of the 'war machine'. Questions about the historical veracity of their description of nomads throughout history have no bearing on their theoretical excursus on their concept of 'nomadism'.

7 The game of chess probably originated in the Gupta Empire of India; the four divisions of the Gupta Empire State apparatus – infantry, cavalry, elephants and chariotry – evolved into the pawn, knight, bishop and rook, respectively. The game of go (an abbreviated form of the Japanese word *igo*) originated in China, where it is still known as *Wéiqí*.

Bibliography

Althusser, Louis (2006), *Philosophy of the Encounter: Later Writings, 1978–1987*, London: Verso.
Anderson, Gary (2000), *Literature on Adam and Eve: Collected Essays*, Leiden: Brill.
Anderson, Gary, and Michael Stone (1999), *A Synopsis of the Books of Adam and Eve*, 2nd rev. edn, Atlanta, GA: Scholars.
Angelucci, Daniela (2019), 'Cinema and Resistance', *Deleuze and Guattari Studies* 13(4): 567–79.
Arbel, Vita Daphna (2012), *Forming Femininity in Antiquity: Eve, Gender, and Ideologies in the Greek Life of Adam and Eve*, New York: Oxford University Press.
Artaud, Antonin (1976), *Selected Writings*, trans. Helen Weaver, ed. Susan Sontag, Berkeley: University of California Press.
Austin, J. L. (1975), *How to Do Things with Words*, 2nd edn, Oxford: Clarendon Press.
Aviam, Mordechai (1995), *Survey of Sites in the Galilee*, Jerusalem.
Balch, David L. (2008), *Roman Domestic Art and Early House Churches*, Tübingen: Mohr Siebeck.
Balch, David, and Annette Weissenrieder, eds (2012), *Contested Spaces: Houses and Temples in Roman Antiquity and the New Testament*, Tübingen: Mohr Siebeck.
Barad, Karen (2007), *Meeting the Universe Halfway*, Durham, NC: Duke University Press.
Barber, Daniel Colucciello (2009), 'Immanence and Creation', *Political Theology* 10(1): 131–41.
Barber, Daniel Colucciello (2010), 'Immanence and the Re-expression of the World', *Substance* 39(1): 38–48.
Barton, Stephen, and G. H. R. Horsley (1981), 'A Hellenistic Cult Association and the New Testament Churches', *Jahrbuch für Antike und Christentum* 24: 7–41.
Bauer, Walter (1971), *Orthodoxy and Heresy in Earliest Christianity*, ed. Robert A. Kraft and Gerhard Krodel, Philadelphia, PA: Fortress Press.
Bauer, Walter, Frederick Wm. Danker, W. F. Arndt and F. W. Gingrich (2000), *A Greek-English Lexicon of the New Testament*, 3rd edn, Chicago: University of Chicago Press.
Bergson, Henri (1991), *Matter and Memory*, trans. Nancy M. Paul and W. S. Palmer, London: Zone.
Betz, Hans Dieter, ed. (1992), *The Greek Magical Papyri in Translation including the Demotic Spells*, 2nd edn, Chicago: University of Chicago Press.
Betz, Hans Dieter (1998), *Antike und Christentum*, Tübingen: Mohr Siebeck.

Bird, Michael F. (2006), *Jesus and the Origins of the Gentile Mission*, London: Continuum.
Bogue, Ronald (1989), *Deleuze and Guattari*, London: Routledge.
Bogue, Ronald (2003), *Deleuze on Literature*, London: Routledge.
Bogue, Ronald (2004), *Deleuze's Wake: Tributes and Tributaries*, Albany, NY: SUNY.
Bollmann, Beate (1998), *Römische Vereinshäuser: Untersuchungen zu den Scholae der römischen Berufs-, Kult- und Augustalen-Kollegien in Italien*, Mainz: Philipp von Zabern.
Bouaniche, Arnaud (2007), *Gilles Deleuze: Une introduction*, Paris: Pocket.
Bouaniche, Arnaud (2014), '"Faire le Mouvement": Deleuze lecteur de Kierkegaard', in Jean Leclercq (ed.), *Kierkegaard et la Philosophie Française: Figures et Receptions*, 127–50, Louvain: Presses universitaires de Louvain.
Boundas, Constantin (1996), 'Bergson-Deleuze: An Ontology of the Virtual', in Paul Patton (ed.), *Deleuze: A Critical Reader*, 123–32, Oxford: Blackwell.
Boyarin, Daniel (2004), *Border Lines: The Partition of Judaeo-Christianity*, Philadelphia: University of Pennsylvania Press.
Braidotti, Rosi (2001), 'Becoming-Woman: Rethinking the Positivity of Difference', in E. Bronfen and M. Kavka (eds), *Feminist Consequences*, 393ff, New York: Columbia University Press.
Braidotti, Rosi (2019), 'Affirmative Ethics and Generative Life', *Deleuze and Guattari Studies* 13(4): 463–81.
Brakke, David (2010), *The Gnostics: Myth, Ritual, and Diversity in Early Christianity*, Cambridge, MA: Harvard University Press.
Bremmer, Jan, 'Scapegoat Rituals in Ancient Greece', *Harvard Studies in Classical Philology* 87 (1983): 299–320.
Bryden, Mary (2001), *Deleuze and Religion*, London: Routledge.
Buchanan, Ian (2008), *Deleuze and Guattari's Anti-Oedipus*, London: Continuum.
Buchanan, Ian, and Nicholas Thoburn (2008), *Deleuze and Politics*, Edinburgh: Edinburgh University Press.
Burkert, Walter (1979), *Structure and History in Greek Mythology and Ritual*, Berkeley: University of California Press.
Burkert, Walter (1985), *Greek Religion*, trans. J. Raffa, Cambridge, MA: Harvard University Press.
Burridge, Richard (2004), *What Are the Gospels? A Comparison with Graeco-Roman Biography*, 2nd edn, Grand Rapids, MI: Eerdmans.
Calhoun, Craig J. (2002), *Classical Sociological Theory*, Oxford: Wiley-Blackwell.
Chalier, Catherine (2002), 'Levinas and the Talmud', in Simon Critchley and Robert Bernasconi (eds), *The Cambridge Companion to Levinas*, 100–18, Cambridge: Cambridge University Press.
Cimatti, Felice (2019), 'Deleuze and Italian Thought', *Deleuze and Guattari Studies* 13(4): 495–507.

Clough, P. T., and J. Halley, eds (2007), *The Affective Turn: Theorizing the Social*, Durham, NC: Duke University Press.
Colebrook, Claire (2001), *Gilles Deleuze*, London: Routledge.
Colebrook, Claire (2020), 'Extinction, Deterritorialisation and End Times: Peak Deleuze', *Deleuze and Guattari Studies* 14(3): 327–48.
Colombat, André Pierre (1997), 'Deleuze and the Three Powers of Literature and Philosophy: To Demystify, to Experiment, to Create', *South Atlantic Quarterly* 96: 579–97.
Colombat, André Pierre (1999), 'Deleuze and the Three Powers of Literature: To Demystify, to Experiment, to Create', in Ian Buchanan (ed.), *A Deleuzian Century?*, 199–217, Durham, NC: Duke University Press.
Crockett, Clayton (2002) 'Gilles Deleuze and the Sublime Fold of Religion', in Philip Goodchild (ed.), *Rethinking the Philosophy of Religion*, 267–80, New York: Fordham University Press.
Crockett, Clayton (2010), 'Post-Secular Spinoza: Deleuze, Negri and Radical Political Theology', *Analecta Hermeneutica* 2: 1–13.
Crockett, Clayton (2011) *Radical Political Theology: Religion and Politics after Liberalism*, New York: Columbia University Press.
Crossan, John Dominic (1991), *The Historical Jesus: The Life of a Mediterranean Jewish Peasant*, San Francisco, CA: HarperSanFrancisco.
Crossan, John Dominic (1994), *Jesus: A Revolutionary Biography*, San Francisco, CA: HarperSanFrancisco.
Danker, F. Wm., W. Bauer, W. F. Arndt and F. W. Gingrich (2000), *A Greek-English Lexicon of the New Testament*, 3rd edn, Chicago: University of Chicago Press.
Deissmann, G. A. (1995), *Light from the Ancient East: The New Testament Illustrated by Recently Discovered Texts of the Graeco-Roman World*, trans. Lionel R. M. Strachen, 4th edn, rev. and expanded, Peabody, MA: Hendrickson.
Deleuze, Gilles (1968), *Différence et répétition*, Presses Universitaires de France.
Deleuze, Gilles (1972), 'Interview with Catherine Backès-Clément', *Revue L'Arc – 2eme trimestre 1972*, no. 49, Librairie Duponchelle.
Deleuze, Gilles (1986a), *Cinema 1: The Movement-Image*, trans. H. Tomlinson et al., Minneapolis: University of Minnesota Press.
Deleuze, Gilles (1986b), *Foucault*, Paris: Éditions de Minuit.
Deleuze, Gilles (1988a), *Bergsonism*, trans. Hugh Tomlinson and Barbara Habberjam, New York: Zone Books.
Deleuze, Gilles (1988b), *Foucault*, trans. Seán Hand, Minneapolis: University of Minnesota Press.
Deleuze, Gilles (1988c), *Spinoza: Practical Philosophy*, trans. Robert Hurley, San Francisco, CA: City Lights Books.
Deleuze, Gilles (1989), *Cinema 2: The Time-Image*, trans. Hugh Tomlinson and Robert Galeta, Minneapolis: University of Minnesota Press.

Deleuze, Gilles (1990), *The Logic of Sense*, ed. Constantin V. Boundas, trans. Mark Lester, New York: Columbia University Press.
Deleuze, Gilles (1991), *Coldness and Cruelty*, New York: Zone Books.
Deleuze, Gilles (1992), *Expressionism in Philosophy: Spinoza*, trans. Martin Joughin, Brooklyn: Zone Books.
Deleuze, Gilles (1994), *Difference and Repetition*, trans. Paul Patton, New York: Columbia University Press.
Deleuze, Gilles (1995), *Negotiations: 1972–1990*, trans. Martin Joughin, New York: Columbia University Press.
Deleuze, Gilles (1997), *Essays Critical and Clinical*, trans. Daniel W. Smith and Michael A. Greco, Minneapolis: University of Minnesota Press.
Deleuze, Gilles (2001a), *Empiricism and Subjectivity*, trans. Constantin V. Boundas, New York: Columbia University Press.
Deleuze, Gilles (2001b), *Pure Immanence: Essays on a Life*, trans. A. Boyman, New York: Zone Books.
Deleuze, Gilles (2003), *Francis Bacon: The Logic of Sensation*, trans. Daniel W. Smith, Minneapolis: University of Minnesota Press.
Deleuze, Gilles (2006), *Nietzsche and Philosophy*, trans. Hugh Tomlinson, New York: Columbia University Press.
Deleuze, Gilles (2007a), *Desert Islands and Other Texts 1953–1974*, trans. David Lapoujade, ed. Michael Taormina, Los Angeles: Semiotext(e).
Deleuze, Gilles (2007b), *Two Regimes of Madness: Texts and Interviews 1975–1995*, trans. Ames Hodges and Mike Taormina, ed. David Lapoujade, New York: Semiotext(e).
Deleuze, Gilles (2008), *Proust and Signs*, trans. Richard Howard, London: Continuum.
Deleuze, Gilles (2015), *Lettres et autres textes*, ed. David Lapoujade, Paris: Éditions de Minuit.
Deleuze, Gilles, and Félix Guattari (1972), *Capitalisme et Schizophrénie, tome 1: L'Anti-Œdipe*, Paris: Éditions de Minuit.
Deleuze, Gilles, and Félix Guattari (1980), *Capitalisme et Schizophrénie, tome 2: Mille plateau*, Paris: Éditions de Minuit.
Deleuze, Gilles, and Félix Guattari (1983), *Anti-Oedipus: Capitalism and Schizophrenia*, trans. Robert Hurley, Minneapolis: University of Minnesota Press.
Deleuze, Gilles, and Félix Guattari (1986), *Kafka: Toward a Minor Literature*, trans. Dana Polan, Minneapolis: University of Minnesota Press.
Deleuze, Gilles, and Félix Guattari (1987), *A Thousand Plateaus: Capitalism and Schizophrenia*, trans. Brian Massumi, Minneapolis: University of Minnesota Press.
Deleuze, Gilles, and Félix Guattari (1994), *What Is Philosophy?*, trans. Janis Tomlinson and Graham Burchell III, New York: Columbia University Press.
Deleuze, Gilles, Félix Guattari, Claire Parnet and André Scala (1978), 'The Interpretation of Utterances', in Paul Foss and Meaghan Morris (eds), *Language, Sexuality and Subversion*, 141–158, Darlington: Feral Press.

Deleuze, Gilles, Félix Guattari and Charles J. Stivale (1984), 'Concrete Rules and Abstract Machines', *SubStance* 13(3): 7–19.

Deleuze, Gilles, and Claire Parnet (2007), *Dialogues II*, revised and translated by Barbara Habberjam, Eliot Albert and Janis Tomlinson, New York: Columbia University Press.

Deleuze, Gilles, and Claire Parnet (2012), *Gilles Deleuze from A to Z*, trans. Charles J. Stivale, Los Angeles: Semiotext(e).

Delpech-Ramey, Joshua (2010), 'Deleuze, Guattari, and the "Politics of Sorcery"', *SubStance* 39(1): 8–23.

Derrida, Jacques (1974), *Of Grammatology*, Baltimore, MD: Johns Hopkins University Press.

Derrida, Jacques (1978), *Writing and Difference*, trans. Alan Bass, Chicago: University of Chicago Press.

Derrida, Jacques (1990), *Limited Inc.*, trans. Samuel Weber, Evanston, IL: Northwestern University Press.

Didi-Huberman, Georges (1995), *Fra Angelico: Dissemblance et figuration*, Paris: Camps Arts.

Dosse, François (2010), *Gilles Deleuze & Félix Guattari: Intersecting Lives*, trans. Deborah Glassman, New York: Columbia University Press.

Droit, Roger-Pol, and Jean-Philippe de Tonnac (2002), *Fous comme des sage. Scènes grecques et romaines*, Paris: Seuil.

Ehrman, Bart D. (1998), *The New Testament and Other Early Christian Writings: A Reader*, New York: Oxford University Press.

Ehrman, Bart D. (2003), *Lost Christianities: The Battles for Scripture and the Faiths We Never Knew*, New York: Oxford University Press.

Engels, Frederick (1972), *The Origin of the Family, Private Property and the State*, trans. Alex West, New York: International.

Faber, Roland (2002), 'De-Ontologizing God: Levinas, Deleuze, and Whitehead', in Catherine Keller and Anne Daniell (eds), *Process and Difference*, 209–34, Albany: SUNY Press.

Fitzgerald, F. Scott (1945), *The Crack-up: With Other Uncollected Pieces*, ed. Edmund Wilson, New York: New Directions.

Flieger, Jerry Aline (1999), 'Overdetermined Oedipus: Mommy, Daddy and Me as Desiring-Machine', in Ian Buchanan Buchanan (ed.), *A Deleuzean Century?*, 219–40, Durham, NC: Duke University Press.

Flusser, David (2001), *Jesus*, 3rd edn, Jerusalem: Magnes Press, Hebrew University of Jerusalem.

Foucault, Michel (1970), *The Order of Things*, New York: Pantheon.

Foucault, Michel (1972), *The Archaeology of Knowledge*, New York: Pantheon.

Foucault, Michel (1977a), *Discipline and Punish: The Birth of the Prison*, trans. Alan Sheridan, New York: Pantheon.

Foucault, Michel (1977b), *Language, Counter-memory, Practice*, ed. Donald F. Bouchard, trans. D. F. Bouchard, Sherry Simon, Ithaca, NY: Cornell University Press.

Foucault, Michel (1980), *Power/Knowledge: Selected Interviews and Other Writings, 1972–1977*, ed. and trans. Colin Gordon et al., New York: Pantheon.

Foucault, Michel (1990), 'Nietzsche, Freud, Marx', in Gayle L. Ormiston and Alan D. Schrift (eds), *Transforming the Hermeneutic Context*, 59–67, Albany, NY: SUNY.

Foucault, Michel (1998), *Aesthetics, Method, and Epistemology: Essential Works of Foucault 1954–1984*, ed. James Faubion, trans. Robert Hurley, New York: New Press.

Foucault, Michel (2000), *Ethics: Subjectivity, and Truth*, ed. Paul Rabinow, trans. Robert Hurley, London: Penguin Books.

Frazer, James (1915), *Golden Bough: Vol. 3. The Scapegoat*, 3rd edn, London: Macmillan.

Gager, G. (1972), *Moses in Greco-Roman Paganism*, Nashville, TN: Abingdon.

Genosko, Gary (2008), 'A-signifying Semiotics', *Public Journal of Semiotics* 2(1): 11–21.

Genosko, Gary (2002), *Félix Guattari: An Aberrant Introduction*, London: Continuum.

Giofkou, Daphne (2015), 'The Writer as an Acrobat: Deleuze and Guattari on the Relation between Philosophy and Literature (and How Kierkegaard Moves in-between)', *Transnational Literature* 7(2): 1–10.

Girard, René (1986), *The Scapegoat*, trans. Y. Freccero, Baltimore, MD: John Hopkins University.

Girard, René (1987), *Things Hidden Since the Foundation of the World*, Stanford, CA: Stanford University Press.

Gros, Pierre (1997), 'Maisons ou sièges de corporations? Les traces archéologiques du phénomène associatif dans la Gaule romaine méridionale', *Comptes-rendus des séances de l'Académie des Inscriptions et Belles-Lettres* 141(1): 213–41.

Goodchild, Philip (1996a), *Deleuze and Guattari: An Introduction to the Politicis of Desire*, London: SAGE.

Goodchild, Philip (1996b), *Gilles Deleuze and the Question of Philosophy*, Madison: Farleigh Dickenson University Press.

Goodchild, Philip (2001), 'Why Is Philosophy So Compromised with God', in Mary Bryden (ed.), *Deleuze and Religion*, 156–66, London: Routledge.

Gorelick, Nathan (2011), 'Life in Excess: Insurrection and Expenditure in Antonin Artaud's Theater of Cruelty', *Discourse: Discourse Berkeley Journal for Theoretical Studies in Media and Culture* 33(2): 263–79.

Gros, Pierre (1997), 'Maisons ou sièges de corporations? Les traces archéologiques du phénomène associatif dans la Gaule romaine méridionale', *Comptes-rendus des séances de l'Académie des Inscriptions et Belles-Lettres* 141(1): 213–41.

Grosz, Elizabeth (1993), 'A Thousand Tiny Sexes: Feminism and Rhizomatics', *Topoi* 12: 167–79.

Grosz, Elizabeth (2012), 'The Body of Signification', in John Fletcher and Andrew Benjamin (eds), *Abjection, Melancholia and Love: The Work of Julia Kristeva*, Routledge, pp. 80–103.

Guattari, Félix (1984), *Molecular Revolution: Psychiatry and Politics*, trans. Rosemary Sheed, New York: Penguin.
Guattari, Félix (1995), *Chaosmosis: An Ethico-aesthetic Paradigm*, trans. Paul Bains and Julian Pefanis, Sydney: Power.
Guattari, Félix (1996), *The Guattari Reader*, ed. Genosko, Gary, trans. Sophie Thomas, Oxford: Blackwell.
Guattari, Félix (2006), *The Anti-Oedipus Papers*, trans. K. Gotman, New York: Semiotext(e).
Guattari, Félix (2008), *The Three Ecologies*, trans. Ian Pindar, Paul Sutton, London: Continuum.
Guattari, Félix (2009), *Chaosophy: Texts and Interviews 1972–1977*, ed. Sylvère Lotringen, trans. D. Sweet, Los Angeles: Semiotext(e).
Guattari, Félix (2011), *The Machinic Unconscious: Essays in Schizoanalysis*, trans. Taylor Adkins, Los Angeles: Semiotext(e).
Guattari, Félix (2012), *Schizoanalytic Cartographies*, trans. Andrew Goffey, New York: Continuum.
Guattari, Félix (2015), *Psychoanalysis and Transversality: Texts and Interviews 1955–1971*, trans. Ames Hodges, South Pasadena: Semiotext(e).
Habermas, Jürgen (1988), *On Logic of the Social Sciences*, trans. Sherry Weber Nicholsen and Jerry A. Stark, Cambridge: Polity Press.
Hallward, Peter (2006), *Out of This World: Deleuze and the Philosophy of Creation*, London: Verso.
Hardt, Michael (2015), 'The Power to Be Affected', *International Journal of Politics, Culture, and Society* 28(3): 215–22.
Harl, Marguerite (2001), 'La Bible D'Alexandrie 1: The Translation Principles', in B. A. Taylor (ed.), *The Tenth Congress of the International Organization for Septuagint and Cognate Studies, Oslo, 1988*, 181–97, Atlanta, GA: SBL.
Harman, Graham (2002), *Tool-Being: Heidegger and the Metaphysics of Objects*, Peru, IL: Open Court.
Hayden, Patrick (1998), *Multiplicity and Becoming: The Pluralist Empiricism of Gilles Deleuze*, Peter Lang.
Heidegger, Martin (1998), *Pathmarks*, ed. William McNeil, Cambridge: Cambridge University Press.
Hennecke, Edgar (1963), *New Testament Apocrypha*, vol. 1, ed. Wilhelm Schneemelcher, 392–401, Philadelphia, PA: Westminster.
Higgins, Luke B. (2010), 'A Logos without Organs: Cosmologies of Transformation in Origen and Deleuze-Guattari', *SubStance* 39(1): 141–53.
Hiller von Gaertringen, F. F., ed. (1968), *Inschriften von Priene*, Berlin.
Hillman, James (1975), *Re-Visioning Psychology*, New York: Harper & Row.
Hjelmslev, Louis (1969), *Prolegomena to a Theory of Language*, trans. Francis J. Whitfield, Madison: University of Wisconsin Press.

Hoheisel, Karl (1978), *Das antike Judentum in christlicher Sicht*, Wiesbaden: Harrassowitz.
Horsley, Richard A. (1986), 'The Zealots; Their Origin, Relationships and Importance in the Jewish Revolt', *Novum Testamentum* 28: 159–92.
Horsley, Richard A. (1984), 'Popular Messianic Movements around the Time of Jesus', *Catholic Biblical Quarterly* 46: 471–95.
Horsley, Richard A. (1995), *Galilee: History, Politics, People*, Valley Forge, PA: Trinity Press International.
Horsley, Richard A. (2001), *Hearing the Whole Story: The Politics of Plot in Mark's Gospel*, Louisville, KY: Westminster John Knox.
Horsley, Richard A. (2003), *Jesus and Empire: The Kingdom of God and the New World Disorder*, Minneapolis, MN: Fortress Press.
Horsley, Richard A. (2010), 'Jesus and the Politics of Roman Palestine', *Journal for the Study of the Historical Jesus* 8(2): 99–145.
Horsely, Richard A. (2012), *The Prophet Jesus and the Renewal of Israel: Moving beyond Diversionary Debate*, Grand Rapids, MI: Eerdmans.
Horsley, Richard A. (2014), *Jesus and Magic: Freeing the Gospel Stories from Modern Misconceptions*, Cascade Books.
Horsley, Richard A., and Jonathan A. Draper (1999), *'Whoever Hears You Hears Me': Prophets, Performance, and Tradition in Q*, Harrisburg, PA: Trinity Press International, 1999.
Hughes, Denis (1991), *Human Sacrifice in Greece*, Cornwall: Routledge.
Irigaray, Luce (1985), *Speculum of the Other Woman*, trans. G. C. Gill, Ithaca, NY: Cornell University Press.
Irigaray, Luce, and G. Howie (2008), 'Becoming Woman, Each One and Together', in Luce Irigaray and S. Pluhacek, *Conversations*, 73–84, New York: Continuum.
Justaert, Kristien (2007), '"*Ereignis*" (Heidegger) or "La Clameur de l'être" (Deleuze): Topologies for a Theology beyond Representation', *Philosophy and Theology* 19(1–2): 241–56.
Justaert, Kristien (2010), 'Liberation Theology: Deleuze and Althaus-Reid', *SubStance* 39(1): 154–64.
Justaert, Kristien (2012), *Theology after Deleuze*, London: Continuum.
Kaestli, Jean-Daniel (19886), 'Response (to Virginia Burrus)', in *The Apocryphal Acts of Apostles*, ed. Dennis R. Macdonald *Semeia* 38: 119–31.
Kaufman, Eleanor (2007), 'Klossowski, Deleuze, and Orthodoxy', *Diacritics* 35(1): 47–59.
Kaufmann, Walter (1954), *The Portable Nietzsche*, New York: Viking.
Kee, Howard Clark (1993), 'Magic and Divination', in Coogan, Michael David Coogan and Bruce Metzger (eds), *The Oxford Companion to the Bible*, 483–4, Oxford: Oxford University Press.
Keller, Catherine (2002), 'Process and Chaosmos: The Whiteheadian Fold in the Discourse of Difference', in Catherine Keller and Anne Daniell (eds), *Process and*

Difference: Between Cosmological and Poststructuralist Postmodernisms, 64ff, Albany, NY: SUNY.
Keller, Catherine (2003), *Face of the Deep: A Theology of Becoming*, London: Routledge.
Kerslake, Christian (2007), *Deleuze and the Unconscious*, New York: Continuum.
Kerslake, Christian (2010), 'Deleuze, Guattari, and the "Politics of Sorcery"', *SubStance* 39(1): 8–23.
King, Karen L. (2005), *What Is Gnosticism?*, Cambridge, MA: Harvard University Press.
Klauck, Hans-Josef (2008), *The Apocryphal Acts of the Apostles: An Introduction*, Waco, TX: Baylor University Press.
Kloppenborg, John (1996), 'Collegia and *thiasoi*: Issue in Function, Taxonomy and Membership', in Steven Wilson and John S. Kloppenborg (eds), *Voluntary Associations in the Graeco-Roman World*, 16–30, London: Routledge.
Kloppenborg, John (2006), *The Tenants in the Vineyard: Ideology, Economics, and Agrarian Conflict in Jewish Palestine*, Tübingen: Mohr Siebeck.
Kloppenborg, John S., and Richard S. Ascough (2011), *Greco-Roman Associations: Texts, Translations, and Commentary. I. Attica, Central Greek, Macedonia, Thrace*, Berlin: De Gruyter.
Kloppenborg, John S. (2019), *Christ's Associations: Connecting and Belonging in the Ancient City*, New Haven, CT: Yale University Press.
Lacan, Jacques (1966), *Écrits*, Paris: Seuil.
Lacan, Jacques (1977), *The Four Fundamental Concepts of Psychoanalysis: The Seminar of Jacques Lacan Book XI*, ed. Jacques-Alain Miller, trans. Alan Sheridan, New York: Norton.
Lacan, Jacques (1988), *The Seminar. Book II: The Ego in Freud's Theory and in the Technique of Psychoanalysis, 1954–55*, ed. Jacques-Alain Miller, trans. Sylvana Tomaselli, Cambridge: Cambridge University Press.
Lacan, Jacques (1992), *The Seminar: Book VII. The Ethics of Psychoanalysis, 1959–60*, trans. Dennis Porter, London: Routledge.
Lacan, Jacques (2002), *Ecrits: A Selection*, trans. Bruce Fink, New York: Norton.
Landolfi, Claudia (2019), 'Beyond the Society of Judgement: Deleuze and the Social Transitivity of Affects', *Deleuze and Guattari Studies* 13(4): 541–51.
Lane, Eugene (1971–1978), *Corpus monumentorum religionis dei Menis*, 4 vols. Leiden: Brill.
Lanzillotta, Lautaro R. (2007), *Acts Andreae Apocrypha: A New Perspective on the Nature, Intention and Significance of the Primitive Text*, Genève.
Latour, Bruno (2005), *Reassembling the Social: An Introduction to Actor-Network-Theory*, Oxford: Oxford University Press.
Lawrence, D. H. (1962), *The Collected Letters of D. H. Lawrence*, vol. 2, ed. Harry T. Moore, New York: Viking.
Lawrence, D. H. (1983), *Tortoises: Six Poems by D.H. Lawrence*, Northampton, MA: Cheloniidae Press.

Leach, Edmund, and D. Alan Aycock (1983), *Structuralist Interpretations of Biblical Myth*, New York: Cambridge University Press.

Lévy, Pierre (2007), *Qu'est-ce que la virtuel?* Paris Éditions de la Découverte.

LiDonnici, Lynn R. (1999), 'The Disappearing Magician: Literary and Practical questions about the Greek Magical papyri', in Benjamin G. Wright (ed.), *A Multiform heritage: Studies on Early Judaism and Christianity in Honor of Robert A. Kraft*, 227–44, Atlanta, GA: Scholars.

Lorraine, Tamsin (1999), *Irigaray & Deleuze: Experiments in Visceral Philosophy*, Ithaca, NY: Cornell University.

Louw, Johannes P., and Eugene A. Nida (1988), *Greek-English Lexicon of the New Testament Based on Semantic Domains*, 2 vols., ed. Rondal Smith et al., New York: United Bible Societies.

Lüdemann, Gerd (1996), *Heretics: The Other Side of Early Christianity*, Louisville, KY: Westminster John Knox.

Lypsius, R. A., and M. Bonnet (1972), *Acta Apostolorum Apocrypha post Constantinum Tischendorf*, 2 vols. in 3, Hildesheim: Georg Olms.

Marks, John (1998), *Gilles Deleuze: Vitalism and Multiplicity*, London: Pluto.

Marx, Karl (1959), 'Manifesto of the Communist Party', in Lewis S. Feuer (ed.), *Marx & Engels: Basic Writings on Politics and Philosophy*, 1–41, New York: Doubleday.

Marx, Karl (1976), *Capital: A Critique of Political Economy*, vol. 1, trans. Ben Fowkes, Harmondsworth.

Marx, Karl (1978), 'A Contribution to the Critique of Political Economy', in Robert C. Tucker (ed.), *Mark-Engels Reader*, 3–8, New York: W. W. Norton.

Massumi, Brian (1992), *A User's Guide to Capitalism and Schizophrenia: Deviations from Deleuze and Guattari*, Swerve edn, Cambridge, MA: MIT Press.

Massumi, Brian (2002a), *Parables for the Virtual: Movement, Affect, Sensation*, Durham, NC: Duke University Press.

McLean, Bradley H. (2002), *An Introduction to the Study of Greek Epigraphy of the Hellenistic and Roman Periods from Alexander the Great down to the Reign of Constantine (323 BCE–337 CE)*, Ann Arbor: University of Michigan Press.

McLean, Bradley H. (2012a), *Biblical Interpretation and Philosophical Hermeneutics*, New York: Cambridge University Press.

McLean, Bradley H. (2012b), 'The Crisis of Historicism and the Problem of Historical Meaning in New Testament Studies', *Heythrop Journal* 53(2): 217–40.

McLean, Bradley H. (2013), 'Lessons Learned from Swinburne: A Critique of Richard Swinburne's *Revelation: From Metaphor to Analogy*', *Toronto Journal of Theology* 29(2): 369–88.

McLean, Bradley H. (2015), 'The Rationality of Early Christian Discourse', *Toronto Journal of Theology*, Supplement 31: 43–65.

McLean, Bradley H. (2017), 'The Rationality of the Miracles of the Apostolic Women: Thekla, Drusiana, and Maximilla as Anti-Function', *Toronto Journal of Theology* 33(1): 73–85.

McLean, Bradley H. (2019), 'Deleuze's Interpretation of Job as a Heroic Figure in the History of Rationality', *Religions* 10(3): 1–8.
McLean, Bradley H. (2020), 'What Does *A Thousand Plateaus* Contribute to the Study of Early Christianity?', *Deleuze and Guattari Studies* 14(3): 533–53.
McLean, Bradley H. (2021), 'Abraham as a Deleuzian Hero of Repetition: The Rationality of the Akedah', in Heiko Shulz and Jean-Pierre Fortin (eds), *A Cruel God? The Binding of Isaac: A Challenge for the Rationality of Judaism, Christianity and Islam*, Berlin: De Gruyter.
Meillassoux, Quentin (2008), *After Finitude: An Essay on the Necessity of Contingency*, trans. Ray Brassier, London: Continuum.
Melville, Herman (1961), *Moby Dick or the White Whale*, New York: Signet Books.
Mengue, Philippe (2000), 'Presentation de Nietzsche et la philosophie', in Yannick Beaubatie (ed.), *Tombeau de Gille Deleuze*.
Milik, J. T. ed. (1976), *The Books of Enoch: Aramaic Fragments of Qumrân Cave 4*, Oxford: Clarendon Press.
Miller, Henry (1961), *Tropic of Capricorn*, New York: Grove Press.
Miroshnikov, Ivan (2018), 'The Gospel of Thomas and Plato: A Study of the Impact of Platonism on the "Fifth Gospel"', in *Nag Hammadi and Manichaean Studies*, vol. 93, 269–73, Leiden: Brill.
Mosser, Carl (2013), 'Torah Instruction, Discussion, and Prophecy in First-Century Synagogues', in Stanley E. Porter and Wendy J. Porter (eds), *Christian Origins and Hellenistic Judaism: Social and Literary Contexts for the New Testament*, 2.523–51, Leiden: Brill.
Nail, Thomas (2017), 'What Is an Assemblage?' *SubStance* 46(1): 21–37.
Neocleous, Mark (2003), 'The Political Economy of the Dead: Marx's Vampires,' *History of Political Thought* 24(4): 668–84.
Nichelsburg, George W. E., and James VanderKam (2012), *1 Enoch: The Hermeneia Translation*, Minneapolis, MN: Scholars.
Niemoczynski, Leon (2013), 'Nature's Transcendental Creativity: Deleuze, Corrington, and an Aesthetic Phenomenology', *American Journal of Theology & Philosophy*, 34(1): 17–34.
Nigianni, Chrysanthi (2009), *Deleuze and Queer Theory*, Edinburgh: Edinburgh University Press.
Paris, Jean (1965), *L'espace et le regard*, Bourges: Éditions du Seuil.
Patte, Daniel, and Aline Patte (1978), *Structural Exegesis: From Theory to Practice*, Philadelphia, PA: Fortress Press.
Pearson, K. Ansell (2002), *Philosophy and the Adventure of the Virtual: Bergson and the Time of Life*, London: Routledge.
Perniola, Mario (2019), 'Becoming Deleuzian?', *Deleuze and Guattari Studies* 13(4): 482–94.
Phillips, Richard L. (2009), *In Pursuit of Invisibility: Ritual Texts from Late Roman Egypt*, Durham, NC: American Society of Papyrologists.

Patton, Paul (2010), *Deleuzian Concepts: Philosophy, Colonization, Politics*, Stanford, CA: Stanford University Press.
Pombo Nabais, Catarina (2013), *Gilles Deleuze: philosophie et littérature*, Paris: Harmattan.
Posteraro, Tano (2016), 'Habits, Nothing but Habits: Biological Time in Deleuze', *The Comparatist*, 40: 94–110.
Powell, Mark Allan (1998), *Jesus as a Figure in History: How Modern Historians View the Man from Galilee*, Grand Rapids, MI: Eerdmans.
Powell-Jones, Lindsay, and F. LeRon Shults (2016), *Deleuze and the Schizoanalysis of Religion*, London: Bloomsbury.
Preisendanz, Karl, ed. (1974), *Papyri graecae magicae: die griechischen Zauberpapyri*, 2 vols. Stuttgart: B.G. Teuber.
Price, S. R. F. (1984), *Rituals and Power: The Roman Imperial Cult in Asia Minor*, Cambridge: Cambridge University Press.
Prigogine, Ilya, and Isabelle Stengers (1984), *Order out of Chaos: Man's New Dialogue with Nature*, New York: Bantam.
Protevi, John (2001), *Political Physics: Deleuze, Derrida and the Body Politic*, London: Athlone Press.
Proust, Marcel (1981), *Remembrance of Things Past*, 3 vols, trans. C. K. Scott Moncrieff and Terence Kilmartin, New York: Random House.
Ramey, Joshua (2012), *The Hermetic Deleuze: Philosophy and Spiritual Ordeal*, Durham, NC: Duke University Press.
Redell, Petra Carlsson (2012), *Theology beyond Representation: Foucault, Deleuze and the Phantasms of Theological Thinking*, Uppsala: Acta Universitatis Upsaliensis.
Redell, Petra Carlsson (2014), *Mysticism as Revolt: Foucault, Deleuze, and Theology*, Aurora, CO: Davis Group.
Ricoeur, Paul (1970), *Freud and Philosophy: An Essay on Interpretation*, New Haven, CT: Yale University Press.
Riley, Gregory J. (2000), *One Jesus, Many Christs: How Jesus Inspired Not One True Christianity, but Many: The Truth about Christian Origins*, Minneapolis, MN: Fortress Press.
Sanders, E. P. (1985), *Jesus and Judaism*, Philadelphia, PA: Fortress Press.
Sanders, E. P. (1995), *The Historical Figure of Jesus*, New York: Penguin.
Sarraute, Nathalie (1963), *The Age of Suspicion*, trans. Maria Jolas, New York: Braziller.
Saussure, Ferdinand de (1976), *Course in General Linguistic*, Oxford: Duckworth.
Schneemelcher, Wilhelm (ed.) (1963), *New Testament Apocrypha*, trans. R. Wilson, 2 vols. Philadelphia, PA: Westminster.
See, Tony, and Joff Bradley eds (2016), *Deleuze and Buddhism*, London: Palgrave Macmillan.
Sellew, Philip H. (2006), 'Jesus and the Voice from beyond the Grave: *Gospel of Thomas* 42 in the Context of Funerary Epigraphy', in Jón Ma Ásgeirsson, April D. DeConick and Risto Uro (ed.), *Thomasine Traditions in Antiquity: The Social and Cultural*

World of the Gospel of Thomas, 39–73, Nag Hammadi and Manichaean Studies 59, Leiden: Brill.

Semetsky, Inna (2010), 'Silent Discourse: The Language of Signs and "Becoming-woman"', *SubStance* 39(1): 87–102.

Sherk, R. K. (1969), *Roman Documents from the Greek East*, Baltimore, MD: Johns Hopkins University Press.

Sherman, Jacob Holsinger (2009), 'No Werewolves in Theology? Transcendence, Immanence, and Becoming-Divine in Gilles Deleuze', *Modern Theology* 25(1): 1–20.

Shults, F. LeRon (2014a), *Iconoclastic Theology: Gilles Deleuze and the Secretion of Atheism*, Edinburgh: Edinburgh University Press.

Shults, F. LeRon (2014b), *Theology after the Birth of God*, New York: Palgrave Macmillan.

Simpson, Christopher Ben (2012), *Deleuze and Theology*, London: Bloomsbury.

Sloterdijk, Peter, and Hans-Jurgen Heinrichs, *Neither Sun nor Death*, trans. Steve Corcoran, Los Angeles: Semiotext(e), 2011.

Small, Alastair (1996), *Subject and Ruler: The Cult of the Ruling Power in Classical Antiquity*, Ann Arbor, MI: Journal of Roman Archaeology.

Smart, Alan, and Josephine Smart (2017), *Posthumanism*, Toronto: University of Toronto Press.

Smith, Daniel W. (2009), 'Klossowski's Reading of Nietzsche: Impulses, Phantasms, Simulacra, Stereotypes', *Diacritics* 35: 8–21.

Spinoza, Benedict de (1985), *The Collected Works of Spinoza*, vol. 1, ed. and trans. Edwin Curley, Princeton, NJ: Princeton University Press.

Theissen, Gerd, and Dagmar Winter (2002), *The Quest for the Plausible Jesus: The Question of Criteria*, Louisville, KY: Westminster John Knox Press.

Thornton, Edward (2017), 'The Rise of the Machines: Deleuze's Flight from Structuralism', *Southern Journal of Philosophy* 55(4): 454–74.

Thrift, Nigel (2008), *Non-representational Theory: Space/Politics/Affect*, London: Routledge.

Tromp, Johannes (2005), *The Life of Adam and Eve in Greek: A Critical Edition*, Leiden: Brill.

Vattimo, Gianni (1991), *The End of Modernity*, trans. Jon R. Snyder, Baltimore, MD: Johns Hopkins University Press.

Vermès, Géza (1983), *Jesus the Jew*, London: SCM Press.

Vermès, Géza (1993), *The Religion of Jesus the Jew*, London: SCM Press.

Vermès, Géza (2010), *Jesus in the Jewish World*, London: SCM Press.

Vernant, Jean P. (1973), *Tragedy and Myth in Ancient Greece*, Brighton: Harvester Press.

Vignola, Paolo (2019), 'Do Not Forbid Nietzsche to Minors: On Deleuze's Symptomatological Thought', *Deleuze and Guattari Studies* 13(4): 552–66.

Villani, Tizianna (2019), 'Gilles Deleuze: Philosophy and Nomadism', *Deleuze and Guattari Studies* 13(4): 516–27.

Virilio, Paul (1975), *L'insecurite du territoire*, Paris: Galilée.

Voloshinov, Valentin N. (1973), *Marxism and the Philosophy of Language*, trans. Ladislav Matejka and I. R. Titunik, New York: Seminar Press.
Watson, Janell (2005), 'The Face of Christ: Deleuze and Guattari on the Politics of Word and Image', *Bible and Critical Theory* 1(2): 1–11.
Wellhausen, Julius (1905), *Einleitung in die drei ersten Evangelien*, Berlin: Reimer.
Whitehead, Alfred North (1978), *Process and Reality*, New York: Free Press.
Williams, Raymond (1977), *Marxism and Literature*, Oxford: Oxford University Press.
Žižek, Slavoj (1992), *Looking Awry: An Introduction to Jacques Lacan through Popular Culture*, Cambridge, MA: MIT Press.
Žižek, Slavoj (1997), *The Plague of Fantasies*, London: Verso.
Žižek, Slavoj (2016b), *Disparities*, London: Bloomsbury Academic.
Zourabichvili, François (2004), *Le vocabulaire de Deleuze*, Paris: Ellipses.

Index

Abraham 51, 167, 224, 230
absence 125
  positivization of absence 22, 102
abstract machine (*machine abstraite*) 8, 11, 51, 69, 73, 77, 85–8, 90–7, 114–15, 120, 154
affect (*affectus*) 26, 63, 146, 147–56, 161, 175, 199, 213
aleatory alliances/events/forces 14, 45, 59, 162, 167, 173–4, 206
Althusser, Louis 211, 212
animality 165–6, 172, 206
anomalous individual/point of a pack 166–70, 173, 183, 190, 206, 230
arborescence, arborific structures 3, 8, 45, 57, 66, 193
Ark of the Covenant 137
Artaud, Antonin 38, 67
  and the judgment of God 67
assemblage (*agencement*) 8, 48–9, 73–81, 88–89, 145, 171–2, 220, 232
  collective assemblage of enunciation 114, 139
  biform social assemblage 77, 81–8, 107, 114, 119, 200, 220
  machinic assemblage 30, 86, 228
  social assemblage 8, 27, 30, 65, 87–8, 90, 92, 110, 118, 120, 203
autoproduction 37–44

Bacon, Francis 149, 227, 228
base-superstructure schema 14, 25, 211, 213, 219, 221
becoming 8, 9, 26, 33, 36, 145, 157–8, 174
  becoming and multiplicities 158
Bergson, Henri 7, 213, 229
betrayal 116, 133–40, 176
  double betrayal 67, 119, 141–3, 205
bifurcation, bifurcate 9, 43, 105, 111, 117, 195, 216, 228

body without organs (*corps sans organes*) 8, 37–44, 73, 109
  attractive body without organs 42–3
  paranoiac body without organs 41–2

conjunctive synthesis 39–40, 43–4
connective synthesis 39–40, 42–3
contagion 29, 166–9, 170, 173, 196–7, 206–7
content plane 57, 82–9, 94, 96, 106–7, 109, 114, 124, 157, 171, 195, 202, 211, 220, 221, 224
crucifixion 51, 119, 132, 141, 176–8, 182–3, 204, 226, 228

de Saussure, Ferdinand 82–3, 211, 220, 225
debt 68–9, 182, 200, 218, 223
Derrida, Jacques 82, 223
desire 21–8
  desire-as-lack 23, 28, 104, 106, 111, 202
  desiring production (*production désirante*) 21–8, 32
despot-god (*dieu-despote*) 23, 66, 69–74, 105, 116, 119, 125–42
despotic signifier (*signifiant despotique*) 23, 66–72, 95, 105, 125–30, 137, 141, 160, 163, 186, 199, 200, 204–5, 218, 225
despotic socius 66–71, 95, 115, 126, 131, 199–200, 218–19
destratification 8, 72–3, 75, 92–3, 97, 105, 108–9, 186, 201
destruction 95, 140, 172, 185, 208
deterritorialization 8, 23, 28, 45–9, 52–61, 73, 75, 86, 92–7, 105–6, 116–21, 125–9, 132–3, 137, 139, 141, 161, 163–6, 169, 171–3, 176–9, 185–6, 192, 198–201, 206–7, 217
  absolute 51, 56, 58, 177, 179, 186, 207

diagrammatic 49, 51, 55, 72, 95–7, 117–20, 201, 203
generative 50, 121, 125, 129, 132–3, 136
machinic 51–2, 195
typology of deterritorialization 49–52
diagram (as abstract machine) 87–9, 94, 96, 120, 148, 183, 222
power/knowledge diagram 51–2, 77, 86–93, 96, 108, 110, 114–15, 120, 201–2, 204
difference 2, 5–6, 25–7, 30, 32, 34, 36, 57, 154–5, 157–9, 172, 175, 178–9, 188, 195, 204, 207–8, 211, 214, 215, 221, 222
differentiation 155, 162–3, 215
disjunctive synthesis 30–2, 35–6, 39, 40–3, 69, 169, 197–8, 214–16
Emmanuel Kant 215
Duns Scotus, John 196, 214

Ebionites (Adoptionists) 12, 32, 120
ecumenon 8, 73, 92–5, 105, 110, 114–15, 201, 222
Engels, Frederick 69, 219
errors of desire 100–4, 109, 201–2, 223
essence 3, 26–7, 30, 33–5, 40, 66, 94, 138, 142, 147, 178, 192, 196
eternal return (*see under* Nietzsche)
ethics 106, 146, 185
event 30, 33, 35, 48–9, 59, 61
exegesis 16, 18–19, 89, 96, 113–14, 123–4, 127, 152, 205
Exodus 49, 137, 198
expression plane 57, 82–9, 94, 96, 106–10, 114, 121, 124, 154, 202, 211, 220–1, 225
exteriority 6, 13, 23, 27, 80, 94–6, 104, 116, 118, 150, 153, 184, 189, 203

faciality 116, 123, 125–30, 132–3, 136, 139
abstract faciality machine 123, 125, 127, 130, 139
end of faciality 139–40
faith 2, 41, 61, 91, 106, 108, 182, 188, 218, 224, 231
familialism 167, 173, 206
familialist territory 46, 50

force (*puissance*) 39, 44, 62, 87, 146, 148, 154, 161, 222, 227
Foucault, Michel 1, 24, 87, 128, 188, 209, 210
autonomous subject 230
interpretation 28
lost origins 3
mechanism (*dispositif*) 220
NFM construct 124
panopticism 87
power/knowledge 88
regime of truth 7, 9, 114–15, 120, 202
Freud, Sigmund 32, 154, 214
libidinal drives 24–5, 213
unconscious 24–5

gaze 21–2, 101, 212
gender 4, 47–8, 50, 52, 58–9, 60, 157, 159–60, 163, 186, 194, 205–6, 229
gnostics 4, 12, 24, 32, 35, 120, 177
group subjectivity 25, 213
guilt 68, 100, 102–3, 110, 118, 200, 202, 223

Hebrew God 50, 136–7, 139, 141, 204
Heidegger, Martin 209, 214
heretic, heresy 119, 121, 225
Paul as heretic 12
historical-libidinal materialism 24–6
Hjelmslev, Louis 82–3, 88, 220–1, 225
form-substance complexes 82–3

ideal-ego 223, 217
Idea(s) 94, 214, 215, 222
idealization 22, 102–3, 110, 202, 218
of lack 67, 101–2
of law 67, 102–3
of language 67, 103–5
imaginary order/register/regiment 69, 74, 99, 200, 217
immanence 26–7, 34, 37, 166, 196, 209, 215
incarnation 126, 130, 158, 163, 175, 178–9, 214
inter-religious dialogue 4
interative group/social practices 12, 48, 51–2, 79, 81, 85–5, 90, 93, 114, 200–1
interpretation 52, 88, 115, 125, 127–8, 130, 133, 140, 151, 182, 192, 198

Jesus movement 3, 182–4, 189–90
  Jesus-in-movement 183, 188
judgment 66–8, 71, 135, 178–9, 207
  and the Lobster God, 67
  judgment of God 38–9, 67, 73, 75, 200

Kafka, Franz 78, 151, 158, 166, 184, 220
Kant, Emmanuel 215
Kierkegaard, Søren 2, 224, 227
kingdom of God 29, 168, 224, 227
  and the parable of yeast and leaven 29, 168, 173, 196, 206–7
Klossowski, Pierre 223

Lacan, Jacques 154, 214
  absent Other (*Autre*) of signification 225
  daddy–mommy–me triangle 215
  desire and transgress 218
  desire-as-lack 23, 104, 202, 212
  divided subject 103
  imaginary order (*imaginaire*) 69
  impossible real (*réel impossible*) 104, 213
  lack (*manque*) 101–2
  Law 102
  object of desire (*objet a*) 21–22
  Other (*l'Autre*) 102, 125, 223
  phallus 229
  real (*réel*) versus reality (*réalité*) 213
  reterritorialization 217
  structure of fantasy 212
  symbolic order (*symbolique*) 69
  territorialization 217
lack (*manque*) 21–3, 67–8, 100–5, 109–11, 114, 126–7, 129, 168, 188, 199–202, 223
language (*langage, langue*) 125, 220, 223
LGBTQ 159
lines in literature, lines of writing (*lignes d'écriture*) 55–9
  line(s) of flight 30, 48, 51, 57, 59, 61–2, 95, 136, 139, 162–3, 165, 199, 210
  lines of rigid segmentarity 56–8, 60–2, 186, 199
  lines of supple segmentarity 56–61, 62, 107, 199, 208
  typology of lines 56–62

literary characters 56–7, 62–3, 131, 150–2, 155, 199, 205, 228
literary machine 16–18, 53, 153, 196–6
Lobster God 67
love 12, 25, 115, 138–9, 141, 149, 152–3, 168, 178, 212, 222
  as a war machine 186

machine 1, 6–9, 11–20, 29–42, 48–9, 66, 85, 162–3
  abstract machine 8, 11, 51, 69, 73, 77, 85–8, 90–7, 114–15, 120, 154
  and multiplicities 20, 30–3, 172
  Christ machines 6, 11–12, 15, 19, 24, 28, 30–2, 74, 158, 196–7
  literary/writing machines 16–18, 52, 94, 96, 153
  versus structure 12–14, 19, 56
  scapegoat machine 117–20
  social machines 17
machinic assemblage 30, 86, 228
machinic unconscious 154, 213
magic 170, 176, 177–9, 230, 231
map, mapping 8–10, 19, 30, 36–8, 52, 63, 69, 79, 89, 100, 107, 110, 116–17, 121, 125, 153, 183–4, 187, 190–1, 196, 202–3, 208
Marcionites 12, 32, 120
Marx, Karl 24–5
  Asiatic mode of production 219
  base-superstructure 14, 211, 219
  class interest and ideology 213
  historical materialism 25
  surplus value 219
master signifier 102, 103–4, 125–6
messianic movements 4, 182–3, 187, 190–1
messianism 182, 190–1
micro-cracks (*micro-fêlures*) 59 60
micropolitics 4, 60, 159, 168, 173, 194, 205–7
milieu 45–6, 186, 210, 216
minor literature 151, 166, 220
minoritarian processes/movements 159–60, 184–5, 187
  becoming-minoritarian 160, 187
miraculating pole 41–2, 216
modes of propagation 167–70, 173, 206

molar formations/bodies 8, 39, 44, 46, 56–9, 61–2, 66, 131–2, 146–8, 154, 157–67, 169, 171, 176–9, 199, 201, 204, 207, 213
  molar plane of literature 150–1
  molar subject/subjectivity (*subjectivite molaire*) 57, 131–2, 146, 151, 154, 158–63, 176–9, 204–5, 207
molecular bodies 57, 62
  becoming-molecular 175–6, 205
  lines 199, 210
  molecular forces/processes/events 8, 39, 56–9, 147–50, 161, 169, 172, 178–9, 203, 205
  molecular plane 39, 43, 151–9, 228
  molecular revolution 185
  planes of literature 150–1
molecularity 169, 175
morality 67, 106, 110, 126, 137
Moses 91, 136–42, 170, 181, 184, 230
multiplicity 8, 29–36, 40, 42, 45, 95, 146, 151, 155–8, 161–73, 176, 178–9, 183–4, 190–1, 194–7, 206–7, 222, 227, 230
  of demons 29, 167
  of weeds 29
  of wolves 31
  of yeast 178, 196

Nietzsche, Friedrich 7, 25
  active and reactive forces 26
  affirmative gods 222
  and Kierkegaard 2
  eternal return 27
  grammar of God 100, 223
  'Nietzsche-Deleuze' 147, 213
  will-to-power 24, 147, 227
nomad 183–4, 186–9, 190–2, 208, 232
nomadism 8, 49, 51, 181, 184–6, 188, 190–1, 207–8, 232
nonrepresentational concepts 6, 7–9, 10, 117, 195

object-cause of desire (*objet a*) 21–2, 101, 103, 212
Oedipus 131–2, 154, 204, 214
  oedipal family 217
  oedipal mystification 32, 37
  oedipal statements 32

oedipal subject 104, 123, 202
  Oedipus complex 214
orchid and wasp 49–50, 148, 161–2
order-word (*mot d'ordre*) 16, 138, 142
organism 8, 46, 67–75, 95–7, 101–3, 105, 109–10, 157, 160, 162–3, 184, 199–200, 207
  and the Lobster God 67
origin(s) 2–6, 19, 32, 88, 90, 193–4, 230
Other (*l'Autre*) 21, 46, 102–3, 125–6, 223, 225
outlandish 48–9, 51, 55, 62, 181, 198–9, 216–17, 231
overcoding 57, 62, 66–9, 72, 199

pack 30–2, 137, 158, 165–73, 183, 190
  contagion though a pack 166–7, 170
  of demons 168, 170–3, 229
  of disciples 167, 190–1
  multiplicity as a pack 30, 167–9, 173
  of wolves 29, 31–2, 167
Panopticon, panopticism 87, 220, 221, 222
paradigmatic processes 49, 84, 104, 118, 125–6, 127, 136, 139, 160, 163, 184, 198, 221, 225
paranoiac pole 41–2, 44
particles-signs 13, 86–7, 146, 148, 175, 211
passional subjective regime of signs 50, 117, 135–44
passive syntheses 39–44, 69, 216
patrilineal kinship 167–9, 173
Pauline Christianity 3, 92, 193, 221
Phallus 160, 163, 205, 229
plane of consistency 30, 109, 175
plane of content (*see under* content plane)
plane of expression (*see under* expression plane)
plane of immanence 8, 26–7, 39, 49, 61, 66, 93–4, 104, 121, 128, 131, 136, 149, 196, 201, 207, 210, 213
planes of literature 150–1
plane of organization 8, 33–4, 66, 95, 115, 224, 227
planomenon 8, 73, 92–4, 105–6, 121, 128, 201
plateau 9–10, 38, 56
Plato, platonic 27, 33–4, 37, 86, 198, 210

point of subjectification 50, 115, 136–9, 141–2
post-signifying passional subjective regime (*see* passional subjective regime)
power (*pouvoir*) 87, 148, 161, 171, 227
power/knowledge diagram 52, 77, 86–9, 92–3, 96, 108, 114–15, 120, 147, 202, 204, 222
Prigogine, Ilya, and Isabelle Stengers 216
prohibition 68, 94, 102, 200, 218
prophet 14, 42, 50, 81, 91, 114, 116, 119, 135–7, 140–1, 181–2, 204, 226
  as divided subject 137–9
  as subject of enunciation 103, 114, 138–9, 141–2
  as subject of the statement 138–9, 141
proto-orthodox groups 12, 32, 120
Proust, Marcel 33, 45, 152–3, 197, 228
punishment 7, 42, 58, 77, 88, 102, 200, 212

regime of signs 8, 27, 52, 113–22, 202
  passional subjective regime of signs 135–44
  signifying despotic regime of signs 123–34
  typology of regime of signs 116–17, 152–3, 203
regime of truth 7, 9, 114–15, 120, 202
religion 1–4, 46, 118, 186, 194, 203, 222
  God of religion 8, 94–6, 105, 115, 201
repetition 2, 27, 33, 42, 68, 200, 213, 215, 224
representational concepts/thinking 5–6, 116–17, 150
repression 24–5, 39, 41, 43, 67–9, 105–6, 109, 160, 199, 200, 213, 215
resonance 33, 215
  stratigraphic resonance 67, 74
reterritorialization 8, 48–52, 58–9, 62, 119–20, 136–7, 139, 142, 148, 161–2, 171–3, 178, 198–9, 217
  in Lacan 217
rhizome 4–6, 8, 10, 12, 36, 66, 116, 154, 175–6, 178, 183, 186, 194
rhizomatic model/relations/philosophy 3–4, 6–8, 36, 194, 195, 197

rhizomatics 4, 194–5
rhythms of bodily intensity 146–50, 155, 227–8
Roman Empire 12, 23, 25–26, 38, 40, 65–6, 68, 70–1, 73–4, 81, 93, 95–7, 126, 186–7, 189–91, 199, 200–1, 218
rupture 48, 52–3, 56, 61, 91–2

salvation 160, 162–3, 176, 178, 205, 209, 214, 218, 222, 226
scapegoat 117–19, 121–22, 125, 128–9, 131–4, 136–7, 141–3, 203–5, 224, 226
  faceless 118, 132, 134, 204
  Levitical 117–18, 203
  scapegoat machine 118–20
  scapegoat mechanism 117–19, 121, 136, 203–4
schiz 43, 105, 111, 117, 216
schizo God 8, 94–7, 105–6, 201
schizoanalysis 1, 18, 92, 97, 110, 120, 155, 164, 179, 190, 192, 201, 207, 209
signification (*signifiance*) 5, 67, 74, 95–7, 100–2, 109, 115, 120, 124–7, 155, 160, 163, 185, 199, 202, 218, 221, 225
  and the Lobster God, 67
signifying despotic regime of signs 117, 123–34
simulacra 26, 223
singularities 9, 13, 34, 86–7, 146, 148, 161, 211, 215
smooth space (*espace lisse*) 8, 184–91
social production 16, 23, 25, 39, 67, 69, 72, 74–5, 93, 95–7, 105–6, 186, 199, 201–2, 219, 229
socius 69, 222
  despotic socius 66–74, 95, 115, 126, 131, 199–200, 218, 219
  primitive territorial socius 69, 116
  typology of the socius 69
sorcerer(s), sorcery 49, 168–9, 173, 177, 198, 206, 230–1
Spinoza, Baruch 7, 145–50, 155, 213, 214
  affects if joy and sadness 148–50, 227
stratification 8, 23, 57, 62, 66–9, 71–5, 101, 104, 108, 160, 199–200, 202, 220
stratum, strata 30, 66–9, 73–4, 92–3, 109, 114, 124, 160, 184
  stratigraphic resonance 67, 74

three great strata 66–9, 73, 101, 199
striated space (*espace strié*) 8, 95, 184–90
structure, structural relations 12–14, 19, 47–8, 52, 56, 61, 63, 65, 68, 85, 92, 104, 131, 193–5, 189, 198
   structural function 65, 74, 132, 200, 204, 218, 225
subject 22, 34, 46, 49, 52, 62, 67–8, 101
   divided subject 103, 137–9, 141, 212, 221, 223
   idealization of subject 101–2
   molar subject 57, 131–2
   subject of enunciation (*sujet d'énonciation*) 103, 138–9
   subject of the statement (*sujet d'énonce*) 103, 138–9
subject group (*groupe-sujet*) 106, 109
subjected group (*groupe assujetti*) 105, 109–11
subjectification (*subjectivation*) 50, 67, 95–7, 139, 160
   and the Lobster God 67
subjectivity 22, 25, 61, 73–5, 104, 109, 115
   group subjectivity 25, 213
surplus value (*plus-value*) 23, 40–4, 69–74, 101, 105, 125–6, 129–30, 133, 199, 204
symbolic order/register/regiment 21, 69, 100–1, 103–4, 118, 129, 130, 137, 160, 163, 202, 206, 212, 213
symptoms, symptomology 151–5, 161, 205, 220
synagogue 12, 15, 30, 40, 47, 79, 85, 89, 92, 135, 182

syntagmatic processes 102–3, 125–6, 223, 225

territory 45–9, 92, 165, 172, 181, 189, 198, 207, 210, 224
territorialization 8, 45–54
   in Lacan 217
tracing 3, 32, 116, 193–4
transcendence 2, 26–8, 34, 37, 196, 209, 214, 228
   immanent transcendence 2, 209, 214
transgression 56, 68, 91, 99, 101–4, 108, 200, 218, 222–5
tree-logic (*see* under arborescence)

univocity, univocal being, 26, 34, 37, 196, 209, 214, 228

vertical filiation 66, 69, 70, 73, 105, 123–6, 129, 133, 199, 204
virtual, virtuality 2, 9, 13–14, 17, 32–8, 49, 52, 59, 61, 72–3, 75, 86, 95, 222, 224, 227
voluntary associations 41–3, 70, 79, 84, 88–9

war machine 8, 95, 183–6, 190–2, 194, 207, 208, 232
will-to-power (*see under* Nietzsche)
writing machine, 94, 96

zone of proximity 49, 147–8, 161

www.ingramcontent.com/pod-product-compliance
Lightning Source LLC
Chambersburg PA
CBHW062131300426
44115CB00012BA/1888